Evening Ga

ROBSON AND THE BORO

By Eric Paylor

Juniper Publishing

Juniper Publishing
Liverpool

First Published in Great Britain by
Juniper Publishing
3, Sandy Lane, Melling, Liverpool L31 1EJ.
1996

ISBN 0-9528622-0-4

Typesetting and Origination by: P's & Q's Ltd., Unit 10, Gibraltar Row,
King Edward Industrial Estate, Liverpool L3 7HJ.

Printed and bound by: Albion Graphics, Old Connolly Complex,
Kirkby Bank Road, Knowsley Industrial Park North, Kirkby, Merseyside, L33 7SY

Contents

Introduction and Acknowledgements

I T'S sometimes hard to believe that Middlesbrough Football Club have come so far in such a short period of time.

Only a couple of years ago, the club was languishing in the middle of the First Division, seemingly with a lack of ambition. There was a small squad of players, of mixed talents and abilities, and a sense of frustration among the supporters which was reflected in ever decreasing attendances at an ever ageing stadium.

Since those depressing days, there has been a wonderful wind of change blowing through the football club.

Two years ago Steve Gibson, the club chairman, outlined his intentions to make Boro a great club again, and has backed his promises to the fans with hard cash and positive and adventurous new policies.

Not only have Boro bounced back into the Premiership, but they have stayed there. World class players like Juninho, Emerson, Barmby and Ravanelli have been purchased, and more are on their way.

As the Boro Revolution gathers pace, the club's 92-year-old cultural home, Ayresome Park, has become one of the casualties. It has been replaced by a magnificent state of the art modern stadium which is attracting near 30,000 capacity crowds.

The Cellnet Riverside Stadium, as it will be known for the first ten years of its life, has attracted a hugely lucrative sponsorship deal from Cellnet, the country's leading mobile communications company. It has helped to give the Boro a rich new profile in the community.

Throughout all these impressive changes, there is a shining light portraying the new image of the club and the determination to bring success back to Teesside.

It is the club manager, Bryan Robson, who has been Steve Gibson's catalyst to make the dream a reality. Robson, a former England captain with 90 international caps to his credit, has returned to his native North-east to revitalise the Boro.

Robson has delved into the respect he commands throughout the world of football to entice top quality players to Teesside and build a new team, which promises so much hope for the future.

Not everything has gone perfectly and as planned. There have been one or two hiccups along the way. In fact Boro's return to the Premiership has been very much a learning period for club officials, the players and Robson himself. But the platform has been erected, and it is becoming increasingly solid.

As a result, there is a remarkable story to tell of the rebirth of the Boro over the past two years.

Nobody has monitored the club's success more than the Middlesbrough Evening Gazette, which has always maintained strong links with the football club and the Teesside community at large.

This book is an attempt to mirror the story of Robson's first two years with the Boro, as told through the sports pages of the Evening Gazette.

There are no new revelations, just the original stories as they were exclusively given to the Evening Gazette, but with fresh comment and opinion from the author.

Many thanks are due to Bryan Robson and Steve Gibson for making this book possible, in addition to Viv Anderson and other staff at the club, likewise Nigel Pearson and his fellow players for always taking the time out to be available for interviews.

Thanks are also owed to the fans, for their kind letters of support in the writing of this book. Nobody deserves this new wave of success more than the Boro fans.

In addition, I would like to thank the staff of the Evening Gazette for their help and support, notably editor Ranald Allan for placing the newspaper's photographic library and other important facilities at my disposal. Sports editor Allan Boughey, picture editor David Jamieson, chief photographer Doug Moody and head librarian Barbara Thompson have also given valuable support and assistance.

The photographic team of Colin Robertson, Terry Reed, Ian McIntyre, Steve Elliott and Michelle Maddison, all of whose photographs are featured in this book, also deserve a big thank-you.

I am extremely grateful to Cellnet for their kind and generous offer of sponsorship. Their part in the ongoing success of the football club should not be underestimated.

Finally I would like to thank my colleague **John Wilson** for co-ordinating the printing and publication of this book and also my wife **Brenda**, for her extreme patience and forebearance.

Eric Paylor

A New Era Begins

CHAPTER ONE:

RYAN ROBSON was a manager waiting to happen. As he approached the end of his illustrious playing career with Manchester United, the world was at his feet.

He had already achieved everything as a player, getting his hands on virtually every club trophy and establishing himself as one of the England all-time greats by winning 90 international caps.

As an aggressive ball-winning midfield player, he was both respected and feared by players throughout the country. As a former England World Cup captain, he was admired throughout the world.

At the age of 37 Robson was still a valuable member of the Manchester United first team squad. He was revered by the fans and was held in high esteem by his teammates, and could comfortably hold his own playing against top clubs at any level.

Perhaps there was a slight loss of pace. The old, scarred legs wouldn't always do what was expected of them. But Robson could still hold down a place at Old Trafford on merit, and it was only right that United were ready to offer him a new contract.

Clearly manager Alex Ferguson wanted to hang on to the influential midfielder who had brought so much inspiration to the dressing room and charisma and talent to the playing field. When a player has that much impact on the men around him, you don't want to let go of him.

However, Robson was his own man, and he was becoming restless. He had lost none of his love for Manchester United, nor for the game as a whole, but Robbo was starting to feel that his first team opportunities in the Premiership might be limited in the future, He did not want to take over a supporting part on the big stage.

As a businessman in his own right, Robson did not need to stay in football. He was a partner in a highly successful chain of Birthdays greeting cards shops, and could so easily have decided to concentrate on his business interests.

But football was in Robson's blood and he was determined to prove himself on a new front. Most of his contemporaries had moved into football management or coaching, and Robson had already taken a step in this direction by accepting an invitation from England's director of coaching Terry Venables to take up a part-time coaching post with the international side.

Robson was honoured and delighted to retain an involvement with the England set-up. He had always loved playing for his country and, while relishing the opportunity to work with the top England players again, realised that the coaching job offered a possible future stepping stone to the England managerial hot seat.

If that was to eventually become a reality, Robson needed to prove himself as a manager. He retained plenty of self belief and knew that he could make a success of running a club. One of Robson's strengths was his power of motivation, but he also had a wealth of experience from a 20-year playing career not to mention a long list of top contacts throughout Britain and the world,

Not that Robson had any intentions of hanging up his boots. He could have comfortably played on with Manchester United, so he knew that he could do a good job for any team in the country. He certainly had a lot to offer as a player-manager.

Having finally decided to make the break from Old Trafford, the feelers were put out. Clearly there was no point in Robson accepting a managerial post with a Third Division club. He had spent all his career at the top level and it was important he stayed there.

Naturally, not every club happened to be looking for a new manager, and in any case the handful of big established clubs may have preferred a man with previous managerial experience.

So Robson's best bet seemed to lie with a big club which had been going through a lean spell. He needed a challenging role where he could give new hope by lifting morale, and bringing the best out of a useful squad of players. But most importantly Robson needed to find a club whose ambitions matched his own. The bottom line was that he would not accept second best, wherever he went.

Wolves, looking for a manager to replace Graham Turner, were the first big club to show interest. They were a rich club, thanks to the generous investment of Sir Jack Hayward, who had helped finance the total rebuilding of the ageing Molineux stadium.

The Hayward family maintained strong ambitions for making Wolves one of the top clubs in the country. They had a fine football tradition over the years and were capable of attracting huge crowds. But Wolves were currently idling in the First Division and needed a new injection of lifeblood if they were to return to the Premiership.

It was a job which looked tailor made for Robson, and he went to Molineux for talks. However he did not become their new player manager. The media claimed that Robson's financial demands were too high. Within 12 months, Wolves officials and their supporters were left to regret that they had not moved heaven and earth to get Robson to Molineux, whatever the cost.

BORO Chairman Steve Gibson, the man behind the ambitious plans to build the Cellnet Riverside Stadium and bring Bryan Robson to Teesside as player-manager.

A New Era Begins

Ironically a move to the West Midlands would have taken Robson back to an area which meant a lot to him. He spent the early part of his football career on Wolves' doorstep, with West Bromwich, and had strong feelings for the people who lived there.

Naturally part of Robson's heart was also in the North-east, which was the region of his birth and of his youth. He was born in Chester le Street, a town with magnificent football traditions which has produced so many top players over the years.

As a lad, Robson stood on the terraces at Newcastle United, and shouted on the Magpies. He was a North-east boy with passions for the football on his doorstep. Those passions never faded and Robson was always fully aware of the devout love of the national game by North-east people, even when their regional teams were not living up to expectations.

With his knowledge of the region, Robson was bound to sit up and take notice when he received strong interest from a North-east club. The call came from Middlesbrough, 30 miles or so from his birthplace, who wanted to talk to him about the possibilities of him becoming their player-manager.

Having grown up in the middle of strong Newcastle-Sunderland rivalry, Robson would have regarded Boro as the third of the region's big clubs. They were still capable of pulling in big crowds when they were winning, but Boro were not a club with a history of success, certainly not over the past 40 years.

Boro had been a big club in the past and for many years were one of the First Division giants. But standards had slipped, and the club had been allowed to drift. Now they were nationally renowned as a yo-yo club. They would alternate between the First Division and the Premiership, winning promotion every few years, but never being strong or ambitious enough to hang on to their status before slipping back down again very quickly.

At the time of making contact with Robson, Boro had been back in the First Division for 12 months following their most recent relegation from the Premiership.

Boro had not made much of an impact back in the First Division and the directors had decided to relieve manager Lennie Lawrence of his duties. Lawrence, who had been in charge at Ayresome Park for three seasons, won promotion in his first year on Teesside. He achieved this success with a small squad and limited resources.

However Boro struggled badly in the Premiership and were relegated after just one season back in the top flight.

Despite his sacking, Lawrence still retained a good relationship with Boro directors Steve Gibson and George Cooke and advised them who to try to sign as his successor. He named Bryan Robson.

Coincidentally, Gibson and Cooke were already thinking along the same lines. They were fired by new ambitions, and believed that Robson possessed all the qualities to ignite the fuse. So the scene was set for Boro to approach the Manchester United legend.

Remarkably, it was Lawrence who arranged the meeting between Robson and the Boro directors. The displaced Boro boss drove to Wetherby to meet up with Robbo, and accompanied him to the meeting with Gibson and Cooke on Teesside.

Even so, Robson must have arrived on Teesside very much with an open mind. There was nothing in Boro's recent history to suggest that Boro had the resources or the capabilities to become a big time club again.

Just eight years earlier Boro had reached rock bottom when they went into liquidation. They were saved from oblivion by minutes and, despite a dramatic recovery, had since gone up and down the leagues with amazing regularity.

There was always some measure of ambition about the club,but they had never matched it with financial investment. Boro had tried to build up slowly, but it was a routine which never paid dividends because they always found themselves back at square one again. So Robson needed to know if the Boro directors were finally ready to grasp the nettle at last.

With that in mind, Robson had good reason to be pleasantly surprised when he sat down with Gibson and Cooke, and was given a clear insight of their plans, and their genuine ambitions.

Chairman Steve Gibson, a director since pre-liquidation days, had only recently taken control of the club. A committed Boro fan since he was a lad, Gibson had dreamed of the day when he would be in a position to restore the Boro glory days. Now he had reached that position.

A self made businessman through his company Bulkhaul, Gibson had the financial clout to invest in the club. He realised that the club had to act big and think big, if it wanted to be big. He had the full backing of Cooke, who represented ICI's shareholding on the board.

Gibson had already set the winds of change into motion. With the help and financial assistance of the Teesside Development Corporation the club was about to start work on constructing a grandiose state of the art 30,000 all seater stadium in the Middlesbrough Dock area.

The new stadium, which was replacing the ageing and partially delapidated Ayresome Park, was designed to give Boro a brand new power base and stature with the 21st Century in mind.

The stadium alone was good enough to offer Robson a mouth watering carrot because it would increase the profile of the club, and make it easier to attract top class players. It would also lead to a new surge of interest by the supporters, who would appreciate the new atmosphere and modern facilities, and bring a healthy increase in revenue for the club.

However Robson also needed a few potatoes to go with his carrot. He needed to hear from the directors that they were capable of providing the high finance which would buy the players to enable Boro to compete with the best teams in the country and ultimately the best in Europe.

That vital information was also forthcoming. The Boro directors were ready to provide as much money as it needed for team strengthening as well as financing the new stadium. Gibson and Cooke wanted Robson to have the financial backing to take Boro back into the Premiership at the first time of asking. Within reason, the manager could have whatever money he required, plus the total backing of the board.

So, not only did Robson discover that Gibson's ambitions matched his own, but Gibson discovered that Robson was definitely the man he was looking for to take Boro back into the big time. They also had a liking for each other, which was also vitally important.

It didn't take long to hammer out the rest of the details and on a shake of hands and the promise of a three-year contract Bryan Robson became the new manager of Middlesbrough.

Boro pushed the boat out to meet Robson's financial demands and settled back to let him get on with the job. There's normally a gamble offering any manager his first job in the hot seat, but this gamble was a lot smaller than most.

Robson had no doubts about his immediate target. He had to take Boro back up to the Premiership in his first season in charge on Teesside, so that top flight football and the completion of the new stadium would come together at the same time.

Robson's first job was to appoint an assistant manager with whom he had similar beliefs and theories on how the game should be played. It was an easy choice to make. Robson immediately contacted his former England and Manchester United colleague Viv Anderson, who was manager of First Division Barnsley.

Anderson and his Oakwell assistant, Danny Wilson, had worked hard to establish a new playing pattern in their first 12 months at the helm of the South Yorkshire club.

They were expecting to take Barnsley forward the following season, and so it was not an easy decision for Anderson to make when he was suddenly offered a job elsewhere. In addition, he was managing a club in his own right, and was now being asked to take a step down as far as his title was concerned.

However, after initial talks with Robson, it did not take the 38-year-old Anderson very long to appreciate the huge potential on Teesside. So he agreed to link up with Robson in a new partnership leaving Wilson to move into the hot seat at Barnsley.

While Anderson became assistant manager, Robson was quick to ensure that Lawrence's former No.2 John Pickering, did not leave the club. Pickering, who was immensely popular with the playing squad, was happy to stay on as first team coach. Pickering's speciality was working with the players, and varying training by continually introducing new ideas.

To be fair, Robson still knew little about the vast majority of the members of his squad. He had played against the Boro side two seasons earlier and was familiar with the names, but had not had the benefit of watching the team in action before taking control.

What he was inheriting was a good nucleus of 12 experienced senior professionals, plus a host of promising young players, many of whom had already tasted first team football under Lawrence when the club suffered from a horrendous run of injuries.

There were two full internationals in the squad. Derek Whyte had played both at centre-back and left-back for Scotland, while utility player Chris Morris had played in the World Cup Finals for the Republic of Ireland.

Goalkeeper Steve Pears might also have become a full international had not a fractured cheekbone ended his chances with England, while many people felt that striker John Hendrie was one of the best uncapped Scottish players.

Hendrie formed a strong attacking partnership with fellow striker Paul Wilkinson and the duo were generally regarded as the best forward double act

CLAYTON BLACKMORE, pictured with first team coach John Pickering left, and assistant manager Viv Anderson, was Bryan Robson's first signing for Boro. The Welsh international arrived on a free transfer from Manchester United.

in the First Division. However Boro had very little cover up front in case of injuries.

Behind the front two, experienced winger Tommy Wright had recovered from a bad knee injury, while the Irish lad Alan Moore, who had been converted from midfield to the left wing by Lawrence, was regarded as one of the top young talents in the game.

Craig Hignett, who could play in a variety of positions, including up front or on the wing, was a set piece specialist with a good record for finding the target.

In midfield, Boro were served by the rapidly emerging Jamie Pollock, who was the best home grown player to come through since the club had revamped their youth programme following liquidation. Alongside him was Robbie Mustoe, a Colin Todd signing who was a midfield grafter who seemed to get better every season.

In addition to Whyte and Morris, the defence included Lawrence's last signing, the £750,000 Bishop Auckland-born Steve Vickers, and Irish B international Curtis Fleming who was a crowd favourite at right-back.

Defensively Boro had looked very strong when they fielded Lawrence's first choice side in the previous season. But full strength sides were few and far between as the club was hit by regular

Despite his limited knowledge of the side, Robson was keen to bring in new players quickly and placed the emphasis on experience. His first signing was an international, Manchester United's play anywhere Welshman Clayton Blackmore. Having spent ten successful years at Old Trafford Blackmore was snapped up on a free transfer and was initially signed to play at left-back. But Robson soon realised that Blackmore's excellent passing ability would be better utilised in midfield.

Blackmore was soon followed into the club by Boro's new record signing. Boro forked out £1 million for the first time to bring England Under-21 international defender Neil Cox to Teesside. Cox had been unable to maintain a regular place in the side at Aston Villa, but was regarded as one of the top young players in the country.

Robson identified Cox's best role at right-back, and stressed from the outset that this was the position where he would play most of his football for the club. Boro already had two players who could operate at right-back in Fleming and Morris but, as with any squad, they were going to have to battle for a place in the side.

The next Premiership player to arrive on Teesside was Nigel Pearson, the 30-year-old Sheffield Wednesday centre-back who was the rock around whom Robson's defence would be built.

IF the cap fits, wear it... Bryan Robson snapped up centre-back Nigel Pearson from Sheffield Wednesday for £750,000, and immediately made him club captain.

injuries to key players, and as a result they missed out on the chance of challenging for the play-offs. If the squad had been bigger, it might have been a different story. But Lawrence was often forced to throw in several young players at the same time, and as a result the team struggled to win games in the middle of the season when the injuries were at their worst.

Robson paid £750,000 for the tough tackling player and he must have come highly recommended by Viv Anderson, who played alongside Pearson in his time with the Owls. Many fans thought that Boro might have paid over the odds for a player who was re-establishing himself in the game following two broken legs.

But Pearson made such a huge impact, with his natural determination to win the ball and his inspirational qualities, that Robson got the player on the cheap.

With Robson intending to stamp his own qualities in the centre of the park, the new Boro boss had quickly strengthened both his defence and his midfield. He had done so with the addition of four players, all of whom had plenty of Premiership experience. It was clear that Robson had made his signings with more in mind than simply winning promotion from the First Division.

The manager's next task was to sort out his attack. As far as most supporters were concerned this was the priority problem area because Boro had very little cover should John Hendrie or Paul Wilkinson pick up an injury. Boro had struggled badly up front in the previous season when either, or both, of the players was absent.

Robson solved this little dilemma in an unusual manner. He paid £250,000 to FC Blooming to bring Bolivian international striker Jaime Moreno to Teesside. The 20-year-old became the first Bolivian to play in English football.

Moreno's talents had been initially spotted by Robson on one of the many videos he routinely received from agents. So Bryan brought him over for a trial, which included the opportunity to see Moreno in action in a friendly match against Darlington at Feethams.

Moreno not only produced an impressive individual display but he also scored two of Boro's goals in a 3-0 victory. Robson immediately put the wheels into motion to sign the Bolivian though he knew that Moreno would not be available for the start of the season because of the delay caused by applying for a work permit.

Boro enjoyed a relatively good pre-season. They defeated Torquay and Exeter on a West Country tour, and came home to beat Darlington before setting off for Scotland.

They opened North of the Border with a disappointing 1-0 defeat at Raith Rovers, which was watched by Bryan Robson from the stands, However the manager put his boots back on for the second Scottish game, at Ayr United, and scored both Boro goals in a 2-1 win. The team's pre-season programme was concluded with a 3-1 win at home to Hearts.

Despite the steady build up, Robson still encountered problems in the week leading up to the opening First Division match against Burnley at Ayresome Park. He was without regular goalkeeper Steve Pears who had missed the pre-season action with rib and calf injuries. In addition, reserve keeper Andy Collett had injured his knee in the pre-match warm-up at Raith.

Robson's only other keeper was the untried 19-year-old Ben Roberts, so the manager decided to make another transfer swoop just a few days before the start of the season.

He agreed a £375,000 fee with Arsenal for Alan Miller, who was understudy to England keeper David Seaman at Highbury. Miller had turned down the offer of a new contract to stay with the Gunners because he wanted to try to win a first team place elsewhere.

So this was a dream move for the 24-year-old Miller, who had an early chance to stake his claim for a regular role in the Boro team because he would be pitched straight into the action against Burnley.

As the opening game approached, there was great anticipation throughout Teesside. The arrival of Robson had grabbed the imagination of the Middlesbrough public and a remarkable 23,343 supporters turned up to watch the match against Burnley.

This was less than 1,000 below the total capacity and was good news for everybody at the club, particularly the directors, It was an indication that the fans were ready to respond to the club's new ambitions, while at the same time promising even better support in the future once the new stadium was up and running.

But the game is all about winning as far as supporters are concerned and Robson desperately needed a successful start to his managerial career.

Boro received a late boost when Nigel Pearson passed a fitness test on an injured knee, so Robson's first line up against Burnley was: Miller, Cox, Fleming, Vickers, Pearson, Blackmore, Robson, Pollock, Wilkinson, Hendrie, Moore, Subs, Whyte, Hignett, Roberts.

It was the line-up which Robson had been expected to select and included Curtis Fleming at left-back. Fleming was primarily right footed, and had played most of his football on the other flank. But he had adapted well to the left sided role in pre-season, and so was given the chance to make this new position his own.

The afternoon was very hot but it was no problem for Boro. They were far too good all-round for newly promoted Burnley and won 2-0 with a brace of goals from John Hendrie.

Many members of the crowd had gone along mainly to see Bryan Robson in action, because he was still very much regarded as one of the top players in the country. Robson enjoyed a steady debut, in no way sensational, but did a good job in holding the team together and making good use of every ball which came his way.

Boro were one of the bookmakers' favourites for the First Division title, along with Wolves, who had eventually appointed former England boss Graham Taylor as their new manager. This win consolidated the widely held belief that Boro would be good enough to be heavily involved in the championship race.

But Boro were given a clear indication of the wide gulf in class between the Premier League and the First Division when they were soundly beaten 3-0 in mid-week by Manchester United in Clayton Blackmore's testimonial match. Two goals from Mark Hughes and another from Lee Sharpe was a clear reflection of the difference between the two teams.

Blackmore had virtually completed his testimonial year at Old Trafford when he was transferred to Boro, and it was a fine gesture by the directors to allow him to stage his benefit match at Ayresome. In the event almost 20,000 fans turned up to make it a good night all-round for the Welsh international.

However Boro had better success when they returned to their First Division programme and recorded another 2-0 victory at Southend United. The key to the victory was Boro's solid defence, with the lively John Hendrie once again scoring both goals.

A New Era Begins

TEENAGER Phil Stamp enjoys an early season run-out for the first team in an Anglo Italian match against Piacenza

Any lasting doubts that Robson was not thinking big were permanently dispelled on the Monday after the Southend win, when the manager revealed an ambitious plan to bring Gary Lineker to Teesside. It was to be the first of many similar bold moves to bring top players to the club.

Lineker was contracted to Japanese club Grampus Eight but Robson was keen to sign his former England teammate once his contract in the Land of the Rising Sun ended in December. Lineker was made aware of Robson's interest, and was reported to be giving the matter strong consideration.

However there were other matters on Lineker's agenda. He had been promised a job by the BBC, and did not know if the job would still be open if he spent a spell with Boro first. So the 33-year-old reluctantly turned down Robson's offer and prepared to move into a new career in broadcasting.

Boro could have done with Lineker in their attack when they entertained Piacenza in the Anglo Italian Cup on Wednesday, August 24. Robson made eight changes to give the fringe players a run-out, but it was a hard grind for everybody involved including the generous crowd of 5,348, and the match ended goalless.

It was also an instantly forgettable night for Paul Wilkinson, who came on as a second half substitute and received a red card within 20 seconds of being on the pitch, for kicking an Italian opponent. The good news for Wilko was the two-match ban he received only covered Anglo Italian Cupties, and did not affect league games.

Robson reverted to a full strength side for the home game against Bolton Wanderers on the Saturday. Bruce Rioch's men were another of the promotion favourites and it turned out to be a hotly contested clash. But Boro just had the edge and grabbed all three points when Paul Wilkinson converted a cross from Jamie Pollock.

Robbo admitted: "This was our biggest test so far and I was pleased with the way the lads worked hard, and were patient for the breakthrough. We still have some work to do on our passing, but I'm happy with the three points and another clean sheet."

Boro maintained the momentum in midweek by travelling to Derby County and winning 1-0, courtesy of a Clayton Blackmore goal. So far, Robson's boys had a 100 per cent record in the league and had yet to concede their first goal of the campaign.

It should have been enough to earn Robson the manager of the month award for the First Division. But the football authorities, in their wisdom, decided against making a selection for August.

Robson was forced to make his first change in the league at Watford on September 3. Steve Vickers had picked up a calf strain at Derby, and so Derek Whyte stepped into his place.

The three points seemed to be set up for Boro when Watford goalkeeper Kevin Miller was dismissed in the 22nd minute for bringing down Bryan Robson as the player-manager went around him outside the box. Victory looked assured when Clayton Blackmore fired Boro in front before the interval with his second successive goal.

However Watford's ten men never gave up the battle and Alan Miller was beaten for the first time in league action when a shot from Richard Johnson was deflected wide of the keeper off Nigel Pearson. The match ended 1-1 leaving Boro still unbeaten.

The following week, Boro received official confirmation from the Department of Employment that Jaime Moreno had been awarded a work permit. The 20-year-old striker, who had been kept waiting six weeks for the good news, flew out from Bolivia at once. Robson finally had the cover up front that he had been looking for.

Moreno was introduced to the Boro faithful before the start of the televised derby clash at home to Sunderland on September 11 and received a standing ovation. However he was not fully fit, as a result of his long lay off and was not included in the squad. Steve Vickers returned after injury in place of Derek Whyte.

The match was not the TV spectacular that Robson would have been hoping for. Boro could not put their game together and the Rokermen dominated almost the whole of the match. Sunderland built up a 2-0 lead thanks to a brace of goals from Craig Russell, but missed several good chances to double their score.

Boro then woke up in the final 11 minutes and made Sunderland pay for those missed chances. They reduced the arrears with a terrific solo goal from Alan Moore which was worth the admission money alone, and then skipper Nigel Pearson equalised two minutes later.

The match finished 2-2 and Boro retained their unbeaten record. But Sunderland were treading water at the close and Boro could easily have won it if John Hendrie had been able to convert a late opportunity.

A crucial goal for the Boro as Paul Wilkinson beats his former teammate Alan Kernaghan in the air to score the goal which earned Robbo's men a vital 1-0 win against Bolton Wanderers at Ayresome Park.

PAUL WILKINSON is congratulated by Neil Cox and Clayton Blackmore after scoring the winner against Bolton Wanderers at Ayresome Park.

JAMIE POLLOCK, pictured going past former Boro defender Jimmy Phillips, gets Boro on to the attack against Bolton Wanderers. Pollock went on to become one of the mainstays of Boro's promotion charge.

NEIL COX was Boro's first £1 million signing when snapped up from Aston Villa before the start of the season. Cox is pictured in action in a 1-0 victory in heavy rain at Derby County.

ONE of Boro's most difficult early games under Bryan Robson was at home to neighbours Sunderland. Here, John Hendrie goes on a weaving run against the Roker defence.

Robson told the Evening Gazette: "It was a bit disappointing in the first three quarters of the match because we allowed Sunderland to dominate it. But I was delighted with the way we didn't give up, and the way we came back at the end showed that there is a lot of character in the side. We finished so strongly that we might even have won it."

Boro attracted less than 15,000 fans, almost 5,000 down on their Sunderland crowd, for the following home game against West Bromwich Albion. Clayton Blackmore was injured, but Craig Hignett came in as replacement and turned out to be the match winner.

Robbo's men had to do it the hard way after falling behind to a first half goal from Lee Ashcroft, but Robbie Mustoe came off the bench to equalise and Hignett grabbed the winner from the penalty spot in the very last minute.

Mustoe had come on for Bryan Robson, who was injured in only the first minute when he was kicked on the calf.

The injury forced Robson to miss Boro's next game at Port Vale on September 19. Goalkeeper Alan Miller was also sidelined, so Steve Pears returned for his first taste of competitive action since May. Derek Whyte also came in for Nigel Pearson.

Boro were well in command in the first half and everything was going to plan when Jamie Pollock fired them in front. But Boro showed defensive frailties for the first time after the restart, and ended up losing 2-1.

It was Boro's first defeat of the season in their ninth league and cup match and knocked them off the top of the First Division, with Wolves taking over as new leaders.

Robson admitted: "We should never have lost it. We must have had 70 per cent of the play. We need

to learn to bury sides when we are in that much control."

The manager handed the same line-up the opportunity to restore morale in the Coca Cola Cup second round first leg at Scarborough and Boro quickly took control of the tie by beating the Third Division side by 4-1. All the goals came during monsoon conditions in the first half with Boro scoring through John Hendrie, Jamie Pollock, Alan Moore and Robbie Mustoe.

Boro were now starting to establish a pattern of a reasonably strong defence and a quick breaking attack, with good passing movements in the middle. They got back to winning ways in the league the following Saturday when a lone goal from John Hendrie was enough to bring all three points back from Bristol City.

Hendrie was rested for the second leg of the Coca Cola Cuptie against Scarborough, which enabled Jaime Moreno to make his Boro debut, However it was fellow striker Paul Wilkinson who took the honours with the club's first hat-trick of the season in a 4-1 victory. Moreno still made a good impression, laying on two of the goals, including one for Craig Hignett.

Boro moved into their October programme with everything shipshape and going well. They opened with a home game against Millwall but were without Alan Moore, who failed a fitness test on a groin injury, so Clayton Blackmore returned to the fray.

The fans were also hoping that Bryan Robson might soon be back in action, but the manager was making very slow progress as he battled against his calf injury and was resigned to being out of action for another few weeks.

In the event Boro were doing well with the manager on the sidelines. They missed a chance to take a first half lead against Millwall when Craig Hignett had a penalty saved, but second half goals from John Hendrie, Paul Wilkinson and a Mark Beard own goal gave Boro a convincing 3-0 win.

The following week, Robson paved the way for a reduction in numbers when Tommy Wright was placed on the transfer list. The winger, signed by Lennie Lawrence for £650,000 two years earlier, had not started a league game all season and was struggling to win a place in the first team squad.

Ironically Wright was called up for the Anglo Italian Cuptie at home to Cesena as Robson made eight changes, but it was Jaime Moreno who grabbed the headlines by scoring his first Boro goal in a 1-1 draw.

The eight rested players were all back in action for Boro's home game against fellow promotion challengers Tranmere Rovers on October 8, and Robson was looking for three points.

Clayton Blackmore was switched to the centre of midfield to replace the injured Mustoe for Boro's trip to Luton Town, while transfer listed Tommy Wright was given his first league start of the season on the left flank.

It should have been a routine match for Boro, but it turned out to be nothing of the kind. Boro were absolutely turned over by 5-1. They were never in the game from the start and reached the interval three goals down.

Graham Kavanagh was brought on to strengthen the midfield at the interval, with the unfortunate Wright dropping out. However Boro hardly fared any better at the start of the second half and shipped another two goals before Derek Whyte fired home a consolation.

Robson told the Evening Gazette: "We played badly, but it was out of character with what has gone before this season. Luton were really fired up

ROBBIE MUSTOE has long been one of Boro's most consistent players. The midfield grafter is pictured in action in the 3-0 home win against Milwall.

Boro proceeded to produce their best attacking display of the season so far and pounded the Tranmere goal for long periods. But they could not score, and suffered a frustrating 1-0 defeat when John Aldridge headed a late winner for the visitors.

The disappointment was compounded when it was revealed that hard working midfielder Robbie Mustoe who picked up a thigh injury in the closing minutes, would be out of action for three weeks.

Robson immediately tried to plug the gap by offering to take Manchester City's former England international midfield player Steve McMahon on a month's loan, but City turned down the idea. McMahon later joined Swindon Town as player-manager.

from the start and it's important that we learn to deal with sides who really want to beat us because of where we are in the table."

It was important for Robson that he didn't allow his players to dwell on this defeat. He decided to opt for togetherness, and took most of the first team to Udinese for the Anglo Italian Cuptie. Paul Wilkinson was left behind because he was suspended, John Hendrie was playing in Gavin Oliver's testimonial match at Bradford City while Jamie Pollock was rested.

Any plans Robson held of giving the rest of the first team regulars a run-out at Udinese backfired when Derek Whyte, Clayton Blackmore and Craig Hignett all picked up minor injuries in training on the morning of the match.

WHEN Bryan Robson arrived at Ayresome Park, he said that he wanted to build a team of internationals. Graham Kavanagh was quick to get in on the act with a call-up for the Republic of Ireland Under-21s which played in Latvia.

In addition, Neil Cox suffered a hamstring injury in the first half of the match, and did not return for the second half. Despite all these setbacks, Boro managed to force a goalless draw.

Robson was still able to call upon most of his squad for Sunday's televised match at Portsmouth, and was demanding a much improved performance following the Luton debacle.

The manager still made changes, bringing in Jaime Moreno for his league debut, while Andy Todd made his seasonal bow in midfield and Alan Miller was back between the sticks in place of Steve Pears.

It was not a happy debut for Moreno who limped off with a thigh strain in the early stages. But Boro still looked a much more determined outfit than at Luton and should have comfortably beaten Pompey. In the end they had to settle for a goalless draw, but the performance was a boost for morale.

Robson said: "I was hoping that Luton was a one-off and I believe that I have been proved right. While I'm happy with the clean sheet, we had four or five great chances to score and this was two points lost rather than one gained."

Boro were now without a win in five games, despite having produced only one under-par display. And they faced a stiff task in their attempts to halt the run when they travelled to Premiership Aston Villa for a Coca Cola Cup third round tie on Wednesday, October 26.

Alan Moore was back in action in place of Moreno, while Andy Todd earned the right to stay in the side following his fine performance at Portsmouth when he marked dangerman Alan McLoughlin out of the game.

Unfortunately Boro did not play particularly well against Villa, even though it was a tight game. Villa eventually won it with a deflected goal, when a shot from Andy Townsend ballooned into the net off the outstretched boot of Derek Whyte.

The defeat left a few question marks against the side. In their past six games Boro had drawn three and lost three scoring only two goals in the process. It was a tricky period for the team and for the manager.

A Winter of Hard Graft

CHAPTER TWO:

BRYAN ROBSON was starting to come to terms with his new way of life by the end of October. The Boro boss was getting his feet under the table and making a fine impression as a manager.

His leadership qualities were never in doubt, particularly on the field. But Robbo had proved that he could handle people off pitch as well, not only with his involvement with the players but with the general public as well.

Bryan had quickly become a popular figure in Middlesbrough and throughout the whole of Teesside. He was a fine ambassador for the club and rarely turned down invitations to appear at public functions and fund raising events, when football commitments permitted.

It was all good publicity for the club, and the fans had responded to Robson's presence and improved performances on the field by raising the average attendance to around a healthy 19,000. Boro had

suddenly become high profile, and this was reflected by the large number of national newspapers who were continually ringing up Robbo and requesting interviews. With his England coaching commitments on top, Robson was a very busy man.

However Robson had lost none of his love for the game and was dedicated to the task of bringing football success back to Middlesbrough. He supervised most training sessions himself, and generally contributed towards maintaining a high level of confidence throughout both the playing and coaching staff.

Even so, by the end of October the team was in need of a pick-me-up. They had gone off the boil a little and had failed to record a win in any of their last six games, including two Anglo Italian Cup ties. The last four of these games had all been played away from home, which was a particular area where Boro were suffering hiccups.

If anything, they were lacking slightly in inspiration on the pitch. Robson himself was sidelined with a calf injury while influential captain Nigel Pearson was still recovering from a minor

NEIL COX races out of the net to celebrate after scoring Boro's first goal, and his first for the club, in a 3-1 home win against Swindon Town at the end of October.

knee operation. But there was still plenty of experience in the side, especially from players like Clayton Blackmore, Paul Wilkinson and John Hendrie.

Robson decided to keep faith with an unchanged side for the home game against Swindon Town on October 29. It was a crucial game, both to get Boro back on to a winning track, and also to keep up the pressure at the top of the First Division. Boro had led the table for the first month, but had since slipped and were now in third position.

Boro were given the start they needed when Neil Cox grabbed his first goal for the club. The £1 million defender had been a permanent fixture in Boro's First Division campaign and had proved himself a hard working player, keen to add to his defensive duties by regularly getting forward down the right flank to support the attack, and fully deserved to break his duck.

Unfortunately Boro were unable to build on Cox's early strike and gradually lost their way. They went through a particularly sticky spell when Norwegian international Jan Fjortoft, who was to join Boro before the end of the season, netted the equaliser. Then Fjortoft's striking partner Keith Scott had what looked a perfectly good second goal disallowed, for offside.

Boro were woken up by the shock of almost falling behind and finished the game very strongly. John Hendrie scored his eighth goal of the season to restore Boro's lead, and then Paul Wilkinson made certain of the points from the penalty spot.

Robson said: "I felt it was just a matter of time before the lads started winning again. We didn't have the run of the ball in October, and were unlucky not to beat both Tranmere and Portsmouth.

"But the lads stuck to the task, especially when Swindon put us under a bit of pressure. Now we need to build on the result and try to put an unbeaten run together."

Three days later Boro made it six points from six at Ayresome Park when second half goals from Alan Moore and substitute Craig Hignett produced a 2-1 win against Oldham Athletic. Boro had moved into second position behind Wolves following their win against Swindon, and this second victory consolidated their position.

However not everybody was happy following the win against the Latics. It was very much a sweet and sour night for Curtis Fleming, who was ruled out for five weeks through a combination of injury and suspension. Fleming picked up a knee injury and a booking which was enough to push him over 21 points and bring a three-match ban.

Naturally the suspension was of little consequence as Fleming battled to recover from the knee injury. His absence was a blow for the team because the Irish lad had settled in really well at left-back.

It was very much a new role for Fleming, specially as he was predominantly right footed. However he attacked the job with his usual whole-hearted commitment, and it was this 100 per cent contribution which made him a popular man in the stands.

Curtis was just as disappointed by the booking as he was by the injury. He said: "I knew that I had to be careful, but the ball was there to be won. I didn't think it was that bad a challenge. It's the inconsistency of the refs which is the most annoying. You just wish they would react the same way every time."

Fleming joined an injury list which included Chris Morris and Robbie Mustoe in addition to Robson and Pearson. Morris and Mustoe were both suffering from thigh injuries and had recently taken the unusual steps of visiting a decompression chamber at the Multiple Sclerosis Therapy Centre at South Bank to aid their rehabilitation.

A Winter Of Hard Graft

Goalkeeper Steve Pears also continued to have problems with his niggling calf injury. The injury flared up from time to time, and Pears had made two visits to a specialist to try to get to the root of the problem, without success. Pears had been on the bench against Swindon, but was still having problems and handed over the substitute goalkeeper's jersey to Ben Roberts for most of the rest of the promotion campaign.

Craig Hignett's fine second half performance against Oldham earned him a place in the starting line-up as Boro chased their third win in eight days at Grimsby Town. Hignett's arrival allowed Clayton Blackmore to switch to left-back in place of the injured Fleming and adopt one of the roles he had undertaken so well during his time at Manchester United.

In the event it was not a very enjoyable game for Blackmore or the rest of the Boro defence. In fact Boro found themselves 2-0 down after only 12 minutes when Neil Woods and Jim Dobbin netted during a torrid spell of early Mariners pressure.

Robson said: "We paid the penalty for being caught cold at the start of a match just as we were at Luton last month. We need to learn to be fired up from the start especially as sides are fired up against us. They want to beat us because we are at the top of the league."

There was a boost for Robson at the beginning of the following week when Nigel Pearson, Robbie Mustoe and Chris Morris all returned to full training after injury. Pearson, whose determined tackling and will-to-win was a big inspiration on the pitch, had been particularly missed by the rest of the team.

There was also good news that week for Jamie Pollock. The Boro midfielder, who had earlier been placed on stand-by for England Under-21s' match against the Republic of Ireland at Newcastle, was informed that he had been officially promoted to the squad.

Pollock had begun the season well for Boro and was an ever present in the First Division. He was another player who had benefited from the arrival

GOALKEEPER Alan Miller, who enjoyed an excellent season in helping Boro to win promotion, produced one of his best performances against Grimsby Town at Blundell Park in November.

Boro struggled all the way until the interval, but managed to avoid falling further behind largely due to the brilliance of goalkeeper Alan Miller. The former Arsenal keeper had regained his place and taken his chance with both hands, going on to make the No.1 jersey his own until the end of the season.

Bryan Robson's half time dressing down clearly paid dividends because Boro were a completely different side in the second half. But all they could do was halve the deficit, when Craig Hignett scored from the spot 17 minutes from time after Alan Moore had been brought down inside the penalty area. It was the first time that Miller had been on the losing side for Boro in a league game.

of Robson. Pollock had terrific engines and his ubiquitous running regularly took him to every corner of the pitch.

Despite the boosts in the dressing room, Boro's first team squad still faced a blank weekend. The match at Reading on November 12 had been postponed for some time because the home side had two players called up for international duty.

Central defender Adrian Williams had been called up by Wales, while Jimmy Quinn was also included in the Northern Ireland squad, despite the fact that he had missed Reading's previous few games through injury and was ruled out for at least another couple of weeks.

If Quinn was injured then he could not be included in the Irish squad. It meant that Reading had only one player officially on international duty and under those circumstances the league match against Boro at Elm Park should go ahead.

Boro were well aware of the circumstances and were angry that the league game was postponed. Their suspicions were justified when Quinn withdrew from the Irish squad because of injury, on the same day that the Reading-Boro match was due to take place.

Quinn's withdrawal led to Boro making an official protest to the Football Association. Assistant manager Viv Anderson told the Evening Gazette: "I wasn't the least bit surprised when Quinn pulled out because we believed him to be injured. We have made our feelings known by letter to the FA."

Jamie Pollock was afforded a bit of match practice the following Tuesday when he made his England Under-21 debut. Jamie was brought on as a second half substitute in the 1-0 victory against the Republic of Ireland at St James's Park. It was a proud

wanted the competition to continue. However, continue it would, though Boro were spared the dubious delights of playing in the Anglo Italian Cup the following season following their promotion to the Premiership.

The one bonus was that Boro were able to use the opportunity to give fringe players and youngsters some valuable experience. In fact seven of the players on duty in Ancona were aged 20 years or younger.

Boro also took the opportunity to give Robbie Mustoe and Chris Morris a run-out after both had recovered from thigh injuries. Morris had not yet established himself in the Boro first team, though Mustoe had taken over from Robson, when the player manager was injured in September, and had been missed when he got injured himself.

It was no surprise to see Ancona win 3-1, though Boro's young side could hardly have battled any harder, in fact they took the lead with a brave header from Morris after only ten minutes and held the advantage for 55 minutes before Ancona finally broke through for the first of their three goals.

GORDON McQUEEN was a valuable addition to the coaching staff at Boro. The former Scottish international, who was appointed reserve team coach, is pictured with some of his young charges. Left to right, Graham Kavanagh, Keith O'Halloran and Wesley Byrne.

night for Boro because Alan Moore and Graham Kavanagh also played for the Irish.

At the same time Boro had flown out a virtual reserve team to Italy for their final Anglo Italian Cuptie at Ancona. There was no way that Boro could qualify for the next stage of the competition, even if they won in Ancona, which was a relief for Bryan Robson because he did not need the distraction from this unpopular event.

The official attendance at Ancona was given as 1,500, hardly an indication that Italian supporters

Morris who banged his head in the back of the Ancona net after scoring his goal, was an outstanding Boro man of the match. Yet, as a result of the head blow, he couldn't remember anything about the match afterwards!

Fortunately Morris made a quick and full recovery, which was just as well because he was back in the first team on the Saturday. Morris was needed at left back because of Curtis Fleming's injury and suspension, while Robbie Mustoe was also drafted straight back into the line-up in place of Andy Todd.

A Winter Of Hard Graft

It was a good game to return in, because Boro were playing their top of the table showdown against First Division leaders Wolves. The match was shown live on TV and was Boro's biggest game of the season so far. Victory would take them back to top spot.

The two teams had been neck and neck at the top for most of the season so it was no surprise to see 19,953 fans packed into Ayresome Park. It was the biggest attendance at the stadium since the opening match against Burnley in August.

In the event, it turned out to be a cracking game as well though only if you were a Boro fan. Bryan Robson's men were in virtual control throughout and Wolves had a nightmare afternoon.

Even so Boro missed a handful of excellent scoring chances and eventually had to settle for a one-goal victory when Paul Wilkinson set up John Hendrie, whose shot was deflected past Wolves goalkeeper Mike Stowell off the outstretched boot of Geoff Thomas.

A measure of Boro's command was illustrated by their 21 shots against Wolves' four and their 16 corners against Wolves' two.

Robson admitted: "I was surprised that we dominated Wolves so much. I had expected an end to end match, but the !ads proved me wrong. It turned out to be our best performance of the season."

Boro were now two points clear at the top after 17 games played, though it was still very tight in the battle for the one automatic promotion spot. The chasing pack, led by Bolton and Tranmere, were only a further two points adrift of Wolves.

Ironically Boro's hold on the top position lasted only four days because Wolves beat Bolton 3-1 at Molineux in mid-week.

However, the see-sawing continued on the Saturday when Boro went to Charlton Athletic and won their first away game for more than two months by 2-0. The same afternoon, Wolves suffered a shock 2-0 home defeat at the hands of Derby County.

Another big bonus for Boro was that skipper Nigel Pearson bounced back after injury and had a happy return. Robson operated with three central defenders, with Pearson playing alongside Derek Whyte and Steve Vickers and the system worked a treat. Boro were very solid and won comfortably with a goal in each half from John Hendrie and Jamie Pollock.

The bad news was that Jamie Pollock picked up a booking which took him over 21 penalty points and brought a three-match ban. Assistant manager Viv Anderson remained philosophical, saying: "It's disappointing but we can cope. We've no complaints about the ban. Midfielders who make tackles are bound to pick up bookings."

The following week Boro added to their senior squad by making a new signing. They swooped for 21-year-old Chris Freestone who had scored 27 goals so far this season for Northern Counties East side Arnold Town. Boro paid £15,000 for Freestone, who was described as "one for the future" by Bryan Robson.

Having won three of their four league games in November, Robson called for his players to produce another series of consistent performances in December. The manager wanted to see his team battle to increase the daylight between themselves and their rivals to try to gain a commanding position by the turn of the year.

Boro could hardly have produced a better response by hammering Portsmouth by 4-0 at Ayresome Park on December 3. Craig Hignett and Paul Wilkinson grabbed a brace apiece.

Nigel Pearson was rested against Pompey to give him the chance to ease himself back in gradually. But the skipper was quickly back in action the following Tuesday for the rearranged game at Reading. The Berkshire club were handily placed in the leading pack and so it represented a tough game.

It became tougher before the interval when Robbie Mustoe was sent off for the first time in his career following two bookable offences, neither of which came from malicious fouls.

However the ten men stuck to their guns and had the chance to take the lead when awarded a penalty in 71 minutes when Keith McPherson impeded John Hendrie inside the penalty area. McPherson was shown the red card for his misdemeanour.

Paul Wilkinson duly rammed home the spot kick and afterwards Boro looked to be coasting towards the final whistle. Unfortunately a misplaced pass by John Hendrie in the closing minutes led to Reading mounting a last ditch attack, and they grabbed the equaliser.

Worse was to follow on the Saturday when Boro lost 2-1 at home to struggling Southend United. Boro went into the match with a few changes to their line-up with Andy Todd replacing the suspended Jamie Pollock, Alan Moore returning for the injured Craig Hignett and Neil Cox operating on a new role on the right flank.

At the same time, the changes were no excuse for such a poor all-round team performance. Boro never threatened to move out of first gear, and were struggling when Jason Hails and Phil Gridelet both scored for Southend from outside the area. In the event, the best that Boro could manage was a late consolation goal from John Hendrie.

To add insult to injury Bolivian striker Jaime Moreno picked up a pulled hamstring after coming on as substitute, and was ruled out of Boro's Christmas and New Year programme.

It was tough luck on the 21-year-old who was still finding his feet in English football. It was his second frustrating injury since joining Boro at the start of the season, and now Jaime had it all to do again to force himself back into the first team reckoning after the turn of the year.

Boro were down in the dumps the following week, with Bryan Robson stressing: "It was a poor performance and we didn't deserve anything out of the game, even if Southend's two goals were out of the blue. We know we can do a lot better, and we need to put things right in our next match at Burnley."

Boro needed a boost for their next match, which was being broadcast live on TV from Turf Moor on Sunday, December 18. They got it, in the form of Robson who was back in action for the first time since September. The player manager had been fighting a long battle to shake off a calf injury but was finally fit again.

CURTIS FLEMING was one of Boro's top men before being struck down by injury.

A Winter Of Hard Graft

Curtis Fleming was also back in action after recovering from a knee injury while Derek Whyte, who had missed the Southend match, resumed in the heart of the defence.

The Boro team had a much stronger look about it and so it proved. While Robson was the inspiration John Hendrie was the executioner, and the Scot grabbed a hat trick in Boro's 3-0 win. It turned out to be Boro's biggest away win of the season The team on duty that day was: Miller, Cox, Fleming, Vickers, Pearson, Whyte, Robson, Mustoe, Wilkinson, Hendrie, Moore. Subs: Kavanagh, Blackmore, Roberts.

In the build-up to Christmas Jamie Pollock was strongly linked by the tabloid press with interest from Blackburn Rovers. However Bryan Robson was quick to scotch the rumours of Pollock's alleged impending departure by stressing: "Jamie is going nowhere."

Boro were also reported to be keen on making a signing of their own and were connected with an interest in 22-year-old Norwegian World Cup striker Sigurd Rushfeldt, who was rated at £700,000 by his club Tromso. However Boro did not follow up their interest. In the meantime Boro were building up to their Christmas programme. Robbie Mustoe had an unwanted Christmas off, due to suspension, so Graham Kavanagh was called up for his first league start of the season to play alongside Robson in midfield for the difficult test away to Sheffield United on Boxing Day.

There was little Christmas cheer for Boro at Bramall Lane. It was a rough and tumble match, which threatened to turn ugly when the home fans were incensed by the dismissal of United defender Paul Beesley for a second bookable offence six minutes before the interval.

As often happens on these occasions, the ten men took the lead when Glyn Hodges scored in 68 minutes. Fortunately Boro were level five minutes later when substitute Craig Hignett, back from injury, volleyed home after Paul Wilkinson had headed down a cross from Neil Cox on the right.

Boro were four points clear at the top as they prepared for their next game against bottom club Notts County at Ayresome Park.

Bolton were now Boro's major rivals, having moved on to 40 points as a result of their 1-0 victory against Tranmere at Burnden Park. Tranmere were third on 39 points while Barnsley had 38, and Wolves, Sheffield United and Reading all 37. However Boro's match against County was effectively a game in hand, so it offered them a great opportunity to widen the gap at the top.

Midfield men Jamie Pollock and Robbie Mustoe were back for Boro after suspension while Bryan Robson rested Steve Vickers and reverted to a 4-4-2 formation, which created an opening for Craig Hignett to return on the flank. John Hendrie, who picked up a dead leg at Sheffield United, was passed fit to play after the injury had responded to an ice pack.

County, who had scored just once in their last six games, included £110,000 new signing Devon White from Queen's Park Rangers. White made a habit of playing particularly well against Boro.

However Robson was in no mood to accept any mistakes from his team, and demanded that his players pulled out all the stops to ensure that they continued to pull away at the top of the First Division.

He told the Gazette: "We have to keep striving to pull away. It's the best thing for us and it's the worst thing for all the other teams in the promotion race.

"We have the comfort of being able to afford a slip up and stay top, but that is not my way of thinking. We must widen the gap."

A crowd of 21,558, which was the second highest Ayresome Park crowd of the season so far, turned up on a wet and windy night and a lot of nail-biting went on in the stands, County shocked Boro by taking a 26th minute lead through Gary McSwegan, though goals from Craig Hignett and Nigel Pearson put Boro in front before the interval.

It was a nerve-racking second half, but Boro held on to their 2-1 advantage to move seven points clear at the top.

Unfortunately Boro paid a price for the victory because full-back Neil Cox suffered a fractured collarbone 15 minutes into the second half and was ruled out for two months.

Robson said: "It's a blow for Neil especially as he had been playing well. However we have got a strong squad here and we will cope."

The manager was not too pleased with the overall team performance, adding; "I didn't have to tell the lads that they hadn't done well, but at least they stuck at it and ground out a result.

"We have played a lot better than that and not got the result we deserved so these things tend to even themselves out."

While everybody was delighted with the result it was not a happy night for many fans, Hundreds were locked outside of Ayresome Park when the turnstiles were closed before the kick-off. The total closure of the turnstiles left not only ticket holders locked outside, but season ticket holders as well.

The fans with tickets who went to complain at the main entrance in Warwick Street were admitted but many others, after checking to make sure that all the turnstiles were locked, simply went home in disgust.

One fan, Joan Appleton from Middlesbrough, telephoned the Evening Gazette to say that she got into the ground and reached the top of the North-east corner steps but couldn't force her way on to the terracing because of fans' congestion.

She said: "A policeman told me that I wasn't allowed to stand at the top of the steps, and said that there would be room in the Holgate End, When I went out and walked towards the Holgate, fans coming the other way told me that it was locked, so I just went home. I was so annoyed, especially as I was split up from my family and they all watched the game."

Meanwhile, Boro's hard pressed players were preparing for their third game in six days, because they were due to take on Stoke City at the Victoria Ground on New Year's Eve.

Bryan Robson had been using the sweeper system to good effect away from home, having gone four consecutive games without defeat on their travels. However the manager produced a surprise by resting Derek Whyte and operating with a flat back four.

Robson did bring himself back as an extra midfield player to play in a deep role just in front of the back four, with Alan Moore dropping out. Steve

STEVE VICKERS, another Titan in the side, scored a valuable goal at Stoke City at the end of 1994 which helped to earn a valuable point away from home.

Vickers also returned to action, while Chris Morris stepped up for the injured Neil Cox.

The system seemed to be working when Vickers scored his first goal of the season when heading Boro in front after only ten minutes. But Nigel Gleghorn equalised ten minutes later and Boro spent most of the rest of the match under the cosh.

However Boro held on, thanks to some desperate defending, for a 1-1 draw. With Wolves winning 3-1 at Barnsley, Boro's lead at the top was cut to five points. But it was still a very healthy position to be in at the start of 1995.

There was no time to relax for Boro were soon back in action in a promotion six-pointer at home to Barnsley on January 2. The players were keyed up and so were the fans. A big crowd of 21,224, the third best of the season so far, turned up - but the day turned out to be a disaster for everybody concerned.

It had been a very cold weekend and it was obvious before the kick off that there was frost in the pitch, even though it had been rolled by the groundstaff and was very flat.

Even so Oldham referee Paul Harrison had clearly made a grave error of judgement when he inspected the pitch at 8.30am and declared it fit for play. With the announcement that the match was definitely on everybody made the effort to turn up including hundreds of fans from Barnsley. But they all had a totally wasted journey.

Immediately from the kick off, it was obvious that the pitch was unplayable. Both sets of players regularly fell on their backsides, while it was impossible to turn, difficult to tackle and dangerous to run. The Barnsley players clearly felt they were wearing the wrong footwear and it was quite comical to see then come off in rotation, one by one, to change from studs to trainers.

The switch seemed to work, because Brendan O'Connell equalised an early Boro goal from John Hendrie and the visitors were beginning to look the better side. However it was Boro who took an interval lead when Alan Moore, who was back in the side in place of Bryan Robson, was put through by Jamie Pollock and scored in the last minute of the half.

It also turned out to be the last minute of the game. Mr Harrison finally decided during the interval that it was too dangerous to continue and the match was abandoned, It was the first abandoned match at Ayresome Park for more than 20 years, when floodlight failure had brought a premature end to a First Division match against Leicester City with the Boro leading by 1-0 after 29 minutes.

Mr Harrison said: "Having arrived at 8.30am I satisfied myself that the conditions were acceptable. I checked them every hour and decided to commence the game.

"However it soon became apparent that the players were having difficulty in keeping their feet despite numerous changes of footwear. So, due to the deteriorating ground conditions and ever being mindful of player safety, I decided to abandon the game."

As quite often happens in these situations, nobody at first knew how to react. But there was the threat of a problem for the club when fans interpreted a Tannoy announcement to believe that they were going to receive all of their money back. Certainly most fans believed that they deserved their money back because all they had seen were 45 farcical minutes of play.

IT'S the New Year and Boro start their traditional slide. Viv Anderson and Bryan Robson discuss their plans to get the show back on the road, during a break from training.

However it was not until 40 minutes after the abandonment that Boro released their official statement, which made it clear that supporters would not receive their admission money back. Instead, the club statement revealed that fans who had retained their stubs could buy tickets for the rearranged match at a discount, which later turned out to be 50 per cent.

The whole incident created a lot of bad feeling, especially from those fans who had travelled a long distance. The Evening Gazette was inundated with letters from supporters who felt that they should be fully reimbursed.

However under Football League rules, Boro were under no obligation to repay a single penny, nor did they have to reduce admission costs for the replayed game if they did not wish. The hard facts were that both the club and the fans had been in the hands of the referee whose "match on" decision had created a headache for the club and a lot of wasted time and money for the fans.

As the furore continued during the week, the Boro first team were busy turning their attentions away from the First Division and looking ahead to the FA Cup.

Boro had been drawn away to Second Division Swansea City who had a good record at the Vetch Field. The tie brought back memories of the previous season when Lennie Lawrence's Boro had been knocked out of the Cup by Swansea's neighbours Cardiff who won at Ayresome following a draw in Wales. Little did anybody realise that history was about to repeat itself.

Boro arrived in Swansea to discover that a lot of heavy rain had fallen in South Wales over the past few days and was threatening to turn the playing surface into a quagmire.

Bryan Robson, well aware of the fact that Boro needed to try to avoid the humiliation of a Cup defeat at the hands of the Swans, reverted back to a five-man defence. It meant that Derek Whyte was brought into the back line with Alan Moore stepping down.

For a long time, Boro looked comfortable at the back but they still struggled to put their normal passing game together on the heavy pitch and paid the penalty when Swansea defender John Ford moved forward to shoot his side into the lead after 35 minutes.

Robson needed to provide the impetus for Boro to get back into the tie and so he brought off Whyte at the interval and introduced Moore in an orthodox 4-4-2 formation. The move paid dividends because Boro applied strong pressure in the second half and it was Moore who headed the equaliser to force a replay.

Robson was in the news the following week when he celebrated his 38th birthday. However, in answer to many questions Robbo stressed that he had no intention of hanging up his boots.

Robson admitted: "I try to forget about birthdays these days, but to be honest, age doesn't matter. It's all about what you can do. As long as I feel I am of benefit to the lads I will play on.

"If the standards I have set myself are slipping then it will be different. But I can still get about the park and do a job for the team."

Robson had been able to leave himself out because of the fine continued form of Jamie Pollock

and Robbie Mustoe. The manager added: "I'm picking the team on merit, and everybody in the team knows that if their performances slip they will be left out."

Robson was generally happy with the quality and commitment of his side, but it had been apparent for some time that he was on the look-out to pep up his attack. So Teesside was buzzing when Robson admitted reports that he had made an ambitious move for Spurs' unsettled England Under-21 striker Nick Barmby.

Barmby, whose transfer market value at that time was estimated at £2.5 million by the national media, was said to be unhappy in London and wanted to move nearer his home town of Hull.

Robson's approach was turned down by Spurs, who were keen to hang on to one of the country's most talented young players. But the Boro boss was to maintain his interest over the next few months, and was ultimately to be successful.

The Boro boss summed up the situation at the time by saying: "I have asked Gerry Francis about Barmby and he is not for sale. Obviously I'll continue to monitor the situation. Paul Wilkinson and John Hendrie have done ever so well for us but I've said all along that we need more cover up front in case of injuries."

However Robson did receive some good news on the striking front when Bolivian international Jaime Moreno returned to full training after recovering from his hamstring injury.

Boro were next in action on the Sunday when they visited struggling Swindon Town in a live TV game in the First Division. The Robins were without a win in their last 14 league outings despite having reached the semi-final of the Coca Cola Cup this week when beating Millwall by 3-1 at the County Ground.

There was a blow for Boro before the match when Wilkinson dropped out with a knee injury leaving the team lightweight up front. Robson decided to stick with his five-man defence, with Alan Moore coming back into the starting line-up in place of Wilkinson.

Despite their problems in attack, Boro made the best possible start when Craig Hignett fired them ahead in the 14th minute with his ninth goal of the season.

However Swindon were on level terms nine minutes later when Jan Fjortoft, destined to join Boro two months later, grabbed the equaliser.

Boro's task was made all the more difficult shortly before the interval when Curtis Fleming was dismissed after raising his hands to Swindon's Dutch midfielder Luc Nijholt. The incident earned Fleming a second yellow card, having been booked earlier, and so he was on his way to an early bath.

Once Kevin Horlock had headed Swindon in front in the 57th minute, there was no way back for Boro and they lost 2-1. The defeat cut their lead at the top of the First Division to just one point though they still had a game in hand over second placed Wolves.

Boro were back in action just 48 hours later when they entertained Swansea City in the FA Cup third round replay. Paul Wilkinson was fit to resume, so Robson reverted to a flat back four with Derek Whyte dropping out.

However, the match was a nightmare for Boro and their supporters as they were once again on the

BORO were struggling for victories early in the New Year and ground out a 1-1 draw at home to Grimsby Town in a mudbath. Here Clayton Blackmore sparks another Boro attack.

wrong end of another Cup upset. Boro failed to perform on the night and Swansea emulated their Welsh neighbours Cardiff by recording a 2-1 replay victory.

The Swans were deservedly two goals up after 57 minutes through Steve Torpey and David Penney, and the best that Boro could offer in reply was a late consolation goal from John Hendrie.

Bryan Robson offered no excuses afterwards. He told the Evening Gazette. "We didn't deserve to win it. Our crossing was poor, our passing was poor and our finishing was poor."

There was a glaring need for a new striker to provide competition up front and the latest player connected with Boro interest was Norwegian international Jan Fjortoft. The Swindon striker had netted 36 goals in the calendar year, including two against Boro this season.

One media report claimed that Boro had already lodged an official bid of £1.5million with Swindon, but assistant manager Viv Anderson denied the report and told the Gazette; "We have inquired about Fjortoft, but then we have inquired about a lot of players."

Boro had a quick opportunity to wipe away the memory of the Swansea defeat because they were due to entertain Grimsby Town in a First Division game on the Saturday. Robson moved to bring a bit more experience into his side by recalling Clayton Blackmore whose previous appearance had come at Grimsby on November 5. Blackmore took over from Alan Moore.

Unfortunately the weather did Boro no favours. Continuous heavy rain on the day of the match left the Ayresome Park pitch looking like a quagmire, with pools of water lying all over. It made it very difficult for the team to play their normal passing game.

That's how it proved, because Boro struggled all the way through. They didn't help themselves when Craig Hignett had a penalty saved by Grimsby goalkeeper Paul Crichton on the hour after John Hendrie had been brought down inside the area and were made to pay for that miss when Neil Woods fired the Mariners ahead eight minutes later.

However Boro continued to persevere and were rewarded when Robbie Mustoe grabbed the equaliser just four minutes from time. There was a price to pay for the hard earned point because Nigel Pearson limped off with a knee injury 18 minutes from time and was ruled out for the next two weeks.

At the end of the game came an unexpected but thoroughly welcome revelation over the Ayresome Park Tannoy system. Announcer Mark Page revealed that Boro had finally ended their search for a new striker.

Uwe Fuchs, a 6ft 2in centre forward from German club Kaiserslautern, was joining Boro on loan until the end of the season. While the fans were delighted with the news, they would have been crying tears of joy if they had realised the dramatic contribution which Fuchs would eventually make to the promotion campaign.

The German breezed into Ayresome Park on Monday, January 23 and made it clear from the start that his ambition was to play well enough to earn a permanent move to Teesside.

The 28-year-old, who had been recommended to Robson by his former England colleague Tony Woodcock, said: "I'm very excited about playing in England. It will be a new experience for me but I feel that I will fit into the English system. I want to help the club to win promotion to the Premier League and win a contract here."

Woodcock, who was coaching in Germany, said: "Uwe is regarded in Germany as a typical English centre forward so I don't think he'll have any problem adapting. He is good on the ball, he holds it up well, brings other players in and is always looking to have a crack at goal."

He added: "The great thing about Uwe is his attitude. He is a 100 per cent player."

Bryan Robson said: "I've been trying to find another striker for a long time but I've regularly been quoted between £3-4million for players from English clubs. It's ridiculous.

"So the obvious thing to do was to look abroad. I contacted Tony Woodcock and he recommended this lad. He looks very impressive on the video, so now we'll have a look at him and see what he can do for us."

The manager added: "I've still got money to spend but it's not burning a hole in my pocket. I know the type of players I am looking for and if the right one comes along at the right price then I'll try to buy him."

Boro received more good news during the week when goalkeeper Steve Pears revealed that he had finally found the answer to his niggling calf problem, which kept recurring and putting him on the sidelines.

A visit to the Bimal Clinic in London had done the trick. The specialists at the clinic had worked out the nature of the problem and stressed that it could be kept at bay by a series of special exercises and regular massages. The same clinic had been responsible for saving Tony Mowbray's career a couple of years earlier when he was hit by a pelvic problem.

Pears said: "The massaging has solved it already. It's a big weight off my mind because I was starting to think that we might never solve it. Now I'm looking forward to playing again in the knowledge that it is all behind me "

Boro had been hoping to play their outstanding match against Barnsley on Saturday, January 28, because both sides were out of the FA Cup. However, the weather intervened once again. Hard frosts made Ayresome Park unplayable and this time the match was postponed before it was allowed to start.

Heavy rain followed the frost over the next couple of days, and Boro were struggling to get in any decent match practice as they built up to the important six-pointer against promotion rivals Reading at Ayresome Park the following Saturday.

Bryan Robson organised a full scale practice match for his first team squad on the Tuesday at Hall Drive. There was a qualified referee and linesmen officiating. The main plan was to give Uwe Fuchs his first taste of competitive action and get to know the players around him. Unfortunately the ground was very heavy and it was virtually impossible for Boro to play their normal passing football.

The Boro boss said: "A few of the lads were in need of a game and this was one way of providing it. There were also a few things we needed to run through in match competition, in addition to the benefits of giving Uwe the chance to see how we play."

The Reading game that weekend was both an important and a special day. Boro stalwart George Hardwick, England's first post-War captain, celebrated his 75th birthday at Ayresome Park that day.

Hardwick was treated to a surprise party at the ground, and the major guest was Middlesbrough's favourite son Brian Clough. The party guests, who also included Mick Fenton and Wilf Mannion, were introduced to the fans before the kick off and Clough received an extra-special ovation when he went to salute the Holgate End faithful before the kick off.

Boro, desperately needing a win, went into the game without the injured Curtis Fleming, who had suffered an injury near his hip in training. Derek Whyte took over at left-back.

Unfortunately the party celebrations off the pitch were not repeated on it. Boro were completely out of sorts and lost 1-0 to a goal scored early in the

BACK at the Boro, and as happy as a lark. Brian Clough gives his backing to Boro before the home game against Reading when he returned for George Hardwick's 75th birthday party.

second half by Paul Holsgrove. Uwe Fuchs who had scored on his debut for the reserves in midweek, came on as substitute for the last 30 minutes but made little impact.

The defeat was a disaster and was Boro's sixth game without a win. It also knocked Boro off the top of the First Division. Bolton were the new leaders on 50 points while Tranmere were second on 49, pushing Boro into third place on goals scored. However Bryan Robson's men still had the bonus of a game in hand over both of the top two clubs.

By the middle of the week Boro were in a slightly stronger position when Bolton dropped two points when held to a 1-1 draw at struggling Notts County.

Even so, there was plenty of pessimism on Teesside because the players knew that they were not playing well. Robson admitted: "The time has come to turn things around. I want to see the players playing with a swagger again. They must pick things up and play with confidence.

"We need to get back to playing the way we did when we started the season. We had a lot of self belief and we went out determined to make it hard for the opposition. There's no reason why we can't go out and play with the same attitude."

He added: "Naturally we are not right because we wouldn't have gone six games without a win. But it's just a few small things we need ironing out.

"We have to remember that we are in a position where we can go to the top of the league if we win our games in hand. We have to want to do it."

Robson had some good news to announce during the week when top scorer John Hendrie signed a new contract. The 31-year-old Scot, who had scored 15 goals so far this season, was now contracted to the club until the summer of 1997. It was a good bit of business for Boro, because Hendrie had lost none of his zest or ability, and was a livewire up front who was clearly feared by opposing defenders. He also made things happen for his teammates.

The Boro boss said: "It was not a difficult bit of business, John wanted to stay and we certainly didn't want to lose him. He's enjoying another good campaign and he's a good character to have around the club."

Boro still needed a boost on the pitch, and failed to get it the following Saturday when their match at Oldham Athletic was postponed at the last minute because Boundary Park was flooded by continuous heavy rain. It was another setback to morale.

The players were now at their lowest point in the season, and Robson wasted no time in trying to lift spirits. He booked the team on the next flight to Malaga for a few days training under the Spanish sun in the holiday resort of Marbella.

Not everybody made the flight. John Hendrie stayed behind to have treatment for a knee ligament injury. He had a scan which showed scarring around the medial ligament. Curtis Fleming was having trouble with a twisted muscle at the top of his thigh and also stayed at home.

Jamie Pollock missed the trip to fulfil another Continental date. He flew out to Italy with the Endsleigh League Under-21 side for a clash against their Italian counterparts in Andria.

Unfortunately the setbacks continued even while Boro were in Spain. It was revealed that Bryan Robson had offered a Boro club record £2.3million for Dutch international winger Glenn Helder, but had been beaten to the punch by Arsenal.

Helder's club, Vitesse Arnhem, had accepted Boro's offer and the player was reported to be keen. But then Arsenal stepped in at the last moment to snatch Helder from under Boro's noses.

It was a huge setback for Robson, who desperately wanted to complete the signing to give his ailing side new impetus. And it was all the more galling because the Boro boss had believed that the deal was cut and dried before Arsenal's 11th hour intervention.

THE new boy in action. Uwe Fuchs comes off the bench to make his Boro debut against Reading at Ayresome Park. But the visitors had the last laugh by winning the six-point clash by 1-0.

HIP, HIP UWE

CHAPTER THREE:

BRYAN ROBSON was beginning to feel his first real spell of managerial pressure by the middle of February. Boro had not won for six games and the cynics were saying that the bubble had burst, just as it seemed to do at the same time of the year, every year.

Robbo's men had been knocked off the top of the First Division table and had slipped to third place, while the team had suffered a disastrous FA Cup defeat at the hands of Second Division Swansea City.

It was a similar situation to that which hardened fans at Ayresome Park had experienced many times in their supporting careers.

Robson himself had played in only the first game in the disappointing run of six, and was having occasional injury problems, while Curtis Fleming was now sidelined with a thigh problem. But the injury list was not a long one, and the Boro boss could not blame it on the loss of form.

The major problem, now, was that confidence in the dressing room was starting to suffer. The players knew that they had lost their way somewhat and, as always happens in these situations, needed a bit of extra help from elsewhere to get themselves back on the rails.

HEADS up! Nigel Pearson and Chris Morris leap high to win the ball in the air during the important home game against Charlton Athletic.

UWE Fuchs, who grabbed the all important winning goal on his full Boro debut against Charlton Athletic, battles for possession.

Such was the task facing Robson at this crucial stage of the season. The manager had to prove that he had both the motivational ability and tactical awareness to turn things around and get the team firmly back on the promotion trail.

Robson rightly retained plenty of confidence in his squad, because he knew that his players were as good as any others in the division. But the proof of the pudding was in winning games.

The team's major problem was up front, where the chances were not being put away. Robson had made no secret of the fact that he had been trying to sign an attacking player for some time, but so far he had failed to make a big transfer breakthrough.

Chairman Steve Gibson had made it clear that there was money to spend, but at the same time Robson stressed that it was not burning a hole in his pocket. He was keen to spend the money and improve his attack, but only if the right player came along. So far, he had failed to secure the men at the top of his list.

In fact it was his failure to make a permanent signing which had taken Robson into the loan market. He had been in touch with his former England colleague Tony Woodcock, who was now coaching in Germany, to tell him of his dilemma. It was a good move because Woodcock had come up trumps and told Robson that he believed he knew of the right man to shoot Boro into the Premiership.

The result was that Boro snapped up one Uwe Fuchs on loan until the end of the season from Kaiserslautern. Fuchs, who made an immediate impression with his formidable frame, had a good goalscoring record in Germany and was described as a typical English centre forward.

Even so, Fuchs was very much an unknown quantity because he had no previous experience of English conditions or the type of football played in this country. But Robson had scoured the domestic market without success and felt that foreign players offered the way ahead. Robson had already broken new ground by bringing the first Bolivian footballer to play in England in the form of Jaime Moreno, and was happy to bring in another overseas player.

So, it was to Fuchs that Robson looked for some attacking inspiration when he handed the German the No. 9 shirt for the crucial home game against Charlton Athletic on February 18.

The player who was left out to accommodate the new boy was Paul Wilkinson, who had been a permanent fixture in the side since completing a £500,000 move from Watford in 1991. Wilko had paid back every penny of the transfer fee and more, but he had not scored for two months, and paid the price.

It was a bodyblow to Wilkinson to find himself omitted because the striker had a lot of personal pride and a belief in his ability to do the job. Several other players had also been off form recently, but it was the need to score goals which had led Robson to make the change up front.

To make matters worse, Wilko's regular striking partner John Hendrie failed a late test on a knee injury, leaving Fuchs as the lone attacker in the line-up. However midfielder Jamie Pollock was pushed forward into a new role, operating just behind Fuchs and in a position where he could run at the Charlton defence.

There was another crucial change, because Robson brought himself back into the action. Boro always seemed to play better when the gaffer was in the side. A further change saw Clayton Blackmore return for Craig Hignett, who had gone down with glandular fever.

Such was the situation as Boro prepared for a game which they not only could not afford to lose, but needed to win. The thing they needed most of all was a goal to settle them down, and it came after only 16 minutes - courtesy of the golden boot of Fuchs.

Robson started the move by knocking the ball forward for Blackmore to hit a first time pass to the feet of Fuchs. The German knocked the ball to his left and instinctively struck home a low drive from ten yards which flew into the Charlton net.

Suddenly Boro looked like the side which had dominated the First Division before the New Year. With Robson encouraging and leading from midfield, Boro battled and scrapped to hold on to their advantgage and grabbed a First Division victory for the first time since beating struggling Notts County on December 28.

The win lifted a cloud from the dressing room and left Boro in a healthy position, just two points behind leaders Bolton Wanderers with two games in hand.

Robson told the Gazette: "It was important to beat Charlton because the lads were being constantly reminded that they had gone six games without a win. The main thing was that we were very solid and I was especially pleased with Uwe and Jamie.

"Uwe is working very hard to regain full match fitness. He holds the ball up very well and that's what we need. Jamie also worked very hard and covered a lot of ground."

Fuchs revealed: "There's a big difference between the game in Germany and the game in England. I had to do a lot more running. I was very tired after 50 minutes but I kept going. It was very important for me to score a goal and very important for the team to win the game."

There was another important reason for winning the game. Boro were due to visit their big rivals Wolves in a promotion showdown at Molineux the following Tuesday and needed to go to the Midlands on the back of a victory.

Both sides had been up at the top of the First Division since the start of the season and generally regarded each other as the main threat to their own title aspirations. They were also the bookies' favourites to finish in the coveted top spot.

When the teams first met at Ayresome Park in the November, Boro were clearly the best side on the day and had won 1-0 thanks to a goal from John Hendrie. But it was a different proposition going into the Wolves' lair in front of a packed house.

Wolves, who had their own high profile manager in former England supremo, Graham Taylor, were currently in fourth place in the First Division. They were two points behind Boro with the same number of games played, and therefore would leapfrog above Boro if they were to win at Molineux.

In the event, the night turned out to be one which Boro fans would remember for many years to come. Boro were the better side throughout and stunned the huge 27,611 crowd into relative silence by winning 2-0. From a psychological point of view, it was one of the results of the season, specially as Wolves suffered particularly badly afterwards and never really got back to the forefront of the promotion race again.

Even so, there was an element of good fortune about Boro's opening goal when Wolves goalkeeper Paul Jones allowed a long, looping header from Steve Vickers to escape from his grasp and drop into the net.

The goal virtually settled the issue, for Wolves were punchless in attack, but Boro made sure with

THIS is how you do it... Boro's goalkeeping coach Mike Kelly gives a lesson to Alan Miller, foreground, watched by Steve Pears, Darren Naisbitt and Ben Roberts.

a second goal nine minutes from time. Jones came racing out of his area to try to clear a through ball from Clayton Blackmore, but only succeeded in kicking it against the onrushing Uwe Fuchs, who sidestepped Andy Thompson before rolling the ball into an empty net.

It might have been an even bigger victory, but Chris Morris had a penalty saved by Jones in the closing minutes after Jamie Pollock had been brought down inside the area.

The victory thoroughly restored every bit of morale to the Boro dressing room and took them into second place in the table, one point behind new leaders Tranmere Rovers, who won 1-0 at Charlton Athletic on the same night. However Boro were still in the strongest position because they had two games in hand on Rovers.

Bryan Robson said: "The lads thoroughly deserved their win. We took the game to them in the first 25 minutes and kept it going. We defended as a team and we attacked as a team. The formation really tightened us up.

"Jamie Pollock did extremely well and Uwe showed a great attitude, especially as he was playing up front by himself. He battled all the way and deserved to grab a goal. His two goals in two games have been a big bonus for us."

Fuchs said: "I was happy with my performance but I want to set the standard a little bit higher. If I can work harder and have a bit of luck, then I will be happy.

"But the main thing is for the team to win. I want the team to get back to the top of the table. If I score a goal as well, fine."

There was a new air of self belief at Ayresome Park the following week, and the players could hardly wait to get back on to the pitch. Boro's next game was a TV match at Millwall on Sunday, February 26, and Bryan Robson had the luxury of being able to name an unchanged line-up.

Boro were desperate to win but, on a hard, bumpy pitch, it was difficult to put any decent attacks together and the match finished goalless. Boro's brave attempt to win all three points was summed up in the closing minutes when Robson threw himself at a ball he could not win and picked up a nasty gash above his left eye.

The player-boss left the field with blood streaming from the wound, which needed 12 stitches. The scar has remained with him and is still visible just above his eyebrow.

There was a further problem when Jamie Pollock limped off with a hamstring problem in the early stages, though it did give Neil Cox the opportunity to come off the bench and have his first taste of action since dislocating his shoulder in December.

The clean sheet at Millwall was Boro's third in a row, so it was fitting that goalkeeper Alan Miller should be named Wilkinson Sword protector of the month for the First Division during the week. Miller had adapted superbly to his first full season in league football, and was now firmly established as an important last line of defence.

Boro received more good news when Steve Pears, Neil Cox, Craig Hignett and Jaime Moreno all successfully came through a reserve game at Sheffield Wednesday after recovering from illness and injury. However the squad was reduced in size when Robson arranged for Andy Todd to go on loan

to Swindon Town until the end of the season. The young defender, who had also done well in a run of games in midfield earlier in the season, had not figured on the Boro first team scene since early December.

Robson might have been happy to take a back seat for a while as a result of the gash above his eye, but the injury to Pollock forced the player-boss to leave himself in the line-up for Boro's home game against Bristol City at the beginning of March. But Robson still needed to protect the injury, and played the match wearing a bright red headband.

Jaime Moreno was called up in place of Pollock, while Robson was forced to make a second change because Chris Morris picked up a thigh strain in training. Morris' injury gave Cox the opportunity to resume at right-back.

Boro were really flying at this stage of the season and the changes made not the slightest of difference to their performance. Robson's men controlled the game throughout and won 3-0 thanks to a memorable hat trick from Uwe Fuchs.

The industrious German needed only ten minutes to fire Boro in front, and he completed his hat trick with two further pieces of lethal finishing in the 48th and 65th minutes.

Fuchs said: "I was really pleased to score a hat trick in my fourth game but I was more pleased for the team. We played really well and with a lot of spirit."

The match was not without a scare for Boro. Influential defender Steve Vickers picked up a shin injury and was taken to hospital for an X-ray. Fortunately there was no damage other than bruising, and Vickers was given the green light to play in Boro's second home game in four days against Watford on the Tuesday.

Boro went into the game three points behind Tranmere, who continued to set a tough pace at the top following a 1-0 win at Sunderland. With Jamie Pollock fully fit again following his hamstring injury, Robson took the opportunity to rest himself.

It was a very cold night, and Boro struggled for a time to find top gear against the Hornets. However their spirits were lifted by a stunning goal from Robbie Mustoe, who ran with the ball from his own half before blasting a 25 yards shot into the top right hand corner of the net. It was a remarkable goal which would have graced any pitch anywhere in the world.

That man Uwe Fuchs also got in the act again and added the clinching goal in the second half. Even so, Boro had to rely on a couple of crucial late saves from Alan Miller before they could be absolutely sure that the three points were in the bag.

With Tranmere losing 2-0 at Sheffield United on the same night, Boro were now level on points with the leaders, but still in second place on goals scored.

Boro were clearly now the form team in the First Division and, with Fuchs in such superb goalscoring form, were a threat to anybody they came up against.

The big German had quickly become a huge favourite with the fans because of his uncanny ability to put the ball in the net with the minimum of fuss. Fuchs had also responded to the fans' support, and a strong rapport was already built up.

HIP, HIP UWE

It was only natural that the fans wanted to see Uwe's loan spell at Ayresome Park turned into a permanent move with the offer of a contract. However Robson insisted that Boro would honour the loan agreement until the end of the season before reassessing.

It had not been publicly revealed, but Boro had already paid a six-figure sum to Kaiserslautern as part of the loan deal, and this would be taken off the transfer fee of £500,000 should Boro decide to sign Fuchs permanently. Clearly there was no need to rush through any decision. One thing Robson did need to know was which division Boro would be playing in next season before sitting down and finalising his team plans.

However there was one new contract signed at Ayresome Park that week. Curtis Fleming, who was still struggling to shake off his niggling thigh injury, signed a two-year deal which committed him to the Boro until the summer of 1997.

Finnish striker Mixu Paatelainen.

The nearest Boro came to salvaging a point was when Robson hit a post in the first half. Unfortunately Robson missed the whole of the second half because of calf trouble, while Boro's problems increased when Clayton Blackmore picked up a groin strain.

Another two points went begging the following Tuesday, when Boro finally played their twice postponed match at home to Barnsley and were held to a 1-1 draw. Jaime Moreno, back in the side for John Hendrie, scored his first league goal of the season but Boro old boy Andy Payton headed Barnsley's second half equaliser.

Worse was to follow at the end of the week for Boro crashed 4-2 at home to Derby County. With Derek Whyte failing a late fitness test, Robson reshuffled his defence and handed a league debut at right-back to Irish teenager Keith O'Halloran.

STRIKING out for the Boro. Bryan Robson unveils his transfer deadline day signing Jan Fjortoft, who was snapped up for a club record £1.3 million from Swindon Town

Boro, with five clean sheets in a row under their belts in a run which had included four wins and a draw, were once again preparing for one of the season's crunch games, at Bolton Wanderers.

Bryan Robson recalled himself to the action to add steel to the Boro midfield, taking over from Jaime Moreno, while Boro also had top scorer John Hendrie back in their starting line-up. The Scot, who had missed the last five games with a knee injury, returned in place of Alan Moore.

It was a big game for both promotion chasing sides, but it was not a happy afternoon for the Boro. They lost 1-0 to a 14th minute goal from the

However O'Halloran was often left exposed by his teammates and Derby took advantage by running rampage down Boro's right flank in the first half. At half-time the Rams were 3-0 up and Boro were struggling to gather their senses.

Robson had to put the accent on attack if Boro were to have any chance of getting back into the game, so Moreno came on for O'Halloran at the interval and Boro played throughout the second half with only three men at the back.

It paid early dividends when goals from Uwe Fuchs and Jamie Pollock brought Boro right back into the game. But then Marco Gabbiadini broke away to score a remarkable solo goal for Derby, and Boro's brave resistance died. Bolton's 1-0 win at Millwall the following day pushed Boro down to third place in the table.

Bryan Robson told the Gazette: "I would like to think that the game was a one-off at Ayresome Park. We had a similar experience at Luton, but this is the first time it has happend at home.

"To be honest, I've never known the wind have such an effect on a game. We were pinned back in the first half and Derby could hardly get out of their own half in the second."

Suddenly, after reviving the season with their five match unbeaten run, Boro found themselves looking for new inspiration after failing to win any of the last three. However the games were coming thick and fast and Boro had no time to dwell on their situation before preparing for a derby battle against Sunderland at Roker Park.

Sunderland were struggling at the wrong end of the table and so it was a match that Boro were well capable of winning, despite the old adage that derbies are great levellers.

Boro had Derek Whyte back in action and looked strong and solid from the start. In fact they rarely looked likely to concede a goal in a game which was scrappy all-round. Boro finally broke through for the goal which brought a 1-0 victory when Jamie Pollock forced the ball home from close range after being put through by Robbie Mustoe.

The match was not without disappointment, because Mustoe received a fractured cheekbone which signalled the end of his contribution to Boro's promotion campaign.

The midfielder was caught by Sunderland defender Richard Ord's elbow as early as the third minute, but played on throughout the match despite the pain. His loss was a big blow, and Boro could certainly have done with his steadying influence in midfield in the promotion run-in.

The three points at Sunderland were still crucial to Boro and assistant manager Viv Anderson said: "We had a couple of bad results at home, so we had to bounce back in an away game. Everybody played well, though I thought the back four and manager Bryan Robson were outstanding.

"We got the goal at the right time and although it was scrappy, with Jamie stumbling a little before scoring, he claims he was always in full control!"

It was transfer deadline week, and within 24 hours of the victory at Sunderland, Bryan Robson had added to his numbers by forking out a club record £1.3 million. The new man was Swindon Town's Norwegian international striker Jan Aage Fjortoft, who had scored 25 goals for the Wiltshire club that season.

Boro clearly needed more options up front and Robson had been working towards that end for several months. Fjortoft had the right pedigree because he was by far the most prolific goalscorer in the First Division and was also an experienced international.

With Fjortoft joining Uwe Fuchs, John Hendrie, Paul Wilkinson, Jaime Moreno and Craig Hignett, Robson now had real competition for places up front in the promotion run-in.

Fjortoft said: "I'm glad to be at Ayresome Park. There is a lot of excitement up here and a lot of potential. And of course Bryan Robson is a great attraction. He is a living legend."

The living legend moved again the following day - which was transfer deadline day - to pull off his second signing. This time he added to his defensive strength by paying Ipswich Town £300,000 for 22-year-old central defender Phil Whelan.

However, there was a big hitch. Although Boro did their best to rush through the necessary documentation, the Football League insisted that the full and correct papers did not arrive until after the official deadline of 5pm. They had been faxed ten minutes late, even though Boro had informed the league some time beforehand that the papers were on their way.

Boro worked hard to argue their case, but the League would not budge. Whelan was a Boro player, because they had completed all the transfer signing formalities, but it meant that the 6ft 4in player was ineligible to play in any of Boro's remaining games because he had been officially signed after the transfer deadline.

It was a blow for Boro, because they had good reason to believe that they were going to need an extra man at the back over the next few weeks. But it was a bigger blow for the player, who found that he had left Ipswich's struggle to stay in the Premiership for Pontins League football with Boro reserves.

Boro also successfully completed an outgoing transfer on deadline day when goalkeeper Andy Collett moved to Bristol Rovers for £50,000. The home grown player was third in line behind Alan Miller and Steve Pears, and so a move was sensible if he was to realise any ambitions of playing regular league football.

Portsmouth were also reported to be very keen to sign Boro striker Paul Wilkinson before the deadline. However, despite plenty of media reports to the contrary, the move did not materialise.

Fjortoft was unable to make his Boro debut at home to Port Vale the following Sunday because he was on international squad duty for Norway's match against Luxembourg. However Boro made one change with Clayton Blackmore returning after injury for Robbie Mustoe.

Boro followed up their win at Sunderland with a comfortable 3-0 victory in the televised game. The match was most notable for Bryan Robson's first goal for the club, which came when he picked up a square pass from Derek Whyte before striking a strong low drive into the corner of the net. The goal was naturally greeted with more than the usual gusto by the home fans.

Steve Vickers added a second goal four minutes later and Uwe Fuchs, whose place seemed to be in jeopardy following the arrival of Fjortoft, grabbed his eighth goal in ten games.

Robson revealed afterwards that a new pair of size seven New Balance boots were responsible for his goal-den touch. He said: "My old boots split at Sunderland, so I had to put on a new pair.

"As soon as I put them on I felt as if it might be my day. Obviously I'm delighted to score my first goal for the club, but the three points were more pleasing."

Not everybody was delighted with Robson's goal. Ladbrokes had been offering 14-1 against the Boro boss scoring the first goal against Port Vale and had lots of takers at their betting kiosks within the stadium. In fact Ladbrokes made an estimated loss

IT'S another one for Uwe. The German striker turns in the net after scoring Boro's third goal at home to Port Vale.

of around £13,000 on the afternoon. Several lucky punters had paired Robbo's first goal with the final score of 3-0, which was a very lucrative double bet paying odds of 100-1.

Boro's win had taken them on to 69 points and enabled them to go four points clear at the top of the league. However second placed Bolton, on 65 points, had a game in hand and fourth placed Wolves, with 63 points, had two games in hand. The promotion battle was very clear. It was going to go all the way down to the wire.

Bryan Robson's men had eight games left to play, only three of which were at home. And three of the last four, against Sheffield United, Barnsley and Tranmere, were against sides who held promotion or play off aspirations of their own.

The season was now moving towards April, and Boro welcomed Jan Fjortoft for his debut at West Bromwich Albion on April 1. However the Norwegian was not the only player called up for his senior debut for the club.

Assistant manager Viv Anderson, 38 years young and a few months older than Bryan Robson, was pushed into competitive action for the 593rd game of his remarkable career which stretched over 21 seasons.

Anderson was needed in an emergency to deputise in the heart of the defence for suspended skipper Nigel Pearson, whose place would naturally have gone to Phil Whelan if Boro had completed his transfer from Ipswich in time.

Fjortoft was drafted in alongside Uwe Fuchs, which meant that top scorer John Hendrie was the man who had to drop down to the bench.

In the event, Anderson had a terrific game and was one of the candidates for man of the match. But he was just upstaged by Irish attacker Alan Moore, who won the game virtually single handedly in a remarkable ten minute spell in the second half.

Boro trailed 1-0 at half-time and Robson, looking for a fresh bit of inspiration, informed Moore early in the second half that he was about to be substituted.

Moore's response to Robson was both immediate and out of the text book. He raced through several attempted tackles to set up a dramatic equaliser for Jamie Pollock, flashed over a low cross which was turned into his own net by West Brom defender Paul Raven, and then put Boro 3-1 up with a terrific solo goal. The game was transformed by the 67th minute and Boro found themselves cruising to victory.

Robson told the Gazette: "I know that young lads' form goes up and down. They are not as consistent as experienced players. Alan didn't play well in the first half, but we know what he is capable of and I was absolutely delighted with his response in the second half.

"We had a laugh about it on the pitch. When Alan scored his goal, he gave me a wry grin. I was happy with that as well."

It was all about games at this stage of the season, and Boro had toned down their training programme to keep everybody as fresh as possible as the battles came thick and fast.

Skipper Pearson was quickly back in action for Boro's second away game in four days at Oldham Athletic. The hard working central defender returned in place of Anderson, who could hardly have done a better job on his Boro debut.

However it wasn't a great night for Pearson, or for the Boro. They suffered a blow after 32 minutes at Boundary Park when Bryan Robson limped off with a new calf injury, yet still looked to be heading for a goalless draw until it all went horribly wrong in the last few minutes.

Pearson suffered a bout of concussion after being caught by the elbow of Andy Ritchie a few minutes from the end, and was wandering around the pitch in a dazed state when Ritchie popped up with the winning goal for Oldham in the very last minute.

Despite the defeat, Boro were still four points clear at the top. However they now had to rely on their opponents dropping points. The placings were: Boro pl 40, pts 72; Tranmere pl 39, pts 68; Bolton pl 38, pts 68; Wolves pl 38, pts 67.

The following day, Robson revealed that his new calf injury would rule him out of the action for at least two weeks. It immediately led to speculative stories in the national newspapers that the Boro boss had kicked his last competitive ball.

However Robson told the Gazette: "It's all rubbish. I have certainly not called it a day and I've no intentions of hanging up my boots. This is a new injury on my left leg and not the calf strain that affected me before. It will clear up and I will be back."

There was a change to the club staff before the next game, which was at home to Stoke City on Saturday, April 8. Mark Nile left the club and was replaced as senior physiotherapist by Bob Ward, who was previously physio at Chelsea. Ward was also a teammate of Robson's when they were young players with West Bromwich Albion.

While one of Ward's first jobs was to get to grips with Robson's calf problem, there was another blow for Boro when Uwe Fuchs was ruled out of the match against Stoke with a hip injury. Their places went to Graham Kavanagh and John Hendrie, while Craig Hignett also returned to the side in place of Clayton Blackmore.

It was a crucial game for Boro because they needed to go all out for maximum points from their three remaining home matches. In the event they were given a flying start when Nigel Pearson scored from close range after only 13 minutes.

However Boro never looked completely happy, and paid the penalty for some promotion nerves when conceding an equaliser to Paul Peschisolido on the half hour. The game then moved into the second half with Boro struggling to create chances.

Fortunately they were saved by another remarkable solo goal from Alan Moore, who had won the game at West Brom the previous weekend. The Irish lad ran at the Stoke defence, played a one-two with Jan Fjortoft, who was making his home debut, and then slipped the ball home from the edge of the six yard box.

It was a golden goal, which was greeted with much relief by Moore's colleagues, and left Boro still four points clear as they prepared for the Easter programme.

The day after the win against Stoke, there was a shot in the arm for the Boro squad when their playing talents were recognised by their colleagues in the Professional Footballers Association. No less than four Boro men -Neil Cox, Jamie Pollock, John Hendrie and Jan Fjortoft - were named in the PFA First Division team, which is selected by the players themselves.

During the week there was a slice of good fortune for the squad when major rivals Bolton Wanderers were held to a goalless draw at home to Luton Town. Boro's lead at the top was cut to three points as a result, but now Bruce Rioch's men had only one game in hand.

Within three days, Bolton were in further trouble when they lost their six-pointer at Tranmere on Good Friday. Boro were now one point ahead of Tranmere with the same number of games played. It was tighter than ever, but Boro were still on top.

Boro were away to bottom of the table Notts County on Easter Saturday and really needed to make their extra ability count by taking all three points. Uwe Fuchs was fit again, and everybody expected the big German to be restored to the

ANOTHER bit of magic from Alan Moore as the tricky Irish forward bursts through the Stoke City defence to score the crucial winning goal at Ayresome Park.

JAN Fjortoft was in Boro action for the fourth time at Notts County, but could not break through on this occasion.

HOW about that then? Uwe Fuchs salutes his adoring fans after grabbing the equaliser at Notts County.

BORO had to work hard to grind out a share of the spoils at struggling Notts County. Neil Cox is pictured in the thick of the action.

starting line-up at Meadow Lane. In fact Bolivian striker Jaime Moreno was preferred, in place of the injured Alan Moore, and Fuchs had to settle for a place on the bench.

Around 5,000 fans travelled from Teesside to watch the game, and were in good cheer before the kick off. However they were given very little to cheer during most of the proceedings, especially when lacklustre Boro fell behind to a goal from Devon White after 73 minutes. The much travelled White always caused huge problems for Boro and it was cynically predictable that he would score.

Bryan Robson desperately needed something to spark the Boro attack, and Fuchs was pitched into the action even before White scored. In the event the German popped up with a remarkable equaliser just as the game seemed to have slipped away from Boro with only six minutes left on the clock.

Neil Cox sent over a deep cross from the far post and it dropped perfectly for Fuchs to scoop it back across goal and into the top right hand corner of the net for his ninth Boro goal.

The goal was greeted by huge scenes of delight and celebration by the Boro fans, several of whom invaded the pitch to mob Uwe. It was yet another priceless goal from Fuchs, who was idolised by the supporters.

Robson told the Gazette: "Uwe's goal was crucial to us, but even so the lads were disappointed only to get a point at Notts County because they desperately wanted to win it. However, in the end, it was a valuable away point, especially as we came home from Nottingham still top of the table."

Boro were in action again within 48 hours when entertaining Sheffield United at Ayresome Park on Easter Monday, and the match attracted a huge crowd of 23,225.

Not surprisingly Fuchs was restored to the starting line-up, though it did not turn out to be a memorable afternoon for Uwe because he ended up being sent off seven minutes from time. It wasn't a great result for the Boro, either, because they were held 1-1.

Boro had been given the perfect start when a clinical finish gave Jan Fjortoft his first goal for the club. But Nathan Blake equalised 11 minutes later and that was the end of the scoring.

However it was not the end of the action. It was an ill-tempered and scrappy match, which was littered with fouls and disputed decisions. The whole thing boiled over in the closing minutes when Fuchs was sent off for taking a wild kick at United full-back Kevin Gage.

A few minutes earlier Fuchs had taken a kick on the knee from United's Glyn Hodges, which Scarborough referee Bill Burns had deemed accidental. It was one of many heated incidents which were largely ignored by the referee, and the resulting lack of control created a lot of bad feeling from both sides both during and after the game.

In fact Bryan Robson risked an FA rap afterwards when he claimed: "The referee did not want us to win the game."

United boss Dave Bassett joined in the war of words by calling Jan Fjortoft and Uwe Fuchs cheats.

Fuchs had no arguments about his red card, but insisted: "My tackle wasn't correct. But I was amazed three minutes earlier when I had a big kick on the knee. That was a real red card."

Despite dropping two home points, Boro were still two points clear at the top of the First Division with only three games left to play. Their chances of holding on to the automatic promotion spot were boosted by the fact that all their main challengers were also starting to feel the pressure, and were struggling to win. The points situation at the end of the Easter programme was: Boro pl 43, pts 77; Bolton pl 42, pts 75; Tranmere pl 42, pts 74; Wolves pl 42, pts 72.

There was a blow for Boro after the Sheffield United match when Nigel Pearson was ordered to rest by a specialist, and was ruled out of Saturday's trip to Barnsley.

Pearson had suffered a further bout of concussion against United, when heading the ball, and was sent to hospital for a scan. Twelve days earlier he had been concussed in a match at Oldham. Fortunately the scan showed that there was no serious problem, but a short period of rest was advised.

At the same time, Pearson's absence left Boro with several selection problems, particularly in defence. They had a dearth of central defenders and were also without the suspended Derek Whyte, who had been the team's most consistent player at left-back over the past couple of months.

The only answer was to give Viv Anderson another taste of league action, ironically at the club which he used to manage. However, it was never going to be a gamble because Anderson had already proved that he could still do a very good job at this level, and he went on to enjoy another good game.

Boro had sold their whole allocation of 4,300 tickets, and the vast majority of fans were seated in the open end at Oakwell. It wasn't the best place to be that afternoon because the heavens opened and there was torrential rain all afternoon. Barnsley were selling plastic macs at £1 each, but these quickly sold out and most of the Boro fans ended up thoroughly soaked to the skin.

Jan Fjortoft gave the saturated fans something to shout about with a glorious goal shortly before the interval. But Barnsley equalised early in the second half and Boro had to settle for their third 1-1 draw in a row.

The point was still enough to enable Boro to continue to hang on to top spot in the First Division. With only two weekends left in the season, it was still anybody's title. The crunch was coming.

WORKING for fitness, that's Boro defender Curtis Fleming as he battles to shake off a troublesome hip injury,

Promotion and Speculation

CHAPTER FOUR

BRYAN ROBSON had cut his managerial teeth, but was now facing the ultimate challenge. He had two games left in which to keep Boro in the First Division's sole automatic promotion spot, and thus guarantee a place in the Premiership.

It was by no means a foregone conclusion, because Boro did not hold their future in their own hands. Bolton Wanderers, managed by former Boro boss Bruce Rioch, still held the whip hand if they could win their game in hand.

In addition, Boro's remaining programme included a particularly tough match. After concluding their Ayresome Park fixtures by entertaining Luton Town, Boro faced a daunting trip to fellow promotion chasers Tranmere Rovers on the final day of the season.

So, Robson still had it all to do despite having guided Boro to top spot. He had done well so far, having had cash to spend but having used it wisely. Players like Nigel Pearson and Neil Cox had been brought in, not just with promotion in mind, but also to try to make an impact in the Premiership should Boro get there.

When Robson had needed some inspiration in the second half of the season he had found it with Uwe Fuchs, the on-loan German striker whose nine goals had enabled Boro to stay in top spot. And Robson had continued to strengthen his attack by paying a club record transfer fee of £1.3 million to bring in Norwegian international Jan Fjortoft from Swindon Town.

His success in building a side capable of winning promotion was also matched by his motivation qualities. Robson was highly respected by the players and they had gone out and done the business on the pitch.

Not all of Robson's tactical decisions had produced dividends, but then the manager had shown that he was not at all frightened to experiment with systems and formations from match to match. One or two individual selections had also not worked out, but for the most part Robson had got it right and made good use of a committed and workmanlike squad.

Ironically the team had always looked most comfortable when Robson was on the pitch alongside them, but groin and calf injuries had played havoc with his season and for the most part the players had done the business themselves.

Robson's arrival on Teesside had created a huge wave of expectation, and the squad had done well to cope with it. However the pressure was increasing all the time as the season moved towards its climax, and the players were finding that they had to dig deeper than ever to grind out results.

The outcome was that Boro had put together a succession of draws in the promotion run-in and, while they had lost just once since the middle of March, they had been fortunate that their major rivals seemed to be struggling badly to cope with the pressure.

Certainly Boro could count on a lot of character in the dressing room, and high spirits, and it was these qualities which were shining through at such a crucial time.

Even so, the pressure could not have been higher as Boro approached their big game against Luton, which was being played on Sunday, April 30. The players were well aware of the fact that they would probably end up in the promotion play-offs if they were to lose the game. And the pressure was doubled by the fact that this was the last competitive game at Ayresome Park, and therefore was being treated as a special occasion and a showpiece match by the club.

In this respect the players knew that they were expected to rise to the occasion, play their part in the lavish celebrations by making it a match to remember, and still make sure of the three points. Fortunately this was allied to a great determination from within the dressing room to win the promotion battle, not to mention the minor fact of avenging their 5-1 drubbing at Luton earlier in the season.

Naturally every supporter who had ever seen the Boro play wanted to be at Ayresome Park for the final game. Many supporters had taken advantage of the club's special offer midway through the season by buying season tickets, mainly with a view to making sure of their seats for the final match at the much revered stadium.

When the match tickets had gone on sale to the general public, they were snapped up very quickly, and without many of the problems which had plagued the club before all-ticket matches in the past. These problems were to return later in the week, but for the time being, everybody was reasonably happy with the arrangements - especially those fans who managed to get tickets.

Some of the fans who missed out initially got lucky, when Luton returned 1,400 of their 2,200 allocation of tickets. These went on sale at the Ayresome Park ticket office on the Wednesday and were snapped up very quickly.

The match was naturally being hyped up by the media, but Bryan Robson worked hard to make sure that the players were kept away from the razzamatazz and enjoyed a quiet build up. However

PAINTING the way for Boro to beat Luton. These young fans are thoroughly behind Bryan Robson's lads.

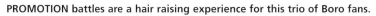

PROMOTION battles are a hair raising experience for this trio of Boro fans.

it was a hectic time for three members of the squad. Alan Moore and Graham Kavanagh had a tough work out for the Republic of Ireland Under-21s in a 1-1 draw against Portugal in Dublin, while Jan Fjortoft played in Norway's European Championship qualifier against Luxembourg.

The Evening Gazette continued with its build up to the big occasion, and told of lifelong Boro fan Joseph Boyle of Fulbeck Road, Netherfields, who had marked the closure of the stadium in a unique way. He had named his nine weeks old son Matthew Luke Ayresome Park Boyle. Proud dad Joseph said "I'm trying to keep the name alive."

Many fans were already looking beyond the last home match against Luton and wanted to make sure of their place at the final game of the season at Tranmere on May 7, especially as it could yet be the game to decide Boro's future.

However tempers flared when the 3,200 tickets for Prenton Park went on sale at Ayresome Park. The tickets sold out in just two and a half hours, but many of the club's 9,500 season ticket holders queued for hours without success.

Afterwards, the Evening Gazette was inundated with telephone calls from angry supporters. They were upset because they claimed they had seen many fans leaving the ticket office with handfuls of tickets, and some 'fans' were opening toutly the tickets to people in the queue who were clearly going to miss out.

Boro sold tickets only to supporters who had the relevant season ticket vouchers, and revealed that one fan had produced 25 vouchers to buy the same number of tickets. A spokesman defended the club's policy by saying: "We wanted season ticket holders at work or school to still have the opportunity to get tickets. When demand exceeds supply you are always going to have some disappointed people."

There was a special boost for Boro just before the game when Middlesbrough-born goalscoring legend Brian Clough telephoned the Evening Gazette to say, "I'll be rooting for the players. I'd love to see them back in the Premier League next season."

Clough revealed that he had turned down an official invitation from the club to join the 100 former Boro players who were due to be entertained at Ayresome Park and then introduced to the fans before the kick off.

He said: "They don't need me there. This a very important game for the players and they have enough to think about without me getting in the way. I just want them to concentrate on the game and win it."

On the day before the match, Bryan Robson stressed that there would be no problems with concentration, or commitment. He said: "My players will be fired up. They will go out there and do themselves justice. They know what's at stake. It's a big game that we need to win."

The manager announced that he had recovered from his calf injury and was ready to pitch himself back into the action. Skipper Nigel Pearson and Derek Whyte were also returning for the crucial game. Pearson had been resting after a bout of concussion, while Whyte had served a one-match suspension.

The players were keen to see the carnival atmosphere was not allowed to interfere with their pre-match preparations. Top scorer John Hendrie told the Gazette: "It's important that the players are kept apart from all the razzamatazz.

"We've spent the whole season having a low key build up towards games. It's helped us with our

BACK at the Boro! That's former Great Britain captain George Hardwick and another of the club's popular skippers Tony Mowbray during the parade of the Boro greats before the match against Luton Town.

ACTION from the match at home to Luton Town as Jamie Pollock beats David Preece in an aerial battle.

concentration and we've got good results as a result.

"We don't want to have to go into this game with it all hyped up for us. This isn't a party for the players. It's a very big game for us and we want to make sure that nothing stands in the way of us winning it."

The supporters must have sympathised with Hendrie, and held the same mixed feelings. However, after 92 years of football at Ayresome Park, it was only natural to want to give the old stadium a proper send-off. There was a pervading sense of deep reverence for the stadium and, at the time, most fans did not want to see Ayresome Park die.

So, despite the sense of great loss, it was time to party. In fact all the talk of promotion and the Premiership tended to take a back seat as the fans came to pay homage to a stadium which had dominated their lives throughout their football supporting careers.

voted for the new name from four selected by the club - Erimus, Riverside, Middlehaven and Teesside stadiums. Erimus came from Middlesbrough's coat of arms and Middlehaven was the new name for the area chosen by the Teesside Development Corporation, who had devised extensive plans to develop the whole of the docklands site. The other two names were self explanatory.

There had been no plans to use the title 'New Ayresome' as one of the names, and this was a wise direction, both to preserve the memories of the current stadium and also to give Boro a new future on a new site elsewhere in the town. In the event, the clear winner in the fans' voting was Riverside, and this was to be the name which was to take the club forward into the 21st Century.

It was very hot on the pitch, and it was clear that the humidity was going to add to the pressure facing both teams. The game kicked off amid terrific noise from the packed stands and terraces,

FANS for the memory... the massed ranks of the Holgate End salute the end of league football at Ayresome Park as Boro prepare to meet Luton Town in their final home game.

Nobody wanted to miss a minute of the occasion, and most of the 23,903 crowd were in the stadium more than an hour before the kick off. There were several celebratory events, the most emotional of which was the singing of You'll Never Walk Alone. This was led by Normanby born soprano Suzannah Clarke, and had every man, woman and child in the stadium on their feet, with scarves aloft and voices high .

Dozens of former Boro stars were warmly received by the fans as they paraded around the pitch before the kick off. Then, they all gathered in the centre circle to witness the official unveiling of the name of the club's new stadium at Middlesbrough Dock.

Boro's fans had earlier been given the opportunity to choose the new name themselves. They had

and Boro immediately took up the running. However, as much as Boro came forward, they could not get the ball in the net.

It was just before half-time when the breakthrough came. John Hendrie created space for a shot from the edge of the box, and his effort was deflected into the net off the boot of Dwight Marshall.

Boro seemed more concerned about preserving their lead rather than adding to it in the second half, and paid the penalty for this complacency when John Taylor headed the equaliser in the 63rd minute.

Legs were starting to tire in the intense heat, but Boro gathered themselves for one last all-out assault on the Luton goal. They were rewarded with what proved to be the winner when Jamie Pollock and Derek Whyte combined to set up a second goal for Hendrie.

This time there was no way back for Luton, and both Jan Fjortoft and Hendrie missed chances in a strength sapping final ten minutes which could have comfortably avenged the five goal defeat at Kenilworth Road.

However this victory was sweet, both in leaving Ayresome Park on a high note and putting the pressure on their fellow promotion rivals. But Boro had not yet secured the Championship, or the automatic promotion which came with it.

However, the situation was now very clear cut. Only Bolton Wanderers could overhaul Boro at the top. Bruce Rioch's men had two games left to play, and the first of them was a potentially difficult trip to Stoke City on the Wednesday night. If Bolton failed to win at the Victoria Ground, then the title belonged to Boro.

made the trip to the Victoria Ground to give their local support to the home side.

In the event, a lot of nervous energy was expended for nothing. Bolton rarely looked capable of winning the match, and it ended 1-1. Boro were in the Premiership and the memorable evening of May 3, 1995, was carnival night on Teesside. The rejoicing and the celebrations went on long into the early hours.

Many supporters felt a need to be at Ayresome Park in a kind of spiritual togetherness and the scenes of jubilation and relief were probably stronger in Warwick Street than anywhere else.

Bryan Robson, having achieved success in his first season in management, told the Evening Gazette: "I'm absolutely delighted for everybody at the club. All the staff and players have worked very hard to bring this all about.

"Promotion is what we set out to achieve at the start of the season and I don't think there's any

GOLDEN goal time for John Hendrie as he slots home Boro's second and clinching goal against Luton Town. It was the very last goal scored in competitive action at Ayresome Park.

The build up to the Stoke-Bolton match was a nail-biting affair on Teesside, specially as everybody wanted to see promotion assured without having to worry about Boro's final game at Tranmere. Whatever happened elsewhere, it was a very important game from Tranmere's point of view because they still needed at least a point against Boro to be certain of a play-off place.

In the hope of making it easier for Boro fans, the local radio stations in Middlesbrough and Stockton decided to send reporting teams all the way to the Potteries to relay live broadcasts of the match back to the North-east.

Even then, the thought of sitting nervously around the radio all night was a daunting prospect for some of Boro's edgy fans, and many of them

doubt that we have proved ourselves the best team in the division."

The triumphant players, who had been due to have their regular training session on the Thursday, were given the day off. Not surprisingly they had some celebrating of their own to do, and a few crates of drinks quickly materialised in the dressing room.

So the Ayresome Park party started before lunch and went on long into the evening. Remarkably, every member of the squad was back in for training the following day.

With the celebrations in full swing, the media wasted no time in linking Bryan Robson with a series of targets for the next season. It was no secret that Robson would be given plenty of money

ALL set for promotion. Bryan Robson salutes the crowd following the victory against Luton Town along with inspirational skipper Nigel Pearson and top scorer John Hendrie.

TWO of the main men in the downfall of Luton Town. John Hendrie, left, scored the two goals and Derek Whyte earned the impressive man of the match award.

HOW about a bit of bubbly gaffer? Bryan Robson gets the treatment from his players after Boro made certain of promotion following Bolton's midweek draw with Stoke City.

to spend to strengthen his squad so that the club could make an impact in the Premiership, and this sparked a guessing game which was to continue right up until the new season in August, and beyond. It was the beginning of the summer of speculation.

The first names on the alleged hit list were England stars Paul Gascoigne, who was reported to be terminating his contract with Italian club Lazio, and Nick Barmby of Tottenham.

Robson was quick to knock the Gascoigne rumours on the head, probably because of the huge gamble which might be involved in bringing the temperamental and potentially injury prone midfielder back to the North-east. But the Boro boss was particularly keen on Barmby, especially as he had already made a positive inquiry about the 21-year-old striker during the promotion campaign.

A third player linked with Boro at the time was Newcastle United midfielder Lee Clarke, though Robson again denied that he had made any move to try to sign the player.

Despite all the speculation and counter speculation, Boro still had to concentrate on completing their First Division programme. The edge had now been taken off the final game at Tranmere because there was nothing at stake from Boro's point of view.

The match was live on TV, but that did not prevent any of the 3,200 Boro ticket holders from making the trip to Birkenhead. They were keen to celebrate the promotion success by giving the team a great send off. Many fans had been in party mood all week and the sense of fun was reflected in the large number of supporters who turned up wearing fancy dress, including vikings and nuns.

Robson could have been forgiven for resting his tired players and giving the kids a chance, but the manager kept his changes to a minimum. Robbo still took the opportunity to rest himself, along with Clayton Blackmore and Alan Moore, while Jamie Pollock was injured.

So 23-year-old Craig Liddle, a former Aston Villa trainee who had been plucked out of non-league football with Blyth Spartans by Boro, was handed his league debut in midfield, and talented teenager Philip Stamp was also called up.

The team which was on duty for the final time in the First Division was: Miller, Cox, Whyte, Vickers,

READY for take off! Jan Fjortoft celebrates his equalising goal for Boro in their final First Division match at Tranmere.

UP he goes! Derek Whyte comfortably wins a heading duel in Boro's game at Tranmere.

Pearson, Liddle, Stamp, Morris, Fjortoft, Hendrie, Moreno.

Robson said: "I'm pleased to have the chance to bring in a couple of young lads and I'm tempted to play more of them, but then that wouldn't be fair on the lads because they need plenty of experience around them.

"This way we are fielding a strong side and I'm looking to win the game. It would be easy for us to go to Tranmere for the ride, but that's not the way we do things at Middlesbrough. We are playing without any pressure, so we can enjoy the game and try to finish the season on a high note."

In the event, Boro gave a thoroughly professional display and dominated the first half. However they could not get the ball in the net and fell behind on the stroke of half-time when Kenny Irons scored for Tranmere. Six minutes after the interval, Jan Fjortoft grabbed the equaliser, and the match ended 1-1.

With the season out of the way, Robson revealed his plans for the Premiership. He said that he was looking to make three or four summer signings to give his squad extra quality and depth.

It was estimated at the time that Robson might have up to £8million to spend, which was a staggering amount of money considering that Boro's previous record signing was £1.3million striker Jan Fjortoft. It was all the more remarkable when one considered that Boro were currently constructing a new £16million stadium and obviously had to find that money from somewhere.

However, Boro knew that they could generate millions of pounds of extra revenue following promotion to the Premiership. Much of this would come from season ticket sales and admission money, specially as it was anticipated that the building of the new state of the art stadium alone would give attendances a big boost.

With TV money and Premiership cash on top, in addition to extra commercial activity, Boro would have few problems in vastly increasing their annual turnover. So much of this new revenue could be pledged to Robson for team strengthening.

Before making any new signings, Robson's first job was to announce his retained list. Three players were made available. Forwards Paul Wilkinson and Craig Hignett were open to offer, while winger Tommy Wright was handed a free transfer. All three players were out of contract during the summer.

Wilkinson, signed for £500,00 from Watford by Lennie Lawrence in 1991, had been an excellent servant, scoring 67 goals for the club, many of them match winners. However, a dearth of goals had led to him losing his first team place in February, and he had failed to figure in any of Robson's starting line ups since. So it was inevitable that Wilkinson would be put on the list.

Hignett, who cost £450,000 when signed by Lawrence from Crewe Alexandra, had enjoyed a bright spell in the middle of the promotion season and was very much part of the side. However a bout of glandular fever cost him his first team place and he struggled to win a place in the side afterwards.

Wright had started just one game for Robson and was virtually certain to be on his way during the summer.

Robson said: "All three players have done well for the club. Paul Wilkinson in particular has done a great job over the years. But I needed to trim the squad to pave the way for bringing in some top quality players who can make an impact for us in the Premier League."

The one name missing from the retained list who the fans desperately wanted to know about was Uwe Fuchs. The German striker was revered on Teesside and was the supporters' choice to lead the Boro attack in the Premiership. Fuchs had scored nine goals in 15 games and nobody was in any doubt that Boro would not have been promoted without him. His contribution had been priceless.

Fuchs had been on loan at Boro for the last three months of the season and was available for £500,000 from his German club Kaiserslautern. In fact Boro had already paid a part instalment of that fee as part of the loan agreement.

Robson's decision was simply whether to complete the deal by making Uwe a permanent fixture with the Boro, or to release him back to his club. Certainly finding the rest of the cash wasn't a problem, but the Boro boss had to decide whether Fuchs could do a similar job for the club in the Premiership.

Whichever way the manager went, he had to back his own judgement. In the event, Robson announced that he had delayed the decision for an another 24 hours until he had the opportunity to speak to Fuchs.

The following day's announcement was a blow to both the player and the fans. Robson revealed that Uwe would not be kept on the payroll, and that his final appearance for the club would come in Steve Pears' testimonial match at Ayresome Park on Tuesday, May 16.

Robson admitted to the Evening Gazette: "It was a very hard decision to make, but I have decided to let Uwe go elsewhere. I know he has done a great job for Middlesbrough. He scored some very important goals and is a big favourite with the fans.

"But I have to pursue other options if I am to bring in the kind of quality players I am looking for next season. I have a lot of money to spend and I am looking for players who have performed at the top level. Time will tell if I have made the right decision."

Uwe, though extremely disappointed, had been half expecting the bad news. He said: "I have enjoyed every minute of my time at the club. I want to thank everybody who has made my time an enjoyable one.I will be sorry to go and leave all my new friends behind, but if possible I would like to stay in English football."

The German striker eventually joined Millwall, but did not enjoy the kind of immediate impact which he made on Teesside. Even so, time may have told that Robson did not make the right decision in deciding against signing Fuchs.

If the truth be known, Robson would have happily signed Fuchs as a squad player, even though he was not in his first team plans. He did not feel that Fuchs' playing style would fit easily into the team pattern he wanted to see from Boro in the Premiership, and felt that it would not be in the German's personal interest to spend month after month languishing in the reserves.

However, if Robson had known that Boro were going to suffer from a horrendous run of injuries in the Premiership, and suffer from a dearth of goals, then he might have acted differently. Unfortunately the ability to see into the future is not a sixth sense bestowed upon football managers.

Robson was at the centre of more activity that same week when he led his triumphant squad to Newcastle for the prestigious Hennessy North-east Player of the Year Awards. During the course of the evening, both Robson and chairman Steve Gibson received standing ovations from the packed hall in the Civic Centre.

And, at the end of the night, there was a personal boost for Boro's Jamie Pollock when he was officially named as runner-up for player of the year behind Newcastle's England international Barry Venison.

There was further good news for Boro's fans when the club announced their prices for seats to watch Premiership football in the new stadium. It was generally accepted that prices would be increased as Boro moved to a brand new all-seater stadium and welcomed back top flight football. But the relatively low increases in the price of the seating pleased most fans.

Individual ticket prices were to range from a minimum of £10 to a maximum of £15 for the regular fan. There were to be 18 Premiership matches at the Riverside Stadium, and season ticket prices ranged from £180 in the North Stand, which was replacing the Holgate as the popular end, to £270 in the upper West Stand, which was the new main stand. Prices for the previous season had ranged from £152 to £225.

While most of Boro's players were easing down and looking forward to a brief relaxing trip to Portugal before Steve Pears' testimonial match, Jaime Moreno was winding up again.

The Bolivan striker, whose first team appearance had been largely restricted by injury, jetted off home to prepare to play for his country in the South America Cup. It was also an opportunity for the

21-year-old to maintain peak fitness during the summer and make a big impact on his return to England.

Boro started the build up to Pears' testimonial by announcing that the First Division Championship Trophy would be paraded by the players during the evening's festivities. Tickets were already selling well, with Boro's fans determined to give a great send off not only to popular goalkeeper Pears, but also Uwe Fuchs. The prospect of seeing the team parade the trophy was another big attraction.

In addition, Boro announced that the 33-year-old Pears was to be awarded a free transfer following the testimonial match, in recognition of his terrific service to the club.

This announcement was appreciated by the fans, but at the same time many were very disappointed to see the final departure of Pears because they felt that he was still good enough to play at Premiership level.

Since joining Boro from Manchester United in 1985, following two loan spells at the club, Pears had been the backbone of the side, making well over 400 appearances. In 1992 his magnificent displays earned him an England call-up by Graham Taylor, but because of a fractured cheekbone, he was unable to take the opportunity and it never came again. The same season Pears was Hennessy North-east Player of the Year.

He had lost his Boro first team place to Alan Miller under Robson, but had also been suffering from a niggling calf injury which took a long time to solve. In the event Pears was eventually snapped up by Liverpool to provide competition for David James.

A huge crowd of 19,000 turned up to give Steve a £120,000 send off at Ayresome Park. The players arrived back from Portugal just in time to do a lap

of honour with the Championship Trophy, which was presented to skipper Nigel Pearson by Mike Naylor, managing director of Endsleigh Insurance, prior to the kick off.

At half-time there was a unique occasion at another player's testimonial match, when Uwe Fuchs came out to salute the crowd. He was rightly given a standing ovation for his terrific contribution to the promotion campaign, and was moved to tears by the scale of the reception from the fans.

Otherwise the night belonged to Steve Pears. The keeper had amassed a team of former Boro stars, who beat Boro 3-1 on the night. As befits a testimonial match, Pears scored the final goal from the penalty spot. It was also the last goal ever to be scored at Ayresome Park in front of a paying crowd.

Steve led a second Boro lap of honour at the end of the night, carrying the trophy around the pitch. He received a standing ovation, which brought the curtain down on football at Ayresome Park.

With the staff and players moving off for well earned holidays, the scene was set for the media to jump in with both feet with renewed speculation about Robson's summer targets. New names linked with the Boro were Portuguese striker Paulo Futre and Danish defender Jacob Lauefen, though both were strenuously denied by the club.

However the Evening Gazette revealed exclusively on May 13 that Robson was very keen to sign his former Manchester United teammate Andrei Kanchelskis. The Russian international was much admired in England and a big name in the game, so it was an exciting time for Boro fans to be connected with such a huge star.

It was no pipedream. Kanchelskis had already created a rift at Old Trafford by publicly criticising manager Alex Ferguson, and the Russian winger

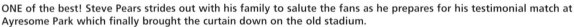

ONE of the best! Steve Pears strides out with his family to salute the fans as he prepares for his testimonial match at Ayresome Park which finally brought the curtain down on the old stadium.

IT'S all ours… Nigel Pearson and Bryan Robson proudly display the First Division Championship Trophy, flanked by Clayton Blackmore, goal ace Uwe Fuchs and Ben Roberts.

DELIGHTED skipper Nigel Pearson shows off his medal and the Championship trophy.

GETTING to grips with the silverware are Jamie Pollock and Phil Whelan as they inspect the FA Carling Premiership Trophy, which was on display at the Dickens Inn in Middlesbrough before the start of the new season.

made it absolutely clear in the media that he felt that his future lay away from Manchester.

Ferguson, while stressing that he did not want to lose Kanchelskis, added that Robson would be kept informed of developments.

Within hours of the news about Kanchelskis, Robson revealed that he was also keen on Dutch international striker Ruud Gullit, who had been released by his Italian club Sampdoria. Gullit, now 32, was one of the top players in the world and news of Boro's interest was quite remarkable for the Boro fans.

Assistant manager Viv Anderson told the Gazette: "We have made an inquiry about Gullit and we are waiting to see what develops. We would like to speak to him and see what his feelings are, and what he is planning to do."

It was obvious that Guillit would make a huge impact on Teesside and lead to a flood of season ticket sales. In fact, bearing in mind that the Dutchman was available on a free transfer, Boro could have covered his signing on fee and his weekly wages by the cash generated by season ticket sales. So any move for Gullit would have been virtually self financing.

The speculation continued thick and fast. Boro were next connected with strong interest in Queen's Park Rangers' England Under-21 winger Trevor Sinclair. However Rangers boss Ray Wilkins was quick to stress that the highly rated player was not for sale.

Boro did make a signing towards the end of May. Talented Irish forward Alan Moore signed a new three year deal with the club.

The month of May was not over before Boro were linked with a handful of other alleged targets, including their former winger Stuart Ripley at

Blackburn, plus Manchester United duo Mark Hughes and Lee Sharpe.

However it was at Glasgow Celtic where Boro first put their money on the table. Robson tabled a bid of £2million for Scottish international John Collins, who was generally regarded as the best player North of the Border. The Boro boss clearly saw Collins as the kind of experienced playmaker who could make his side tick across the middle of the park.

Much to Boro's dismay, Boro's written offer was made public in Scotland. Celtic also revealed that the offer was not big enough to tempt them to sell. Even so, the bid represented a potential record transfer fee for Boro if they could push through a deal for Collins, who still had a year of his Celtic contract to run.

Another Scottish international in the news was Boro defender Derek Whyte, who added a further two caps to his tally. Whyte took part in Scotland's Kirin Cup programme in Japan, where he played in a goalless draw against the host country and a 2-1 win against Ecuador.

It was an opportunity for Derek to stake his claim for further international selection in better known competitions, though the Scottish selectors hardly did him any favours by playing him on the left side of midfield against Ecuador, and then asking him to take the corner kicks.

Back in England, Bryan Robson discovered that he had missed out on one of his targets when Ruud Gullit signed for Chelsea. The word from the Gullit camp was that the Dutchman was keen to come to England, but that he wanted to play only in London.

With that in mind, it was no surprise to see that the Blues had won the battle for Gullit's signature.

Promotion and Speculation

In the event Boro never reached the stage where they could sit around the table with Gullit and tell him what they had to offer.

Viv Anderson told the Gazette: "We were very disappointed to miss out on Gullit, but the fact that we tried to get him has shown people that it wasn't pie in the sky and when we said we intended to bring top quality players to Middlesbrough, we meant it."

Boro were next linked with an interest in Nottingham Forest striker Stan Collymore. Forest had placed a staggering £8.5 million price tag on Collymore's head, which would have taken virtually every penny which Boro could muster at that time.

Clearly it was not impossible for Boro to have moved in for the player, but it would have been a massive gamble to put all their eggs in one basket. In the event, Liverpool were prepared to come up with the cash, and Collymore went to Anfield.

The huge inflated price which was naturally a British record, was a sign that the situation in the

As July arrived, Boro's fans were starting to become restless that the manager had not yet made a transfer plunge. Up the road at Newcastle, Kevin Keegan had pushed through quick deals for Les Ferdinand and Warren Barton, while Chelsea had snapped up Robson's good pal Mark Hughes from Manchester United to add to the signing of Ruud Gullit.

Boro's written bid for Celtic midfielder John Collins remained on the table but there had been no reported progress with this deal since Boro initially submitted their offer.

However Robson had already set his sights in a different direction. Now he was looking towards South America instead of north to Scotland. Robson, carrying out his duties as England coach, had been really impressed by some of the Brazilian players when they played in the Umbro Cup in this country.

The one player who really caught his eye was the diminutive attacking midfield player Juninho. So impressed was Robson, that he decided that he must bring the 22-year-old to Teesside.

IT tickles... Jaime Moreno has his fat levels checked by Boro physio Bob Ward as the players return for pre-season training.

transfer market was changing rapidly and threatening to get out of hand.

In fact Bryan Robson was quick to voice his concerns about the market trends. He said: "The state of the market is making things difficult. It's escalating out of control.

"We're talking about non international players costing millions of pounds and that's not good news for the game. The trouble is that if you don't compete, you are forced to sit back and watch it happening all around you.

"Obviously I have to try to get the quality players I am looking for at the right price, but it is becoming incredibly difficult. The best thing I can do is keep quiet about the players I want because if other clubs show interest, the price starts to rocket."

Without wasting any time, Robson flew out to Brazil to watch Juninho in action for Brazil in a friendly international against Poland. After the match, the Boro boss held talks with the officials of Juninho's Brazilian club, Sao Paulo.

The talks were slow, but Robson saw enough daylight to believe that he might be able to make something happen. In fact he stayed in Brazil longer than he had intended, to try to hammer out a deal with the Sao Paulo officials.

Negotiations were difficult, yet on a shake of hands before he left Brazil, Robson believed that Sao Paulo were willing to sell. However, once back in England, the Boro boss realised that Sao Paulo were not yet ready to release their world class star and that there was still a lot of work to do before he could get Juninho's signature on an official Boro contract.

There was better new at home - temporarily - when Andrei Kanchelskis issued a Come And Get Me plea to Robson through his agent Grigory Esaulenko, who passed on the information via the national newspapers in the North-west.

Esaulenko said: "I think Andrei would sign for Bryan Robson in five minutes. He needs a manager who has a belief in him. We know Bryan well. He is a good man. The two of them were together at United and I think they should stay together. We also think Bryan is going to build a very good team at Middlesbrough."

Robson wasted no time in lodging a written bid for the Russian winger with Manchester United. The Boro boss said: "I've put in my offer and now it's all down to when Alex Ferguson might be prepared to release Andrei. I'm hoping that we will make the breakthrough with Andrei because he is a good player."

no time to sit back and lick his wounds. In fact he quickly turned his attentions elsewhere.

On July 17, the Evening Gazette informed the fans that Robson had renewed his interest in unsettled Tottenham star Nick Barmby. It had become clear that Barmby was determined to leave White Hart Lane and return near to his home town of Hull, and Robson was soon at the forefront of the battle to sign the highly rated young striker.

Robson had already had a £2million offer turned down for the player during the season, but now he would have to pay a far bigger fee if he was to get his man, as a result of the vastly inflated home transfer market. In fact the London newspapers were claiming that Spurs were looking for around £7million for Barmby.

With written bids on the table for Juninho and John Collins, and a firm interest in Barmby, Robson was trying all he could to make the transfer breakthrough. However, as Boro moved into the

IT'S a battle for possession between Steve Vickers and Darlington's Gary Bannister in a pre-season friendly at Feethams.

Boro were reported to have offered £5million for Kanchelskis, but there was ominous news when it emerged that Everton had matched Robson's offer. Within a few days United announced that they were willing to sell, and suddenly Boro found themselves locked in a tug of war with Everton for the signature of Kanchelskis.

Robson had extensive talks with the player and made him, by all accounts, a very good offer. But Everton were soon claiming that Kanchelskis was going to become their player. Within a week, they were proved right.

It must have been a huge blow for Robson at the time, and once again he found himself still trying to make the initial breakthrough. However there was

start of their pre-season friendly programme, the manager was still battling to add his first new face to the squad.

The squad was stronger because Craig Hignett, who had been made available at a fee in Robson's retained list in May, was back in the fold. Hignett had gone to see Robson and asked for a second chance, and was prepared to accept a reduced contract to prove himself. Robson agreed to the player's request and was not to be disappointed, because Hignett not only started the season like a house on fire, but re-established himself as a key member of the team.

Hignett wasted no time in making an early impression by scoring the winning goal from the penalty spot as Boro opened their programme of friendlies with a 1-0 win at Hartlepool.

He was on the mark again as Boro followed up with a 2-1 win at Darlington. Graham Kavanagh scored the Boro winner after Steve Gaughan had equalised for the Quakers.

Boro then packed their bags for a four-match tour to Scandanavia, but had to leave behind Jamie Pollock while the midfielder had treatment for a shin injury.

The first two games were in Sweden, with Boro opening with a comfortable 4-1 win against Rottnerosik with goals from Jan Fjortoft, Robbie Mustoe, Jaime Moreno and Craig Liddle.

The team then wore their new red Cellnet shirts for the first time in their final tour game against Ham Kam, with Robson scoring the only goal of the match.

Boro had only a few days back on Teesside before setting off on another tour, this time to Scotland. However Robson did not waste a minute of his time back in England, and flew down to London for talks with Spurs chairman Alan Sugar about Nick Barmby.

Robson's negotiations with Spurs forced him to miss the start of Boro's Scottish tour, while striker John Hendrie was another who had to drop out. Hendrie stayed behind to have treatment on a groin

READY for the off... Jaime Moreno gets into the action in Boro's friendly match at Hibernian on their pre-season Scottish tour.

Fjortoft suffered a back injury during the match and missed the second game against IF Ornen, which Boro won 5-0. Bryan Robson and Viv Anderson both played in this game but neither got on the scoresheet, the goals coming from Craig Hignett 2, Jaime Moreno 2, and Phil Whelan.

Boro then moved on to Norway, where they didn't find it so easy. They were 2-0 down to Kongsvinger before fighting back for a share of the spoils with goals from Neil Cox and Jan Fjortoft.

strain. On the plus side, Jamie Pollock had made a full recovery from his shin injury, and was back with the squad.

As Boro prepared for their opening game at St Johnstone, Robson broke the news to the Evening Gazette that he had finally made his first big transfer breakthrough. Boro had paid a club record fee of £5.25million for Nick Barmby in a deal which was four times more than the club had paid for previous record holder Jan Fjortoft just five months earlier.

It was a huge outlay, but it was also a sound investment by Robson. Never at any time in their previous history had Boro ever signed a 21-year-old current England international.

A delighted Robson said: "Nick is one of the top five young players in the country, so it has got to be a good signing. He is still young and he will get even better as he gains more experience.

"Nick is also an England international and that's an indication of the direction in which we are heading. We are setting new standards and his arrival here will be a boost for everybody."

Barmby, with two full caps under his belt, oozed quality. He scored goals and was used to playing the kind of pass and run football which Robson was developing with Boro.

The manager added: "Nick was unhappy at Tottenham when they played him as a wide player, but that's not where I intend to use him. He can play up front or just behind the strikers and we'll be looking to use him in one of those roles."

Boro continued to be linked with John Collins, and the Celtic midfielder was sitting in the stands as Boro opened their Scottish tour with a 2-2 draw at St. Johnstone. Two first half goals from Craig Hignett gave Boro a 2-1 interval lead, but the Scots grabbed a late second half equaliser.

As Boro prepared for their second game, at Hibernian, Robson revealed that he was on the verge of completing a second signing in time for the start of the new season.

This time Robson had gone back to his old club, Manchester United, to sign his former colleague Gary Walsh. The Wigan-born goalkeeper had been snapped up for a bargain £250,000 to add competition between the sticks with Alan Miller.

Walsh, who had been understudy to Danish international Peter Schmeichel for several years at Old Trafford, had been keen to leave United and try to make a first team breakthrough elsewhere. If he achieved his ambition with Boro, then they would have to pay United a further £250,000 after 50 first team appearances.

Robson said: "I'm delighted to bring Gary here. He is a very good goalkeeper. We need another experienced keeper to battle with Alan Miller for the first team place, and Gary will give us that competition."

While Walsh was completing his move to Teesside, Nick Barmby made his Boro debut in the goalless draw against Hibs at Easter Road. The record signing enjoyed a bright opening game, but still provided Boro with a scare when he limped off eight minutes from time with a calf injury.

Fortunately Barmby was fully fit to keep his place less than 48 hours later as Boro completed their Scottish programme at Motherwell. Robson's men warmed up for their Premiership programme in great style by crushing the Scots by 4-1.

It was a sparkling performance, especially as Motherwell, who had finished runners up in the Scottish Premier League the previous season, were no mugs. But they were simply torn apart by Boro's terrific attacking play in the second half.

Boro played in their blue and black away strip for the first time, but without the No. 11 shirt, which they had forgotten to pack. As a result, Robbie Mustoe had to start the game with No. 12 on his back.

It was Mustoe who fired Boro ahead before the interval and, although Motherwell equalised from the penalty spot after the restart, a superb hat trick from Craig Hignett sunk the Scots out of sight. Hignett, now working off a reduced contract, had been Boro's top player in pre-season and fully deserved the chance to start the season in the first team.

It had also been a good pre-season for the team as a whole. They had gradually improved, from a slow start, and peaked with their fine display at Motherwell. Now they were ready to test themselves against the top clubs in the country.

FULL BORO RECORD SEASON 1994-95

1994

Aug 13	BURNLEY	2-0	Hendrie 2	23,343
Aug 20	Southend United	2-0	Hendrie 2	6,722
Aug 24	Anglo Italian Cup			
	PIACENZA	0-0		5,348
Aug 27	BOLTON WANDERERS	1-0	Wilkinson	19,570
Aug 31	Derby County	1-0	Blackmore	14,659
Sep 3	Watford	1-1	Blackmore	9,478
Sep 11	SUNDERLAND	2-2	Pearson, Moore	19,578
Sep 14	WEST BROMICH ALBION	2-1	Mustoe, Hignett	14,878
Sep 17	Port Vale	1-2	Pollock	10,313
Sep 20	Coca Cola Cup second round, first leg			
	Scarborough	4-1	Pollock, Hendrie, Mustoe, Moore	4,751
Sep 24	Bristol City	1-0	Hendrie	8,642
Sep 27	Coca Cola Cup second round, second leg			
	SCARBOROUGH	4-1	Wilkinson 3, Hignett	7,739
Oct 1	MILLWALL	3-0	Wilkinson, Hendrie, Beard o.g.	17,229
Oct 5	Anglo Italian Cup			
	CESENA	1-1	Moreno	3,273
Oct 8	TRANMERE ROVERS	0-1		18,497
Oct 15	Luton Town	1-5	Whyte	8,412
Oct 18	Anglo Italian Cup			
	Udinese	0-0		300
Oct 23	Portsmouth	0-0		7,281
Oct 26	Coca Cola Cup third round			
	Aston Villa	0-1		19,254
Oct 29	SWINDON TOWN	3-1	Cox, Wilkinson, Hendrie	17,328
Nov 1	Oldham Athletic	2-1	Moore, Hignett	15,929
Nov 5	Grimsby Town	1-2	Hignett pen.	8,488
Nov 15	Anglo Italian Cup			
	Ancona	1-3	Morris	1,500
Nov 20	WOLVERHAMPTON WANDERERS	1-0	Hendrie	19,953
Nov 26	Charlton Athletic	2-0	Pollock, Hendrie	10,019
Dec 3	PORTSMOUTH	4-0	Hignett 2, Wilkinson 2	17,185
Dec 6	Reading	1-1	Wilkinson pen.	10,301
Dec 10	SOUTHEND UNITED	1-2	Hendrie	16,843
Dec 18	Burnley	3-0	Hendrie 3	12,049
Dec 26	Sheffield United	1-1	Hignett	20,963
Dec 28	NOTTS COUNTY	2-1	Pearson, Hignett	21,558
Dec 31	Stoke City	1-1	Vickers	15,914

1995

Jan 7	FA Cup third round				
	Swansea City	1-1	Moore	8,407	
Jan 15	Swindon Town	1-2	Hignett	8,888	
Jan 17	FA Cup third round replay				
	SWANSEA CITY	1-2	Hendrie	13,940	
Jan 21	GRIMSBY TOWN	1-1	Mustoe	15,360	
Feb 4	READING	0-1		17,982	
Feb 18	CHARLTON ATHLETIC	1-0	Fuchs	16,301	
Feb 21	Wolverhampton W.	2-0	Vickers, Fuchs	26,611	
Feb 26	Millwall	0-0		7,247	
Mar 4	BRISTOL CITY	3-0	Fuchs 3	17,371	
Mar 7	WATFORD	2-0	Mustoe, Fuchs	16,630	
Mar 11	Bolton Wanderers	0-1		18,370	
Mar 14	BARNSLEY	1-1	Moreno	19,655	
Mar 18	DERBY COUNTY	2-4	Fuchs, Pollock	18,168	
Mar 21	Sunderland	1-0	Pollock	16,501	
Mar 26	PORT VALE	3-0	Robson, Vickers, Fuchs	17,401	
Apr 1	West Bromich Albion	3-1	Pollock, Moore, Raven og	20,256	
Apr 5	Oldham Athletic	0-1		11,024	
Apr 8	STOKE CITY	2-1	Pearson, Moore	20,867	
Apr 15	Notts County	1-1	Fuchs	9,377	
Apr 17	SHEFFIELD UNITED	1-1	Fjortoft	23,225	
Apr 22	Barnsley	1-1	Fjortoft	11,711	
Apr 29	LUTON TOWN	2-1	Hendrie 2	23,903	
May 7	Tranmere Rovers	1-1	Fjortoft	16,377	

APPEARANCES

LEAGUE: Vickers 44, Miller 41, Pollock 41, Cox 40, Hendrie 39, Moore 37, Whyte 36, Pearson 33, Wilkinson 31, Blackmore 30, Mustoe 27, Hignett 26, Robson 22, Fleming 21, Fuchs 15, Morris 15, Moreno 14, Fjortoft 8, Kavanagh 7, Pears 5, Todd 5, Stamp 3, Anderson 2, Freestone 1, Liddle 1, O'Halloran 1, Wright 1.

FA CUP: Fleming 2, Hendrie 2, Hignett 2, Miller 2, Morris 2, Mustoe 2, Pearson 2, Pollock 2, Vickers 2, Wilkinson 2, Moore 2, Kavanagh 1, Whyte 1.

COCA COLA CUP: Fleming 3, Pollock 3, Vickers 3, Whyte 3, Wilkinson 3, Hignett 3, Cox 3, Hendrie 2, Moore 2, Mustoe 2, Pears 2, Wright 2, Blackmore 1, Moreno 1, Morris 1, Miller 1, Todd 1.

ANGLO ITALIAN CUP: Stamp 4, Wright 4, Barron 3, Moreno 3, Morris 3, Taylor 3, Todd 3, Cox 2, Kavanagh 2, Liddle 2, Miller 2, Mustoe 2, Vickers 2, Whyte 2, Blackmore 1, Byrne 1, Fleming 1, Hignett 1, Norton 1, O'Halloran 1, Pears 1, Pollock 1, Richardson 1, Roberts 1, White 1, Wilkinson 1.

GOALS

LEAGUE: Hendrie 15, Fuchs 9, Hignett 8, Wilkinson 6, Pollock 5, Moore 4, Fjortoft 3, Mustoe 3, Pearson 3, Vickers 3, Blackmore 2, own goals 2, Cox 1, Moreno 1, Robson 1, Whyte 1.

FA CUP: Hendrie 1, Moore 1.

COCA COLA CUP: Wilkinson 3, Hendrie 1, Hignett 1, Moore 1, Mustoe 1, Pollock 1.

ANGLO ITALIAN CUP: Moreno 1, Morris 1.

Cellnet Step In

CELLNET, the United Kingdom's leading mobile communications company, were revealed as Boro's new official club sponsors in May, 1995.

The announcement was made shortly after Boro had won promotion to the Premiership, and in the wake of the near completion of the new stadium at Middlesbrough Dock.

Cellnet's generous £3 million sponsorship package comprised a ten-year stadium deal, with the newly constructed ground taking the name the "Cellnet Riverside Stadium", and a full range of associated branding, including tickets and signage.

It also involved a three-year shirt sponsorship deal, with an option for another year, and a host of other ancillary and performance related benefits which could potentially increase the value of the package to £4 million over the ensuing four years.

In effect, it was the bonding together of two organisations which were both progressive and ambitious.

In announcing the deal, Paul Leonard, Cellnet's head of marketing communications, said: "Cellnet's strategy for success is to be the best in everything we do. We look for the best from and in our business partnerships.

"Our sponsorship of Middlesbrough Football Club is therefore an obvious partnership. The hiring of Bryan Robson as manager, the promotion to the Premier League after such a tense final few weeks and entering into a new stadium is testament to the club's own strategy for success.

"Cellnet is delighted to be able to contribute to the club's continued success.

"This sponsorship deal will significantly enhance Cellnet's profile in the North-east - which is still an underdeveloped area for the company and for mobile phone usership generally.

"Football is like a religion here and Middlesbrough, having succeeded to the Premier League, provides a strong platform to enhance our local, national and, in the future, international profile.

"While supporting the club, we will also bring major benefits to the local business community and to the general public by offering an unmatched service in mobile telecommunications.

"This major deal perfectly complements our existing range of sponsorships which includes Damon Hill and the English Rugby Union squad. The one thing that links them all is that they are the best."

The ten year stadium deal, which was the largest football stadium sponsorship deal to be signed in Great Britain, and the three year shirt sponsorship were a major coup for the Boro.

It came at a time when Boro's officials were looking to dramatically increase the profile of the club, in keeping with their new status among the country's elite and their magnificent new 30,000 all seater stadium.

Boro chairman Steve Gibson said: "It's been an extremely eventful year for Middlesbrough Football Club, with all our plans now bearing fruit. On behalf of everyone involved with the club I am absolutely delighted to welcome Cellnet as our main title sponsor.

"The financial support of this deal will ensure that the stadium development is a huge success, as well as helping us into the Premier League with a winning team.

"The Cellnet Riverside Stadium is the largest new stadium to be built since the Second World War. It will be something the whole community can be proud of, with facilities that are second to none".

In the first 12 months of the sponsorship deal, the name Cellnet has become synonymous with the Boro. Thousands of shirts have been sold wearing the Cellnet logo, and hardly a major Boro event passes by without heavy Cellnet backing and involvement.

The name Cellnet Riverside Stadium is becoming so familiar, that the stadium is often fondly referred to as the "Cellnet" instead of the "Riverside".

Long may the partnership prosper!

GETTING into gear are Nigel Pearson, Bryan Robson, Alan Miller, Derek Whyte and Neil Cox as they model Boro's new Cellnet kit for the team's return to the Premiership.

Down by the Riverside

CHAPTER FIVE:

THE desperate need to bring football into the modern age by constructing new stadia and rebuilding the old decrepid grounds gathered momentum in the late Eighties and early Nineties.

It quickly became clear that the sport was putting itself at risk by trying to maintain its ancient relics, especially as spectator comfort at many grounds was virtually non-existant.

The damning indictment of the Taylor Report, with its stark relevations on spectator safety, hastened all the big clubs on a rapidly widening course towards putting their houses in order.

Cash which might normally have been used for team strengthening was put aside for the provision of new stands, and huge grants were made available by national bodies. Relocate or rebuild became football's new anthem, and clubs began to take up the battle cry.

And, with the government intervening to ring the death knell for the traditional football terraces at all major stadia, the public face of football was changing forever.

On Teesside, there had been talk of relocating to a new site in the area for several years. But nobody had ever identified a suitable piece of land, and neither had anybody come up with a catalystic plan of how it all might be financed.

Certainly Boro's officials had been unhappy for a long time with the overall delapidated state of Ayresome Park. Over 90 years of wear and tear had taken a heavy toll and the stadium needed much more than a touch of paint every year to keep it habitable.

Hundreds of thousands of pounds had been spent by the directors since 1986 in trying to maintain Ayresome Park in a decent state of repair, and every time inspections were made by structural engineers, there were grave fears that new horrors might be discovered.

The stadium was checked regularly under the building safety regulations, and the club had a legal responsibility to maintain all aspects of the ground if they wanted to be issued with spectator safety certificates by the local authorities.

At the same time, D-Day was forcing itself on the club, and Boro's directors and executive staff had to decide which future route they were going to take for their cultural home.

The first option was to rebuild Ayresome Park, stand by stand. Other big clubs were adopting this route towards the 21st Century, and from Boro's point of view they would be able to undertake the job in stages and thus spread out the cost. In fact the club commissioned a feasibility study to look at every aspect of rebuilding.

Clearly it could be done, but there were potential problems ahead, several of which were probably waiting to be discovered. Every time Ayresome Park had been inspected in recent years, glaring problems had been unearthed, particularly in the foundations.

In fact the whole thing was a minefield. For many years Boro had suffered from access problems, while the long standing question of street parking around Ayresome Park was increasing all the time.

In any case, if the directors were to rebuild Ayresome Park they would want a finished product with which the club and the whole community could be proud. But there was little available space around the boundary of the stadium in which to expand, which meant that Boro would have needed to build small stands rather than big ones, and thus limit the stadium capacity.

The second option was to move to a new site and build a brand new stadium. But where? Boro were potentially in the hands of the local authorities, with all suggested new sites subject to probable objections from nearby communities. Such relocations could not be done easily. And that's not to mention the difficulties which might be encountered financing any move across town.

However, the second option always seemed to offer the best bet for the future of the club. So Boro put out feelers.

Ironically, when it became clear that Boro were considering quitting Ayresome Park, there was a strong groundswell of opinion against the move by the supporters. Most fans had spent their youth on the terraces of the stadium and retained a strong emotional and cultural attachment with the much loved ground.

In many families throughout Teesside, several generations had watched their football at Ayresome Park. Fathers had taken their sons, who in turn had taken their own sons. Watching the Boro play at Ayresome Park was part of their heritage.

The club, while ever mindful of the fans' feelings, were in possession of the sheer hard facts, and this made a difference. Whichever way you shuffled them, relocation remained by far the best of the two options.

At the same time, Boro were mindful that any move must be made with the thoughts of the supporters uppermost. It was pointless moving away from Middlesbrough if you didn't take your grass roots support with you, so the possibilities of moving into the extremities of Teesside could not really be considered.

THIS is a model of the original stadium which was designed for the Middlehaven site. This version, which had four individual stands with scope to fill in all four corners if necessary, was later scrapped in favour of the current design.

Any new stadium needed to be within the boundaries of Middlesbrough, but on a site which was big enough to build a stadium which could regularly hold 20,000 crowds and more.

Crowds at Ayresome Park had dropped to just under 10,000 following Boro's relegation from the Premiership in 1993. This was an alarming trend which worried the directors. Yet they knew that the combination of a successful side and a brand new state of the art stadium would pull the fans back to the club.

It was Boro's search for support in this venture which led them to making the initial breakthrough. The club had talks with leading officers in the Teesside Development Corporation, a government financed body which had set up its headquarters at Stockton.

The TDC was established to rejuvenate the cultural life of Teesside, both in providing the ideas and the plans for massive new social and leisure facilities, and in bringing them to fruition.

WIth huge funds at its disposal, the TDC was in a position to consider all projects which it might be of great value to the life of the community. And, with large confines of land waiting to be snapped up on rundown sites, the TDC did not have to go looking for areas to rejuvenate.

The sting in the tail was that the TDC was the planning authority as far as its own land was concerned. It could start work on any major project which it felt was right for Teesside, without having to do any more than listen to the views of the local authorities and take into account any advice offered. At the same time, the TDC were naturally bound by all the regular building safety regulations.

Bearing in mind their mandate, it was only natural that the TDC were keen to listen to the

Boro. The provision of a grand new sports stadium was the kind of community project which the TDC was in existence to instigate. They could provide the land and the infrastructure, if Boro could finance the building of the stadium.

A working association was quickly bonded between the two bodies and by late summer, 1993, a working party was already looking at all aspects of the feasibility of erecting what was destined to become the biggest new football stadium built in this country since the Second World War.

Boro still had a lot of work to do in finding a way to finance the building of such a stadium. But their new found association with the TDC was manna from heaven. Without such a partnership, it's hard to believe that a super new stadium would ever have been built within the confines of the region.

It was in October, 1993, that details of the negotiations were first revealed. The plan was to erect a 30,000 stadium on TDC land, though the exact location was not announced. The intial plan was to build a £15 million stadium, which was to be an integral part of a much larger leisure complex.

While the TDC was providing the land and the infrastructure, the funding for the construction needed to come from the club and the shareholders, the Football Grounds Improvement Trust and other interested industrial and commercial bodies.

At first, the news was not greeted with much enthusiasm by the fans. Many of them wrote to the Evening Gazette insisting that they wanted to stay at Ayresome Park. There was an opinion by some fans that Boro had not fully explored the possibilities of staying put and that this avenue should be exhausted before relocation was considered.

Down by the Riverside

However the Boro directors knew that the new stadium was a golden opportunity which they could not afford to miss. If Boro stalled at the prospect of relocation at this stage, it might never come again.

So the commitment from the club towards moving to the new stadium was total. They were already moving quickly down the road towards making the dream a reality.

In fact, just before Christmas, 1993, the initial plans for the new stadium were given a media airing. There was a mock-up of what the finished stadium would look like, and the much awaited details of where it would be sited.

Boro had chosen to relocate to a TDC site which was known as Middlehaven. The site was down by the Tees, bordering Middlesbrough Dock, and was close to the famous Transporter Bridge. It was only

know where the Middlehaven site was. It was accessible mainly by driving over the Whitehouse level crossing and the railway line which ran from Middlesbrough to Saltburn. For fans who did have a look at the area, it was impossible to imagine a super new state of the art stadium in existence in this barren area in around 18 months time.

Part of the site housed a tank farm, while there were several other industrial and commercial concerns, including scrap yards. They had already been served notice that they would be expected to quit, but the whole task of clearing the area was clearly going to be a mammoth project, especially bearing in mind the time factor.

In addition, there were obvious access problems for a crowd of up to 30,000. There was a subway, to add to the level crossing, but this hardly looked adequate. At the media unveiling, the TDC admitted

WORKMEN begin site clearing operations.

a couple of miles, as the crow flies, from Ayresome Park. And it was also closer to the original centre of Middlesbrough than Ayresome Park had been when it was opened in 1903.

The cost of building the stadium was now officially revealed as £16 million, which still seemed a huge amount of money to find for a club whose crowds often dipped below 10,000.

However, both the Boro and the TDC were consistent in not only insisting that the funds would be generated, but also that the new stadium would be finished in time for the start of the 1995-96 football season.

As might be expected, it was a very impressive and ambitious project but, such is the nature of the people of Teesside, that they needed to see a few bricks and mortar before they would be fully convinced that the stadium would actually happen.

One problem was that most people did not even

that there was a problem with access, which would be solved by the installation of a new road.

Everything, it seemed, was in hand. Perhaps time remained the biggest problem, because Boro were left with very little leeway in having the stadium built on time, should anything go wrong.

Boro clearly needed a good winter at the end of 1994 if work was to keep up with the deadlines. If the construction was badly delayed by the weather, then it seemed highly unlikely that Boro would have any chance of kicking of the 1995-96 season in a new home.

Towards the end of March, 1994, full details of the plans were presented to Middlesbrough Borough Council for their perusal. It was only a formal presentation to the council, because the plans had already been passed by the TDC. At the same time, five nationally renowned construction companies were invited to tender for the contract.

In the June, Boro announced that the design of the new stadium was now different to that which had been initially envisaged. The original design had consisted of four separate stands with an option to fill in the corners. The new stadium was to be horseshoe shaped.

The horseshoe shape would incorporate three stands, and would face a main stand which was to be divorced from the rest of the construction by two open corners. Apparently the stadium had been redesigned to protect the fans from the bitter winds which blasted along the River Tees.

Details of the constitution of the stands were also revealed. The main stand was to include 20 executive boxes, a function suite, catering facilities, administration offices, state of the art changing rooms and a medical room.

County Council showed that around 4,000 extra spaces were needed for matches attracting 20,000-plus spectators. There were also fears that traffic congestion could lead to parking problems both in North Ormesby and at St. Hilda's.

Councillor Walsh, while welcoming the re-siting of the stadium, said: "A number of concerns should be addressed before the plans are off the drawing board. It would be a shame if people's enjoyment of the new stadium was marred by poor access roads, inadequate car parking and difficulties for public transport access.

"If traffic problems are not addressed now, there could be real problems in the future. What is worrying is that there is no indication of where these numbers could be accommodated."

The TDC replied that they had already carried out traffic research and had informed the County

BORO groundsman David Rigg inspects the condition of the site as preliminary work begins to lay the foundations for the new stadium

It was also announced that the building contract had been awarded to Tilbury Douglas Construction of Birmingham and would create around 250 jobs. Work had already started on the site with the removal of the first of the storage tanks.

However, not everybody was happy at the prospect of a new stadium at Middlehaven. Scrap dealers on the site were angry about the lack of negotiations and were refusing to move out until they had been offered a better deal.

Further problems then appeared in the August when Cleveland County Council stressed that they were very dissatisfied with the lack of provision for match day traffic in the stadium plans. Councillor Dave Walsh insisted that the major traffic problems must be solved before the stadium could be given the go-ahead.

The initial plans for the stadium included only 900 parking spaces. But a survey carried out by the

Council of their findings. They said they were working on problems and looking for solutions.

In the September, the TDC announced that land deals vital to the £16 million development were nearing completion. One of the deals concerned the 25 acres of land between the A66 and the railway line, which had been earmarked to house the main access road to the stadium.

Meanwhile Tarmac Construction had already started work on the other side of the railway line. They were carrying out a £1million earthworks contract, which had been authorised by the TDC.

Tarmac were able to start the work because the TDC had completed settlements with most of the small businesses occupying the land, and site clearance was now continuing at pace. However some of the scrap dealers were still holding out, and this was a matter which the TDC needed to sort out.

Down by the Riverside

The following month, there was a shock change to the building programe when Boro ended their agreement with Tilbury Douglas to construct the stadium.

It had been obvious for some time that timings had not been going too well between the two parties over the complicated contractural arrangements. Contractural wrangles had already led to part of the work being held up, which created fears that the stadium might not be completed on time.

The general theory was that Tilbury Douglas believed that they could not work within the stipulations of the original deal, whereas Boro were insisting that all agreements should be met. So, on October 25, 1994, Tilbury Douglas employees left the site.

For a short time, the fans had good reason to believe that they would not be watching league football at the new stadium the following August. But Boro wasted no time in coming up with a solution to the dilemma. They awarded the contract to Taylor Woodrow, who had initially come a close second to Tilbury Douglas when the contract had been awarded in June.

Taylor Woodrow had their men on the site within days, and progress in preparing the foundations continued as if nothing had happened.

However, just when it looked as though Boro had solved all the problems, there was another blow. Workmen from Tarmac Construction discovered two gun shells as they were excavating the site. The first, which was three feet long, was found on November 2, and the second, a two and a half feet shell which was eight inches in diameter was discovered the following day.

BORO'S new stadium should be a booming success. Lance corporal Allan Chance of 512 EOD (bomb disposal) from Catterick inspects a WWII eight inch shell found at the site of the new stadium.

On both occasions the Catterick Garrison bomb disposal squad had to be called in, leading to fears that more dangerous shells could be lying around the site. Inspector Ian Vickery, in charge of police operations at the site, said: "The area may have been a munitions dump during the War."

Sergeant Ian Brown was one of the men from the bomb disposal squad given the job of inspecting the shells. He said: "While these two shells were harmless, there may be others filled with explosives."

The only answer was to call in an army search team to sweep the site and dispose of any remaining shells. A team from the Royal Engineers was drafted in, but they failed to find any more shells, which was good news for both the club and the work force.

However progress on the earthworks had been hampered by the hold-up, because the workmen had been lying idle while the sweep was carried out. Norman Sturman, the site agent, said: "Work has been delayed, but not too seriously. We have got to excavate only another five per cent of the area."

The stadium continued to attract its fair share of headlines in the Evening Gazette. Business writer Eddie Johnson revealed that new main contractors Taylor Woodrow had awarded the contract to provide most of the steel needed for the stadium to Butlers Engineering of County Laoise in Southern Ireland.

British Steel, the local based company, was being asked to provide just ten per cent of the 2000 tonnes of steel needed to build the framework for the stadium.

The news upset a lot of people on Teesside, many of whom had family traditions linked to local iron and steel works going back through generations, not to mention the hundreds of Teessiders still working in the industry. Many of them, naturally, were current Boro fans and some would be season ticket holders.

British Steel later responded to the news by withdrawing their sponsorship package to the club. BS spokesman Dave Adamson said: "It's very disappointing news when there is a local steel industry about six miles down the road from the new stadium, and they are not using our steel."

However the decision had been made on business grounds by Taylor Woodrow, and Boro were not directly involved. A London based spokesman for Taylor Woodrow said: "Butlers Engineering came very highly recommended. We visited their works in Ireland and were very impressed with the technology they employ."

The argument eventually blew over even if it did leave a bad taste in one or two mouths. Work continued apace, though by the start of 1995 there was still no concrete evidence for the fans to see that the Riverside Stadium would be ready by August.

Clearly, a tremendous amount of work had been completed both in clearing the site, flattening the land and preparing the foundations. But so far there was no sign of the stadium.

Fortunately the winter weather had been excellent so far and had not caused any delays. But all the fans had to view was a few sunken piles and a bit of steel framework.

The framework was for the main West Stand, and was enough to convince the sceptics that the stadium would eventually be built. The fans who had argued that Boro should stay at Ayresome Park were now very much at a minimum, with most supporters enthralled at the prospect of Boro building the biggest new stadium in peacetime.

And, despite the fans' doubts to the contrary, both Taylor Woodrow and Boro officials insisted that the stadium was on schedule for its planned summer opening.

As workmen prepared to start constructing the stadium, there were fresh fears expressed about the lack of match day parking in the plans. In fact a working party of worried Cleveland County and Middlesbrough councillors were formed to look at ways of alleviating the potential chaotic situation on match days.

Other than the 900 parking places which were being provided, it was obvious that there would be few other parking opportunities relatively near to the stadium. The TDC were apparently looking at nearby industrial sites, to see if they were able to make their land available for temporary car parks. But it was most improbable that anybody could provide the extra 5,000 places which councillors were claiming were necessary.

One possibility put forward was that a new railway halt could be installed outside of the stadium or that the former Cargo Fleet station, which was a couple of hundred metres down the track, could be reopened.

The major problem here was that any plans to install a new railway halt involved putting up the money as well, and none of the organisations involved were prepared to stump up the hard cash.

Meanwhile work continued at a merry pace at the stadium and by the beginning of March the whole outline of the new structure was easy to make out through the steel framework.

Hundreds of fans were flocking down to the site every week to monitor the progress of the development. The Boro responded by opening a visitors' centre at the south-east corner of the stadium so that supporters could watch the work progressing in a safe, weather free setting.

The centre was regularly staffed, and contained a virtual reality graphic of what the stadium would look like once it was completed, in addition to detailed drawings and statistical charts.

With the installation of the visitors' centre came a promise from Boro director George Cooke that everything was going to plan. He said: The constructors are happy with the way things are progressing and we are as confident as we ever were that we will be in the stadium for the start of the new season.

"Obviously when you are building the biggest new football stadium in this country since the war, there's always the chance that some things will go wrong during the building programme. But at the moment we've every reason to be very hopeful."

He added: "The wind has held us up a bit and will probably continue to do so on occasions. You can't steel erect in strong winds because it is dangerous. But it's reasonable to assume we are past the months when the weather might cause us real problems."

By this stage, Taylor Woodrow workmen had already installed most of the huge concrete slats into the upper tier of the main West Stand, which was a high, imposing building.

The main stand was due to have a seating capacity of 8,800. Opposite it, work was now underway on the East Stand, which was to have the largest crowd capacity at 11,000. The East Stand was forming the major part of the three-stand horseshoe. It was flanked by the North Stand, housing 5,300 fans, and the South Stand, with a further 4,900 seats. The total capacity was 30,000.

The opening of the visitors' centre created a new flood of inquisitive fans to the site, and Boro were forced to employ stewards to control the crowds. During March, an estimated 1,000 fans a day were flocking to the centre, which naturally created the occasional car parking problems around other industrial premises on the dockside road.

It only served to highlight the car parking worries in the community. North Ormesby councillors Norman Swash and Charles Godfrey, who had been expressing concerns about potential parking hazards for several months, were also ringing alarm bells about the problems which would be posed by the planned new access road.

They stressed that North Ormesby was in danger of getting its own spaghetti junction because of all the elevated roads which needed to be built to provide the feeder roads for a brand new flyover road over the railway line and into the stadium.

They were referring to one of several schemes being considered by the TDC to provide proper access to the stadium. However, by this time, it was already clear that no such road could possibly be in place by August, 1995. For a start, no decision had yet been

BORO director George Cooke promised the fans that the stadium would be completed on time when work seemed to be progressing slowly.

Down by the Riverside

IT'S coming along nicely… Boro's assistant manager Viv Anderson checks on the building work after officially opening the visitors centre at the south-east corner of the site.

THE visitors centre was built with disabled fans in mind.

taken over which road scheme would eventually be selected, so it was clear that the completion of any new road was at least 15 months away.

By the beginning of April, the stadium was taking shape nicely. In fact the only thing missing was a football pitch. However work was now underway to install the drainage system, and this would be followed by the laying of the topsoil. Once this was done, groundsman David Rigg would be in a position to seed the pitch.

Rigg said: "We'll be laying rootzone as the topsoil. It's a mixture of sand, soil and loam, which is ideal for grass seed. We'll also put some fibre sand down in the middle of the pitch and along the sides, where it gets most wear to bind the roots tighter and hold them in place more."

The surface of the pitch would not be exactly level, but would have a slight camber. Laser beam technology was being used to ensure that Boro had a pitch exactly how they wanted it to be.

One thing Boro did not intend to incorporate under the playing surface was under-soil heating. Naturally such a system provided a guarantee that no future games would be postponed because of frost, and bearing in mind that the new stadium was being constructed in one of the coldest areas of the town, it needed to be considered.

However Boro believed that under-soil heating had too many drawbacks. These included the problems caused by the hot pipes burning off the lower roots of the grass and therefore reducing the quality of the turf, in addition to the fact that such pipes made deep spiking difficult.

While everything was fine within the confines of the stadium, the problems continued outside. Discussions between the TDC and Cleveland County Council over the planned new flyover access road were moving at a snail's pace. It was reported in the Evening Gazette that a legal agreement, under which the county council would take over responsibility for the bridge, once it was completed, was the hub of the problem.

The Gazette said that the county council wanted to include a condition under which the TDC would build a new interchange on the A66. The TDC countered that this condition should not be included until the costings and final designs of the interchange were agreed.

Naturally, all of these negotiations were pushing back the starting date of work on the flyover all the time. As a result, the TDC announced that fans would be allowed access to the stadium down the new road from St Hilda's which was being installed for the use of emergency vehicles. The new road was intended to run direct from Dock Street to the Middlehaven site.

The TDC added that coaches would also be allowed down the emergency road, and enterprising pubs were quick to take advantage of the opportunity by offering to run buses from their establishments to the stadium, and back again after the match. It was certainly one method of beating the parking problem.

Pubs such as the Red Rose in Cumberland Road and the Cleveland on Linthorpe Road were popular watering holes before Boro home games at Ayresome Park. Some pubs added around £2,000 to their takings on a match day, so they were keen to hold on to their regulars, and the coaches provided a happy solution for all involved.

The publicans were right to respond to the threat, because the new stadium was a reality. Work was well under way on all four stands and the stadium was now part of the Middlesbrough landscape.

There was another scare however, when construction workers unearthed eight Second World War army shells near to the visitors' centre, in the vicinity of the South Stand.

It was the second time that work needed to be halted on the site because of the discovery of shells. Once again the bomb disposal squad was called in from Catterick Garrison,though again the shells were discovered to be completely harmless.

The following day, on May 25, the stadium - now officially named the Cellnet Riverside Stadium - took a huge step towards becoming a fully fledged football ground.

Groundsman David Rigg sowed the grass seed which was to grow and develop into the pitch on which Boro would play Premiership football in three months' time. It seemed to be a very short amount of time in which to grow a quality playing surface from scratch, but David was happy with his timetable.

He said: "We've used the same mixture of rye grass seed which we always use at Ayresome Park. We'll water it well, and the grass will be through in a few days. It establishes itself speedily, has broader leaves and a stronger root hold."

The supporters' interest in the Cellnet Riverside Stadium was increasing all the time, but there was a new wave of excitement with the eagerly awaited publication of the Premiership fixtures.

On the opening day of the season on August 19, Boro were drawn away from home at Arsenal. This was a Godsend for the contractors because it meant that they had valuable extra time to get the work finished in time. The match at Highbury was later moved back 24 hours for live TV screening, though naturally it did not affect anything that was going on at the Middlehaven site.

Boro's first home game was due to be a mid-week fixture against Southampton on Tuesday, August 22. However the contractors felt that this presented them with too tight a schedule, so Boro made representations to Premiershp officials for the match to be postponed.

The request was granted, and a new date for set for Tuesday, September 12. It meant that the first match at the Cellnet Riverside would be against Chelsea on Saturday, August 26. Clearly it was a more fitting fixture with which to kick off in the stadium, because Chelsea were a more attractive side than Southampton.

Even so, the nearness of the opening game only helped to stress that there was still plenty of work to do to complete the stadium on time. Despite all the promises, it was going to be a close run thing, specially as safety certificates would have to be applied for before spectators could be allowed on the premises.

If nothing else, the building programme would not be held up by the weather. Britain was in the middle of its hottest and driest summers for many years. So the possibility of excessive sunburn was the only threat to the workmen.

THE new stadium starts to take its place as part of the Middlesbrough landscape. The picture also shows the entrance to Middlesbrough Dock.

THE roof of the main West Stand starts to take shape.

AN aerial view of the newly named Cellnet Riverside Stadium in May. The basic construction of the stadium is well under way and the West Stand roof is almost complete.

AS work continues to complete the roofs, the playing surface is levelled and prepared for seeding.

Down by the Riverside

They continued to work flat out, and by the middle of June roof panels were being installed on the stands. Some of the seats were already in place, while the grass was peeping through on the pitch and it was greening over very nicely.

Regular news in the Evening Gazette about the latest developments at the Cellnet Riverside Stadium helped contribute towards a surge of renewed interest in the club. The new construction had grabbed the imagination of the Teesside public, including many who had not been regular attenders at Ayresome Park. The outcome was an unprecedented demand for season tickets.

By the end of June, Boro had processed a club record number of 12,300 applications for season tickets and had many more to deal with. The stadium was clearly the main reason for the demand, because manager Bryan Robson had so far failed to make a breakthrough in the transfer market.

Trinity Crescent, which would provide the stadium with a new flyover road over the railway line.

Unfortunately for the North Ormesby residents, the tide was unstoppable. Boro were soon advertising for staff to man the Cellnet Riverside Stadium. Around 150 catering jobs were up for grabs in the fast food kiosks and bars. More casual work was also made open for stewards, programme sellers, security and commissionaires.

While one building was getting ready to open, another reached the end of its short life. The doors were closed for the final time at the visitors centre to make way for an access road into the south-east corner of the stadium. The centre had been a huge success, having attracted more than 40,000 visitors in five months.

The official opening was now less than a month away, provided everything went to plan. Everything had been rushed through very quickly, that local

HOW about that! The Cellnet Riverside Stadium looks ready for action by the end of July, with the pitch looking very green. However there was still plenty of work to be carried out over the next four weeks.

At this time, the roofing was now in place on all four stands and work was continuing to finish installing the seats. The external structure was virtually complete at this stage, and work was soon to start on the behind the scenes furbishment.

However, not everybody was delighted with the rapid progress being made at Middlehaven. At a meeting of North Ormesby Community Council, residents voted to call on the Boro to postpone opening the stadium until adequate parking and access had been provided.

The residents were fearful that North Ormesby would be jammed solid with supporters' cars on match days. They were also very critical of the plans to build a new interchange on the A66 on land at

councillors remained concerned about the safety of supporters once the stadium was open.

The Middlesbrough and Cleveland County councils commissioned consultants to carry out a risk assessment, focussing on the possible dangers presented by the railway line, the Whitehouse level crossing, pedestrian underpasses and the river and dock.

Bob Pitt, deputy leader of the county council, and councillor Ron Lowes claimed that the pedestrian underpasses beneath the A66 and the railway line were very narrow and may be unable to cope with large numbers of people.

Councillor Pitt said: "The Hillsborough and Ibrox disasters were caused by too many people being in a single area at the same time. The clock is ticking away and we want the risk consultant to look at the pressure points around the stadium and give an independent assessment."

Fears that many fans might try to overcome the anticipated congestion by crossing the railway line on foot were ended when Railtrack announced that a two metres high steel pallisade fence would be erected on either side of the railway line for one and a half miles.

However councillors were still worried that some fans who used the Whitehouse level crossing might still try to cross the railway line when the barriers were down.

The councillors were also fearful of traffic congestion, caused by fans driving down to the stadium in the hope of finding a spare car parking spot. However the police stressed that no cars without the relevant parking discs would be allowed in the vicinity of the stadium.

On August 11, the independent safety consultants revealed their findings. Fortunately they pointed out that they believed the first game against Chelsea should be allowed to take place, as long as a number of safety measures were taken.

Their report, while stressing that crowd safety risks would inevitably exist, said: "Provided the pedestrian flows are properly managed and most of the other suggested safety measures will be in place, the risk to crowd safety should not reach such a high level to justify the cancellation of the first match."

The report focussed on a number of 'pinch points', including the level crossing and the two subways. It pointed out that the pedestrian access in its current form was not satisfactory and called for several measures to be taken to reduce risks.

These included ensuring that the Dockside Road extension was completed in time, that the subways were in good condition and that adequate measures, including the possible use of mounted police, should be used to monitor and manage the traffic flows.

The consultants supported the erection of the high level fencing around the railway line, and also stressed that measures should be taken to reduce demand on the main pedestrian route from the town centre and through the underpasses beneath the A66 and railway line.

The report stated the need for an adequate shuttle bus service from the town centre to the stadium and suggested re-timing a train due to leave the Middlesbrough Railway Station at 2.40 pm to reduce the threat of level crossing problems.

It also suggested that fencing should be erected around the dockside and around any work which was still continuing at the time of the opening games.

Most of the points raised in the report were discussed by council officials, police and TDC representatives, and a general policy agreement was reached. However there was still a sticking point over one of the underpasses, which councillors felt remained dangerous. The Middlesbrough Council leader, Ken Walker, was calling for a ramp to be erected to replace dangerous steps.

There was still a strong level of unease among the councillors, despite the initial agreement. They were still very unhappy at the prospect of many thousands of fans converging on the Cellnet Riverside Stadium, through limited access, at the same time.

And council claims that only 600 car parking spaces were being provided at the stadium also caused annoyance. This meant that an estimated 10,000 cars could be looking for parking spots in North Ormesby and Middlesbrough .

The big test for all the planned safety procedures was now just six days away. Boro kicked off their Premiership season away from home, and earned a 1-1 draw against Aresnal at Highbury.

It was a fine performance by the newly promoted team and increased the sense of anticipation for the 30,000 or so supporters who were looking forward to the opening game at the Cellnet Riverside Stadium against Chelsea. As far as the fans were concerned, the home programme just had to start on time.

Unfortunately, things didn't work out too well for many of the fans who planned to watch the clash with Chelsea. There was a nightmare scenario when thousands of supporters turned up at the ticket office in Ayresome Park Road on the Monday to buy tickets for the game.

The ticket office was simply unable to cope with the demand, reportedly because of the slow process in feeding the information through the electric ticket machines.

Some fans had slept out overnight, but the vast majority arrived very early in the morning. Those arriving in mid morning found themselves at the back of a snaking queue which stretched for hundreds of yards, along Clive Road and beyond.

It was a red hot day, and the queues made painfully slow progress. Stewards were on hand to give advice, and warned of long hold ups. But it was the match that everybody wanted to see, the first game at the Cellnet Riverside Stadium and the supporters waited patiently in the baking sunshine.

Many thousands of fans failed to get to the front of the queue before exhausted ticket office staff finally pulled down the shutters in late evening. The staff had worked as hard as they could, but were restricted in the speed in which they could deal with the heavy demand.

For many supporters, it had been a completely wasted day. Some had lost a day's wages to join the queue and still finished up without a ticket. Ironically, there were still thousands of tickets available for sale, and the fans had no choice but to prepare to queue up again the following day.

The whole situation was a disaster. The club had not been adequately prepared to deal with the demand in one working day. Neither had they been able to differentiate between regular fans, who rarely missed a match, and those who simply wanted tickets because it was a special occasion. A system of vouchers, distributed at the final few games of the previous season, would have solved the problem.

The Evening Gazette was inundated with calls from angry fans who claimed that regular supporters should have been given some kind of priority. Unfortunately the club was in a positon where it was unable to differentiate between the true supporters and those who enjoyed the big match atmosphere now and again.

Down by the Riverside

Many fans queued a second time the following day, and most were successful. However the whole thing left a bit of sour taste, specially in an era where queueing had become a little old fashioned. The modern method of buying tickets was by using plastic cards and telephones, though Boro would have needed 500 phone lines to deal with the demand.

If nothing else, the massive queues indicated to the club that there was a potential level of support on Teesside which must have outweighed previous predictions. The eventual outcome of this, was a total season ticket sell-out before Christmas.

Even so, there was still no guarantee that the fans who had queued for tickets for the opening clash with Chelsea would have a game to watch. A massive army of steel erectors, decorators and electricians were battling against time to try to complete crucial work within the Cellnet RIverside Stadium.

Fortunately the pitch was in excellent shape, and just needed a bit of fine tuning from groundsman David Rigg. There were one of two areas where the grass seed had not come through, so David had been forced to use a few strips or turf to fill the gaps. But it had blended in well, and it was clear that the playing surface would be in a perfect condition come Saturday afternoon.

Most of the work inside the stadium was going on in the executive boxes, the restaurant, installing the TV closed circuit system, erecting the betting kiosks and completing the toilets.

These were the crucial areas, but it was clear even at this stage that part of the furbishment would have to be left over until after the Chelsea game. Some work in the concourses was already being delayed, along with the internal decoration of the administration offices and ticket offices. It meant that most of the office staff would need to continue working at Ayresome Park for a short time until their new working environment was completed.

By the middle of the week, the whole stadium area still resembled a bomb site. To the untrained eye, there seemed no way that workmen could possibly get everything shipshape in time for the stadium to qualify for a safety certificate.

Yet, on the Wednesday, councillors, council safety experts and police representatives arrived en masse to tour the site and decide whether or not to grant the certificate.

It was a crucial day for the club, but club spokesperson Fiona Bell remained very positive, and said: "We have always maintained that the project would not be complete on the day. The offices need refurbishment and that will wait until September. But a game of football will be ready to be played in safety and comfort."

Unfortunately the safety experts visit did not initially bring good news for the club. They discovered that electronic links from the turnstiles to the control box, which monitor how many fans were in the ground, were not in place. They also found that not all the crowd control cameras and signs were installed.

County Council chief executive Bruce Stevenson, while very sympathetic to the club's cause, pointed out that this work needed to be done if they safety certificate was to be issued.

He said: "We need to be satisfied in an emergency that all the exits are clear, everybody knows precisely what to do and they can get the crowd out without anybody getting hurt."

IF you were at the opening game against Chelsea then you are virtually certain to be in this photograph taken by Evening Gazette chief photographer Doug Moody.

THIS picture shows the fans in the concourse before the Chelsea match.

DIDN'T we do well! Boro chairman Steve Gibson and Chief Executive Keith Lamb proudly survey the packed Cellnet Riverside Stadium prior to the Chelsea match.

Down by the Riverside

NIGHT falls at the Cellnet Riverside Stadium. The first floodlit game at the new stadium was against Southampton. Steve Vickers is pictured winning a header.

So, it was impossible for the councillors to make a positive decision, and the awarding of the safety certificate had to be delayed.

Mr Stevenson added that it was obvious that the work was going to go right down to the wire, even though he had been given strong assurances by the contractors that everything would be in place.

The outcome was that the deadline for issuing the certificate was moved back 48 hours to the Friday, when a second inspection would take place. It left Boro with virtually no leeway to put things right if the decision went against them again. In fact it was even suggested in one media report that the game might take place behind closed doors if the stadium was not considered safe for spectators.

When Friday arrived, a continuous stream of lorries was still driving in and out of the stadium site. The area was littered with building equipment and materials, much of which was in use to finish off vital work.

The day started badly for Boro when Teesside licensing justices refused the club a drinks licence. The seven-strong panel discovered that the bar facilities were incomplete and refused to grant the licence under those circumstances.

They also declined an invitation to return on Saturday morning and make a further inspection. Instead, the magistrates adjourned Boro's drinks application until September 7, which meant that there would be no alcohol on sale for the Chelsea match - should it take place.

Fiona Bell said: "We are obviously disappointed and we believe the supporters will be very sympathetic to the fact that not all of the facilities will be in place for the first match. But they will be in place very quickly after that."

However, the drinks licence was a minor problem as Boro nervously awaited the outcome of the final inspection by the council's safety experts. It turned out to be a long drawn out affair and the decision took an age in the making. In fact it was not known by the time the early editions of the Evening Gazette went to press.

It was not until later afternoon that the result of the inspection was announced. It was good news. The certificate had been granted, and the match against Chelsea would go ahead.

The relief was obvious, not only to the club officials who had spent weeks organising the event, but also to the workmen who had slaved long hours to meet tight deadlines. But perhaps the most delighted section of the community were the supporters, who had been building up for the first match at the Cellnet Riverside Stadium all through the summer.

At the same time, a word of thanks was owed to the councillors and safety experts involved in the inspections. It was widely known that many councillors had been angry at the way in which the plans for the new stadium had been bulldozed through, specially without provision for adequate car parking at the stadium or without a new access road for the general public.

But this anger had not developed into bloody mindedness, and when it came down to having the final say on whether the first match went ahead or not, those same councillors gave their blessing to the club, and to its supporters.

There was still a bit of tidying up work to carry out on the site, plus a few minor adjustments, but the opening game came and went without any major problems.

It was a tight squeeze through the underpasses, particularly after the game, and the ban of alcohol posed restrictions for the fans who entered the stadium early, but nobody was complaining.

Even those fans who were expecting a meal in the club restaurant before the match took their big setback in good heart. A sprinkler system went off unexpectedly in the early hours of the morning of the match and ruined all the food which had been stored in the stadium overnight for the restaurant meals. It left one or two red faced club officials, but really they were blameless.

Once up and running, the Cellnet Riverside Stadium quickly became part of the community and an accepted part of the Teesside skyline. Early in September, the licensing magistrates paid another visit and granted the drinks licence. It meant that the bars were officially open in time for the rearranged match against Southampton on Tuesday, September 12.

There were one or two problems after the match, mainly because of the crowd congestion near the subways which led to impatience from some supporters.

Some fans reportedly jumped over the safety barriers and then dropped down into the crowd below, where they collided with other unsuspecting fans. One woman fell over in the melee and broke her wrist.

The police also criticised pub and club regulars, who arrived at the last minute before the kick off, in private coaches, creating a traffic snarl-up. It was the usual night-match situation, where the vast majority of fans arrived late, and the club appealed afterwards for everybody to get there earlier in future.

The following day there was also a warning by the police against parking in unlit, dark streets near the stadium. A dozen cars had been broken into while the game was in progress.

One of the answers to solve all these problems was for the flyover road to be built as quickly as possible, and there were fresh calls from Cleveland County Council for the TDC to start work immediately. The TDC replied that work would start as soon as the necessary paperwork was complete.

Finally, in November the TDC announced that work would start on the flyover after the turn of the year. The £4 million access road would begin at North Ormesby roundabout, span the railway and end at the new roundabout west of the stadium.

One of the hold-ups had been caused by the 16-week notice period which was required because some of the work would be carried out on land owned by Railtrack.

As Christmas approached, and the weather worsened, thoughts that the stadium might be off the beaten track as far as the general public were concerned, were well and truly dispelled.

The club shop was besieged by fans, and chalked up hundreds of thousands of pounds worth of trade. Stewards needed to be brought in to control the crowds, and fans had to be admitted on a rota basis to peruse the merchandise.

With the arrival of Juninho and capacity sell-out crowds every home game, the Cellnet Riverside Stadium was firmly established as a new focal point of the community and a modern new home to take Middlesbrough Football Club into the 21st Century.

Back in the Big Time

Back in the Big Time

CHAPTER SIX:

BRYAN ROBSON'S newly promoted rookies were very much raw recruits in the tough regime of life in the Premiership - but they were keen to adapt quickly alongside the seasoned campaigners.

Their naivety of how to handle life in the hectic and demanding world of top flight football was matched by a determination to establish a niche for themselves.

Not that the team lacked ability. Boro had earned promotion the hard way in one of the most competitive First Divisions for years, and had overcome a mid-season loss of form to come out on top of the class in a hectic finale.

Robson had deliberately built his promotion side with the Premiership in mind, and believed that he had enough quality in his squad for the club to finish comfortably in the top half of the table.

However the pundits, ever mindful of the huge gap between the two leagues and the number of good sides which had failed to bridge the chasm in the past, did not agree. Most of the 'experts' reckoned that Boro, and their co-promoted rivals Bolton Wanderers, were good bets to go straight down again.

Everybody at the new Cellnet Riverside Stadium disagreed, as they would. But they did have an inside knowledge of the strength of their particular squad, and they did have Bryan Robson.

The former England international had spent most of his playing career in the top flight of English football, and knew all about the pitfalls. He believed that he could guide his Boro side not only into a comfortable place in the table, but also to the fringe of European qualification if they had a run of good fortune.

His players were also full of confidence. They foresaw few horrors in the Premiership and could not wait to prove themselves. The season could not start quickly enough.

Not that Robson had rested on his laurels after enjoying the delights of promotion. The Boro boss had spent most of the summer trying to strengthen his squad with big name signings.

Robson had a reported £8 - £10 million to spend in the transfer market and insisted all along that the cash would be spent only on quality players. With that kind of money at his disposal, it must have seemed probable that he would have little trouble getting rid of it.

The opposite proved to be the case. Even though the British transfer market inflated itself three and four times in an amazing three to four months of virtual madness by the big clubs, Robson discovered that the quality players he was seeking were more important to the potential selling clubs than the cash on offer.

So, Boro failed in ambitious bids to bring in international stars like John Collins from Celtic and Andrei Kanchelskis from Manchester United, while the northerly setting of Teesside cost him the chance of signing Dutch superstar Ruud Gullit. Robson had to go to £5 million to try to bring Kanchelskis from Manchester United, only to be pipped at the post by Everton.

These disappointments melted away when Robson made his first transfer breakthrough just before the start of the season. He paid a massive club record fee of £5.25 million for Tottenham's England striker Nick Barmby who, at 21, was one of the country's top young players.

Never at any time in their history had Boro ever managed to get a club to part with a 21-year-old full England international. It was an indication of the club's new ambitious plans for the future, and also the pulling power of Robson.

Not only did Barmby's arrival convince the fans that the club was determined to go places, it also provided a massive boost for the rest of the squad. The players, while full of self confidence, had never doubted the fact that they needed an injection of quality into the dressing room if they were to make an impact in the Premiership.

Barmby provided that initial injection, and the players were buzzing as the season approached.

Their numbers were boosted again, days before the big kick off, when Robson went back to his former club Manchester United to bring in goalkeeper Gary Walsh, to contend the first team spot with Alan Miller. Walsh had been understudy to Peter Schmeichel for several years at Old Trafford, but was highly rated and had experience of European competition.

Barmby and Walsh joined a dressing room at Ayresome Park, where the team continued to train, which contained a lot of good players, though there were only a handful of full internationals, and Premiership experience was sparsely spread throughout the side.

Naturally Robson himself had vast experience of playing at the highest international level with England, but he was never going to play a leading part in Boro's return to the Premiership. He did intend to play occasionally, when he was needed, but a succession of recurring calf strains dictated that he was available a lot less occasionally during the season than he would have wanted.

Boro's most experienced internationals in the dressing room were the Irishman Chris Morris, who

GLAD to be here. Boro's record signing Nick Barmby poses for pictures at
Ayresome Park following his £5.25 million move from Tottenham Hotspur.

had played in the World Cup Finals for the Republic, and the Welshman Clayton Blackmore.

Striker Jan Fjortoft, Norway's current centre-forward, was another with World Cup Finals experience behind him, while the other full internationals at the club were Scottish defender Derek Whyte and Bolivian striker Jaime Moreno.

It wasn't a bad cross section, but it didn't get away from the fact that Boro had few players in their squad who had played much of their careers in the Premiership. Most had some experience, but only Nigel Pearson, Nick Barmby, Blackmore and Robson had played a lot of games at the highest level of English football.

So, how would Boro adapt to the Premiership? Robson clearly had every reason to assume that the team would be all right defensively. He had two good goalkeepers in Alan Miller and Gary Walsh and seemed to be well stocked with defenders.

Skipper Nigel Pearson, who was inspirational in the First Division promotion campaign, was clearly going to make another huge impact. In fact he had a very important role, bearing in mind his previous experience over several years with Sheffield Wednesday.

Derek Whyte, who had suffered as much as his fellow defenders when Boro had been given a hard time in their last visit to the Premiership in 1992-93, had matured into a quality player and was certain to do well.

Steve Vickers remained something of an unknown quantity. Signed for £750,000 from Tranmere Rovers by Lennie Lawrence in late 1993, Vickers had never played in the Premiership. But Robson always maintained that Vickers wouldn't have any problems, and was proved absolutely

right. In fact Steve turned out to be one of Boro's top men over the Premiership season.

Robson could also call upon Phil Whelan, who had been signed from Premiership Ipswich Town, while there were no problems at full-back because the commitment and ability of Neil Cox, Chris Morris and Curtis Fleming would see these players through.

Midfield presented the greatest question marks because of an apparent lack of cover. The three major contenders were Jamie Pollock, Robbie Mustoe and Bryan Robson, though Robson was not going to be available on a regular basis.

Pollock, who had won an England Under-21 cap the previous season, was always going to take to Premiership football like a duck to water, and so too was the hard working Mustoe.

The progressive Graham Kavanagh, still awaiting his first decent run in the side, was certain to be knocking loudly on the door, while Clayton Blackmore could play in midfield and so, too, could Alan Moore, who had been converted into a winger by Lennie Lawrence.

But Boro's midfield was the area of the pitch which seemed destined to come under the greatest scrutiny, mainly because most games were won or lost there.

Up front, Boro had reason for optimism. The lively Barmby would add zest and skill alongside Fjortoft, who had a prolific goalscoring record at Swindon Town.

Robson could also call on Craig Hignett, who was the club's best player in pre-season, and last season's top scorer John Hendrie, whose skill on the ball was a threat for any Premiership defence. In addition, Moreno was also expected to come into his own after problems with injuries in his first season on Teesside.

BRYAN ROBSON swooped again shortly before the start of the season to sign his former teammate, goalkeeper Gary Walsh, from Manchester United.

This was the basis of Robson's squad, though he had made it clear that he still had more cash to spend and intended to spend it when the right player, or players, became available.

It was a different ball game to anything Boro had ever experienced in the past. With £5 million already spent, the club had provided Robson with a similar amount for further team strengthening. Figures of this magnitude were mind boggling to the fans, who had long ceased trying to fathom where the cash was coming from.

But Boro had done their homework. The income potential in the Premiership was light years away from the First Division. The club knew that they could comfortably raise this kind of spending money from massive gate receipts, commercial activities, sponsorship, advertising, TV cash and Premiership hand-outs. They were guaranteed to be able to generate millions of pounds for new players.

This guarantee was backed by the building of the Cellnet Riverside Stadium, which was a magnificent new 30,000 all seater stadium which had taken the club into the modern era.

With Bryan Robson at the helm and a terrific new stadium to house the fans, Boro had moved on to a new level of status, which it was hoped would be the platform to make the club one of the biggest in the country. They were in a different league in two ways, and the cash was set to come flooding in.

Even so, the bottom line was still the quality of the team's performances on the pitch, just as they had always been. Boro needed to build a successful side if they were to maintain their support and their snowballing new levels of income.

And the one thing they needed was a good start to the season, both to maintain the high level of confidence among the players, and to keep away from the pressures of the relegation zone.

It was clear in pre-season that Robson was going to opt for five men at the back, with Nigel Pearson, Steve Vickers and Derek Whyte operating as three central defenders, and the full-backs pushing on to support attacks.

Robson told the Evening Gazette: "You've got to play to your strengths. One of the things we have got is top quality defenders and so it's important that we make good use of them.

"But that doesn't mean that we will be using them in a defensive formation. When you play with an extra central defender you can turn it into a positive system if you operate it properly, and that's what we intend to do."

Robson's new look system was a so-called diamond shape, with Vickers operating slightly behind the other two central defenders, full-backs Cox and Morris pushing on to support Pollock and Mustoe in midfield, and Barmby and Hignett playing behind central striker Fjortoft. It was different to the way Boro had played in the First Division, but this new pattern had produced dividends in pre-season.

With Curtis Fleming and John Hendrie unavailable because of injury, that's the way Boro lined up for their opening Premiership game against Arsenal at Highbury on Sunday, August 20.

The team was: Miller, Cox, Morris, Vickers, Pearson, Whyte, Barmby, Pollock, Fjortoft, Hignett, Mustoe. Subs: Whelan, Moreno, Walsh.

It was a daunting test for Boro on their return to the big-time because the Gunners, managed by former Boro boss Bruce Rioch, had splashed out £12 million to bring in Dennis Bergkamp from Inter Milan and England captain David Platt from Sampdoria. The two men, if playing to their potential, could turn Arsenal from a quality all-round side into a title winning team.

It was a red hot day in London, and Highbury was buzzing with anticipation. As far as the Arsenal fans were concerned, Boro were lambs to the slaughter, and most of the talk was over how many goals the Gunners would score, rather than whether they would win or not.

The truth of the story was totally different. Boro, wearing their new blue and black strip in league competition for the first time, went on to rewrite the script and silenced the 35,000 shirt sleeved crowd over much of the 90 minutes.

In fact Boro took the lead in the 32nd minute when a perfect backheeled pass from Jan Fjortoft released Nick Barmby, who moved clear before beating his England colleague David Seaman with a low drive.

It was a particularly sour goal for the Arsenal fans, because Boro had signed Barmby from their arch-rivals Tottenham. The home crowd had been determined to give Barmby the bird from the start, and wanted to boo him every time he was in possession.

However, they spent much of the time booing Hignett, confusing him with Barmby. It was a confusion which was to continue over the ensuing games as the duo, who earned the nickname the Terrible Twins, were regularly mixed up by fans and reporters alike.

Unfortunately for Boro, they were able to hang on to Barmby's lead for only four minutes. Ray Parlour took advantage of a fortuitous bounce to break through on the right, and he crossed into the middle for England striker Ian Wright to head home.

It turned out to be the only occasion when Alan Miller needed to stoop to pick the ball out of the net. The goalkeeper enjoyed a superb return to his former club and was man of the match.

However it was a thoroughly committed team performance by all of Bryan Robson's men and they made it absolutely clear that they were not in the Premiership simply to make up the numbers. Boro were far from overawed by the occasion and kept Bergkamp and Platt as mere spectators for most of the match.

Robson told the Evening Gazette: "I was delighted for the lads because they battled very hard to deserve the point. We knew it would be hard because Arsenal were among the favourites for the title, but we kept our shape and our pattern.

"It was a new experience for some of our players and it was up to them to prove that they could adapt to the Premiership. They proved that they are a good side."

The fine start to the season increased the high sense of anticipation for the opening game at the Cellnet Riverside Stadium against Chelsea the following Saturday.

Despite doubts that the stadium might fail to qualify for a safety certificate, thousands of fans queued in intense heat for the 13,000 tickets which went on sale on the Monday.

The hard pressed ticket office staff were unable to deal with the huge demand in one day, and many of the supporters had to come back and queue for a second day on the Tuesday. However, over the two days, all the tickets were sold and most supporters who had wanted a ticket managed to get one.

Boro's players also had to build up for the game in the assumption that the safety certificate would be granted, so they continued to train at Ayresome Park.

The former stadium was now being used as a training ground and was absolutely perfect for this purpose because the players had one of the best possible playing surfaces on which to train, in addition to having a gymnasium and full changing and shower facilities at their disposal.

Croatia 93 and the player had agreed terms. Cvitanovic, a full Croatian international, had scored 60 goals in three seasons for his club.

Robson said: "The lad is a good player and I am convinced that he can do well for us. He can play anywhere in the front three, so he will increase our options."

Boro had agreed to pay £350,000 down, rising to £1 million following a stipulated number of appearances. Robson had spotted the player's talents on the many videos he received from agents, and believed that Cvitanovic could prove to be a bargain at the price.

However everything depended on the Croatian receiving a work permit from the Department of Employment. Cvitanovic needed to have played 75 per cent of his country's internationals over the previous two years, and investigations showed that this was not the case.

THE Lion King. Boro mascot Roary meets a couple of young fans at the start of the first match at the Cellnet Riverside Stadium against Chelsea.

Physio Bob Ward and his new assistant Gary Henderson also continued to use the medical room at Ayresome Park.

Remarkably, the Boro squad had not yet officially visited the Cellnet Riverside Stadium. So, on the Wednesday, an organised tour was arranged, and the players also had a brief opportunity to knock the ball around on the pitch.

In many respects, the new stadium would be just as strange for the Boro players as it would for Chelsea, but at least Boro would have the backing of most of the crowd in a near capacity attendance.

With the stadium opening only a couple of days away, Robson revealed that he had signed a new £1 million striker. The Boro boss had been negotiating in secret with 24-year-old Igor Cvitanovic from

At the same time, there were ways and means to get around the stipulations and Boro had to prepare a case to try to convince the D of E that Cvitanovic should be allowed to play football in this country. Boro worked hard to prepare a good case, and the matter dragged on for several weeks. But it was a battle that Boro were destined to lose, and Cvitanovic never kicked a ball for the club.

With Cvitanovic having flown back to Croatia, Robson's main thoughts as the Chelsea match approached were to make sure that his players were properly tuned up for the match.

Boro believed very strongly that the game would definitely take place, and this point was stressed very heavily to the players, and in the sports pages of the Evening Gazette.

But other areas of the media were regularly promoting scare stories, which would be picked up by the players, who must have wondered what on earth was going on. Some stories maintained that the game had no chance of taking place and this was bound to be unsettling for the Boro players.

Bryan Robson told the Gazette: "We could have done without these stories, but to be honest they haven't had any effect. I've told the lads that the game will go ahead and have prepared properly. I want the lads to go out and enjoy themselves in front of a full house. I'll be telling them to express themselves and turn it on for the fans."

In the event, the new stadium was awarded its safety certificate on the Friday afternoon and at last everybody could concentrate all their thoughts on the opening match.

It was going to be a novel occasion for players, fans, club officials, stewards and police alike, and

a new stadium with restricted parking and difficult access, than no new stadium at all.

The police reported that everything went smoothly from their point of view, though there were five arrests on the day for minor public order offences - three from Teesside and two from Chelsea.

There was only one ambulance call, when one unfortunate fan was stung by a bee. But when the ambulance arrived, he refused treatment!

Boro did have one headache, when the sprinkler system turned itself on overnight and destroyed all the food which was intended for the corporate guests, and for the players' pre-match meal.

Sandwiches were brought in for the guests, who accepted the situation in a good natured manner. However it did cause a problem for the players, and club officials had to ring around on the morning to tell them to meet in a nearby hotel for their pre-match meal.

THE big moment arrives. Captains Dennis Wise and Nigel Pearson lead the two teams out at a packed Cellnet Riverside Stadium.

nobody knew how well the carefully compiled pre-match plans would operate. Emergency procedures were all in place, and hopefully all eventualities were covered, though nobody could be certain.

Fans had been warned well in advance that only cars showing permit stickers would be allowed down to the stadium, and most supporters planned to drive into the town centre and then make their way to the stadium either by coach, by taxi or on foot. A fleet of shuttle buses had been set up, and they were allowed to use the new emergency road, along with the taxis and pub coaches.

The people who had forecast traffic chaos were proved wrong, and in the event the whole exercise was a huge success. The fans accepted the circumstances of the situation. It was better to have

It was such a big day in the lives of the fans, that many made their way down to the stadium in early morning and simply soaked up the atmosphere as the kick-off approached. Hundreds of supporters were waiting when the gates opened at 12.30 pm.

In fact the stadium was virtually full by two o'clock, and the atmosphere was electric. Sponsors Cellnet provided a bit of fun by handing out hundreds of foam hands, and also chartered a helicopter to fly a huge Cellnet shirt above the stadium.

Master of ceremonies Mark Page organised a series of Mexican waves, which stalled every time they reached the few hundred Chelsea fans sitting in the South Stand. Many more fans of the Blues were on their way, though they had been delayed by roadworks on the A1.

YES! Craig Hignett gives a double clenched fist salute after scoring the first goal at the Cellnet Riverside Stadium, when putting Boro ahead in the first half against Chelsea.

Around 170 police officers, including dog handlers, mounted branch, air support, British Transport Police and specials, and almost 200 stewards were on hand to make sure that everybody entered the stadium safely and found their seats.

The fans included several from Australia. John Fagan, who had emigrated from Brambles Farm to Perth ten years ago, was there with his wife Ann and sons Jonathan and Matthew, while former Billingham man Roy Stevens from Geelong was also there.

The build up for the players in the dressing room must have been as tense as it was for the fans. In situations like these, when games are treated as a carnival, there's extra pressure on the players to win. Boro knew that they also had more people to please than normal, because the eventual crowd of 28,286 was the biggest home attendance that any of this squad had played in front of.

The team had been boosted during the week when Jamie Pollock made a quick recovery from an ankle injury which he had picked up at Arsenal. It gave Bryan Robson the opportunity to name an unchanged side, though Graham Kavanagh took over from Gary Walsh as one of the substitutes.

Chelsea included their world superstar Ruud Gullit, who had been a summer target for Robson, and Robson's former Manchester United teammate Mark Hughes, who had also been linked with interest by the Boro before electing to join the Blues.

A crescendo of noise greeted the players as they took to the pitch, and continued to increase in volume before the kick off. The match was kicked off by Chelsea striker Mark Stein and both sides were clearly nervous in the opening spell, challenging hard for every ball and burning up the adrenalin which had built up.

There were one or two close calls in both goalmouths before Boro lifted the roofs off the stands by taking the lead six minutes before the interval. The honour of scoring the first goal at the Cellnet Riverside Stadium fell fittingly to Craig Hignett, who had been in lethal scoring form in pre-season and was battling to prove himself a second time with the Boro after signing a reduced contract.

Jan Fjortoft created the opening for the goal by putting Nick Barmby clear in the inside-left position. The England striker had a clear shot at goal, but unselfishly laid the ball square for Hignett to ram it high into the top right hand corner of the net.

The goal lifted a lot of pressure off Boro, and they settled down to control the game. In fact Chelsea rarely looked like getting back into it, and Boro finally made certain of the points in the 74th minute.

Hignett started the move with a break through the middle before laying the ball out to the right for Barmby, whose perfect cross was skilfully driven home by Fjortoft. The Norwegian striker celebrated in style with his aeroplane theatrics and the fans celebrated Boro's return to the big stage.

Bryan Robson told the Evening Gazette: "We wanted to start off with a win in the new stadium and the lads couldn't have worked any harder. We defended patiently and we broke out well.

"We created five really good situations and capitalised on two of them. The main thing was that we chose the right balls at the right time. I'm delighted that we were able to entertain 28,000 fans and send them home happy."

Boro had come through their opening two tests very well, and the pressure was off the team. They showed that they had got what it took to adapt to life in the Premiership and, so far, had been very solid and workmanlike.

However, in their third game back in the top flight, Boro were now facing the ultimate test. They were away to North-east neighbours Newcastle United in the big derby clash at St. James's Park.

The Magpies, hotly tipped by most pundits to win the Championship, had won their opening three games. Manager Kevin Keegan had put the finishing pieces to the team jigsaw during the summer by paying Queen's Park Rangers £6 million for England striker Les Ferdinand, and a further £3 million for French winger David Ginola, who was an unknown quantity in this country, but reckoned to be very quick and skilful on the left flank.

Clearly it was going to be very tough, but Boro went into the match on a high. Robson said: "Newcastle have made a great start, but then we have done well and our confidence is sky high. The lads know already that there is nothing to fear in this league."

Robson was returning to the stadium where he used to stand on the terraces as a boy. He said: "I was a big Newcastle fan, and most of my family still are. But they'll be shouting for my team this time."

Jamie Pollock and Nick Barmby had recovered from ankle injuries picked up against Chelsea, so Boro were again unchanged. Boro had sold their relatively small allocation of 1,826 tickets, but were still assured of a noisy following, even though Newcastle supporters were certain to dominate the air waves in the partially rebuilt and very impressive 36,500 seater stadium.

Shortly before the kick off, the Boro players welcomed a visitor to their dressing room - Middlesbrough born comedian Chubby Brown. He stopped for about ten minutes and cracked a few jokes to try to ease the tension, though skipper Nigel Pearson admitted: "I think Chubby was more nervous before the match than we were!"

The match was as hard as had been expected. Newcastle enjoyed most of the possession, with David Ginola leading Neil Cox a merry dance and sending over a succession of dangerous crosses. But Boro were very strong at the back and limited the Magpies to a series of shots from the edge of the box, which failed to trouble goalkeeper Alan Miller.

By the middle of the second half, it was beginning to look as though Boro might just be good enough to keep Newcastle out. But then the Magpies struck. Ginola got in yet another cross from the left and this time it was perfect for Ferdinand to power home a header from close range.

Boro's chances of getting back into the game looked slim because they had engineered only a few attacks. However, in the very last minute they were denied the most obvious of penalties when Jamie Pollock was barged over by Darren Peacock inside the box. Darlington referee Robbie Hart waved play on, yet TV evidence proved afterwards that it was a foul.

NOT a bad effort from Jan Fjortoft as he goes close for Boro in the derby battle against Newcastle United at St James's Park.

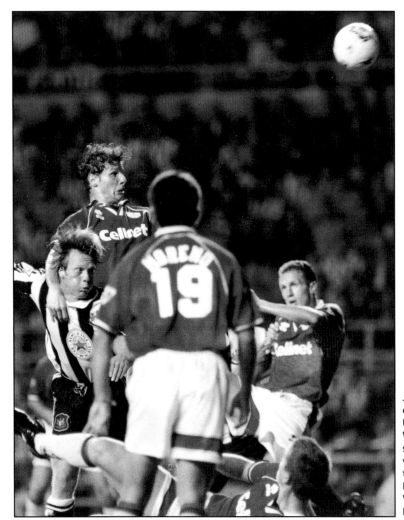

JUMP to it! Neil Cox outjumps Newcastle United defender Warren Barton to send in a header, watched by teammates Jaime Moreno, Steve Vickers and Jan Fjortoft.

So, while Boro could not deny that Newcastle were the better side on the night, they felt aggrieved that justice had not been done at the end of the match.

Bryan Robson told the Evening Gazette: "Everybody in the ground knew it was a penalty. The crowd went silent. They were waiting for the whistle, but it didn't come. However I was still proud of the lads. They worked very hard and on another night they might have got something out of the game".

Boro had the benefit of a blank weekend after the derby battle, because it preceded an international week. So the players had the opportunity to recover from a few bumps and bruises, and enjoy a leisurely build-up towards their next Premiership match at Bolton Wanderers on September 9.

debut, and the former Manchester United goalkeeper did well.

Walsh kept his place in an unchanged team as Boro looked forward to their first night match at the Cellnet Riverside Stadium against Southampton, on Tuesday, September 12. The match had been re-arranged from the first week of the season.

The match attracted a bigger crowd than Boro had drawn against Chelsea, largely because the Saints took up only a fraction of their ticket allocation, and the remainder were sold to Boro fans. So 29,188 supporters turned up to watch the game.

Boro had adopted the modern trend of fixing their floodlights to the front of the stand roofs, with the original floodlight pylons now a thing of the past. The lights gave a good effect, but Boro

IT'S the first meeting of the newly promoted teams at Burnden Park as Nick Barmby shows Bolton and former Boro left-back Jimmy Phillips a clean pair of heels.

Both teams had been promoted together the previous season, though Boro had spent a lot more money and had made by far the better start to their Premiership programme. Even so, with the benefit of home advantage, Bolton were always going to be difficult opponents so early in the season when most teams were still full of confidence.

So it proved. Boro found themselves in arrears from the 24th minute when John McGinlay scored. However Robbo's men hit back in the second half and were rewarded with the equaliser when Craig Hignett netted after being put through by Nick Barmby.

Boro had been forced to make their first change to their starting line up at Bolton because Alan Miller had failed to shake off a groin strain. It gave Gary Walsh the opportunity to step up for his Boro

failed to shine in the spotlight and had to settle for a goalless draw. In fact, but for a couple of missed chances by Southampton, Boro could easily have lost it.

Bryan Robson said: "We didn't play well, but we learned the lesson that there are no easy games in the Premiership. You don't win games if you are not at your best. The consolation was that we got another clean sheet, which was pleasing."

Boro were at home again the following Saturday, when they entertained Coventry City. It was a showdown between Bryan Robson and one of his mentors, Ron Atkinson.

The Coventry boss had been Robson's gaffer at both West Brom and Manchester United, and the pair had a great deal of respect for each other. In fact Robson had regularly contacted Atkinson for

GOALSCORER Craig Hignett is swamped by Nick Barmby, Neil Cox and Jamie Pollock after grabbing the equaliser at Bolton.

DETERMINATION from Jan Fjortoft as he wins a battle for possession in the first night match at the Cellnet Riverside Stadium against Southampton.

advice and guidance since he initially took over the Boro hot seat.

With home advantage, Robson was expected to put one over on his former teacher, and so it proved. However Boro had to do things the hard way after falling behind to a goal from the Brazilian Isaias early in the second half.

The goal sparked Boro to life and they equalised in 58 minutes when Steve Vickers headed in a cross from Nick Barmby. Twelve minutes from time Barmby also set up the winner for Jan Fjortoft.

It was an important win, to maintain morale, and it also lifted Boro back into the top half of the table. However it had been a hard battle, against one of the Premiership's lesser lights, and indicated to the team that they could not relax and needed to battle for every single point in this league.

the first meeting against the Second Division side, but still decided to make a couple of unenforced changes to keep his squad tuned up.

So Phil Whelan was brought in for his first competitive start since joining Boro from Ipswich Town on deadline day last March, while Bolivian striker Jaime Moreno joined the attack. Whelan took over from skipper Nigel Pearson and Moreno replaced Craig Hignett.

At first, the match was plain sailing. Boro took the lead with a strong header from Robbie Mustoe, following a cross by Neil Cox, and Jan Fjortoft added another two mintues before the interval when he flicked home a header from Nick Barmby.

It looked to be all over at this stage, but the tie changed dramatically in first half injury time when the Boro defence was slack and allowed

TAKE THAT! Steve Vickers celebrates his equaliser in the home match against Coventry City.

Despite Boro's encouraging start, Bryan Robson never left any doubts that he was still looking to strengthen his squad, and early the following week Boro were once again linked with Celtic's Scottish international midfielder John Collins. Reports in Scotland claimed that Collins' appearance against Rangers in an Old Firm derby on the Tuesday night would be his last for Celtic.

However Robson, who stressed that he was keeping close tabs on the Collins situation, added that he had been informed by Celtic that they had no plans to sell Collins in the immediate future. At the same time, Robson had asked to be kept informed of all developments.

Meanwhile, Boro had to play their third consecutive home match when they entertained Rotherham United in the Coca Cola Cup second round first leg.

Robson was looking to virtually settle the tie in

Shaun Goater to run in and reduce the arrears.

Rotherham looked a different side in the second half, and urged on by a vociferous following of fans in the corner of the South Stand, they tightened up considerably. The outcome was no more goals, and Boro were restricted to a narrow one-goal first leg lead.

Any worries that Boro might be starting to slacken were dispelled on the Saturday when they won 1-0 away to struggling Manchester City. Pearson and Hignett were restored to the fray and Boro were particularly strong in defence, where they never looked like being breached by City's lightweight attack.

Boro led from the 17th minute when Nick Barmby scored from close range, and might have had another when Robbie Mustoe watched his rocket shot come back off the underside of the crossbar.

Bryan Robson told the Evening Gazette: "I was proud of the lads. They set their stall out to be positive and worked very hard for each other. We should really have got another couple of goals, but you've got to be happy with three points."

One of the individual successes of the side in the opening games had been central defender Steve Vickers. The North-east born player had adapted to the Premiership better than anybody could have hoped and was looking a very good player.

In some respects it was a little easier for the central defenders because Robson was continuing to field five men at the back, but Vickers had stood out with his strength and consistency. His performances were recognised by Robson, who promptly awarded the 27-year-old defender a four-year contract.

Robson said: "Steve deserves this deal because of his contributions so far. He has done particularly well in the Premiership and I believe he is an asset to the club."

Craig Hignett in for the clincher in the second half after having played a one-two with Fjortoft.

It meant that Boro reached the end of September with just one defeat behind them in nine league and cup games. Clearly the strength of the side was in their defensive capabilities, with the extra man at the back paying big dividends. Boro had conceded just five goals in this opening spell, and so far not one side had managed to score more than one goal in any game against them.

However the attack had also done well in difficult circumstances, because Boro were operating without any orthodox wingmen, and relied on full-backs Neil Cox and Chris Morris to get forward when the situation allowed.

Nobody had done better up front than Barmby, who was proving to be a marvellous acquisition. The former Spurs striker had either scored, or set up, every Boro goal in the Premiership and his crucial importance to the side could not be under-

CONCENTRATION from Jamie Pollock and Craig Hignett as Boro battle their way to their first away win in the Premiership at Manchester City.

So much so, that Vickers was being talked of in some reports as a possible England player. Robson said: "That's up to Steve. He has to make people sit up and take note, including Terry Venables."

Vickers was as solid as ever as Boro followed up with another clean sheet in a 2-0 home win against reigning Champions Blackburn Rovers. Roared on by a new record crowd for the Cellnet Riverside Stadium of 29,462, Boro were always half a yard quicker than Rovers, who so far this season had not travelled well.

Robson's men went ahead on the stroke of half-time when Nick Barmby netted after a shot from Jan Fjortoft had been blocked. Then Barmby put

estimated. Not only was he scoring goals, but he was creating them as well.

Barmby took his place as usual in the line-up in Boro's next match at Rotherham United, where Bryan Robson was unable to make major changes because his side held only a slender one-goal lead going into the second leg of the Coca Cola Cup second round tie. However Chris Morris was rested and Phil Whelan played at left-back.

There was a potential upset on the cards if Boro conceded an early goal and lost their first leg lead. But the result was never in doubt as Boro held the Second Division side in a clamp from the kick-off.

I SALUTE YOU! Jan Fjortoft acknowledges Nick Barmby's goal against Champions Blackburn Rovers at the Cellnet Riverside Stadium, while Chris Sutton looks on.

ANY chance of a lift? Chris Sutton from Blackburn Rovers gets tangled up with Nick Barmby.

Any hopes which Rotherham harboured disappeared when they went down to ten men in the 25th minute when Neil Richardson was dismissed for the second of two reckless challenges on Jamie Pollock. Just after the interval, Steve Vickers headed in from a Craig Hignett corner and it was all over as a contest.

Robson admitted: "The sending off ruined the game but there was nothing we could do about that. The lads stuck to their task and have gone through, which is all we could have asked."

Boro had another blank weekend ahead because of international considerations, which gave them time to draw breath.

The club also moved to solve Curtis Fleming's long term thigh problem by sending the full-back for an operation. Fleming had been struggling to shake off the injury since February and every time it looked as though he was recovering, he suffered another setback. Enough was enough, and now the club was hopeful that the operation would solve the problem for once and for all.

Paul Wilkinson was also in the wars, being sidelined for ten days with an ankle tendon injury, while Graham Kavanagh was struggling with a niggling injury on the ball of his foot near to his big toe.

Fortunately Bryan Robson's first choice 11 had so far avoided serious injury, with the only change coming in goal, where Gary Walsh had taken advantage of an unfortunate injury to Alan Miller and was threatening to make the position his own with some solid displays.

So Robson was able to return to full strength, with Chris Morris replacing Phil Whelan, for Boro's televised Premiership match against Sheffield Wednesday at Hillsborough on Sunday, October 15.

Once again Boro were very strong, and grabbed all three points after Wednesday defender Lee Briscoe had needlessly handled in the box. Craig Hignett stepped forward to slam the ball home from the spot and push Boro into fourth position in the Premiership.

It was Boro's sixth win in a row in all competitions, and the players were absolutely brimming with confidence. They had earned a new-found respect throughout the country and their Championship odds had tumbled from 150-1 to 33-1.

Another bonus from the win at Hillsborough was the return to action of John Hendrie, who came on as a second half substitute for Jan Fjortoft. It was Hendrie's first taste of Premiership action following a groin strain picked up in pre-season.

The Scot, who was Boro's top scorer in the promotion season, made an immediate impact on his return by going close on two occasions to making it a goalscoring comeback.

Fjortoft was fit to take his place in an unchanged side as Boro welcomed Queen's Park Rangers to the Cellnet Riverside Stadium the following week. It was a hard competitive match, with Boro winning 1-0 courtesy of a 15th minute penalty from the lively Craig Hignett, who was currently producing some of his best football for the club.

It might have been an easier Boro win if they had not wasted the opportunity of a rather fortuitous second penalty in the 48th minute, when Karl Ready was rather harshly judged to have fouled Nick Barmby inside the area.

Jan Fjortoft elected to take the penalty ahead of Hignett and his powerful shot rebounded off the underside of the bar. Hignett, disappointed to miss out on the chance of a possible second goal, said afterwards: "After I scored the first penalty, Jan asked me if he could take the second penalty and I said he could, not thinking that we would get another one."

Rangers almost made Boro pay for that penalty miss by creating and missing several second half chances, notably when man of the match Trevor Sinclair struck the crossbar and Danny Dichio headed the rebound over an open goal.

Robson, was more concerned about the penalty miss than the three points afterwards, and insisted: "It won't happen again."

The victory was not without a high price because Scottish defender Derek Whyte was stretchered off after suffering a bad tear to his lower stomach.

It was a major blow, because Whyte had produced some sterling performances in the opening couple of months and had proved himself to be a crucial member of the back five. However Boro wasted no time on ceremony. Whyte was quickly rushed into hospital for an operation to repair the tear.

The Boro numbers were further reduced that week when Paul Wilkinson joined First Division Oldham Athletic on a month's loan. The striker was still officially on the transfer list and had so far failed to win a place on the Boro first team sheet during the season.

With seven consecutive wins under their belt, Boro were once again turning their attentions to the Coca Cola Cup. Phil Whelan was drafted in for the injured Whyte in the potentially difficult third round tie against First Division Crystal Palace at Selhurst Park.

It became genuinely difficult when Boro were caught cold from the kick off and found themselves trailing by 2-0 in less than ten minutes through two goals from David Hopkin.

However Boro gathered their senses and got back on level terms very quickly. Nick Barmby reduced the arrears in the 15th minute after good work by Craig Hignett and Jan Fjortoft, and then a long header out of defence by Whelan was flicked on by Fjortoft for Hignett to go clear and equalise in the 20th minute.

Neither side was able to maintain the breakneck start and the game settled down considerably. However Boro were still fortunate to survive when what looked a good goal by Palace striker Leon McKenzie was disallowed in the second half for an unspecified infringement.

Bryan Robson told the Evening Gazette: "We were caught napping at the start but we showed plenty of character to get back into it quickly. In the end we were full value for the draw and it should be a different story at home in the replay."

Now the scene was set for Robson to make his first return to Old Trafford as a manager following his illustrious playing career with Manchester United. Robson was still revered by the United faithful, who would have watched with some satisfaction the terrific progress he had made in just 15 months at Middlesbrough.

In fact there was a strong groundswell of opinion in Manchester that Robson was only on loan with

ACTION from Bryan Robson's return as a manager to Old Trafford. Dennis Irwin takes on Nick Barmby as Jan Fjortoft, pictured right looks on.

Boro, and that one day he would eventually return to Old Trafford as manager once he had served his managerial apprenticeship.

Yet, while Old Trafford was packed to witness the return of the legend, there was also an underlying fear among United fans that Boro might go there and take all three points. Robson's men were now unbeaten in ten league and cup games and were naturally regarded as being a tough, solid side wherever they went.

Even so, the threat posed by Boro to United did nothing to undermine the remarkable reception which Robson received when he walked out from the dressing rooms shortly before the kick off to take his place alongside the Boro party.

In what must have seemed like one of the longest short walks in his life, Robson received a marvellous standing ovation from everybody in the stadium. Robson, who no doubt was mildly embarrassed in addition to proud, responded with several waves to the fans.

The game provided Phil Whelan with his first Premiership start for Boro, in the absence of Derek Whyte, and Robson would have been looking for a good team display from his virtually full strength line-up.

Unfortunately the players failed to do themselves justice on the big stage, and it turned out to be a very disappointing return for the manager, and frustrating for the handful of Boro fans who had managed to find a way around United's ban on away supporters.

Ironically Boro were given a helping hand when United went down to ten men in 30 minutes when Ray Keane was sent off for punching Jan Fjortoft. But Boro never looked like taking advantage.

The writing was on the wall from the moment that Gary Pallister came forward to head the opening goal against his former club shortly before the interval.

Boro clung on during the second half without really looking like scoring themselves, though they should have been awarded a penalty when Jaime Moreno was clearly brought down by Pallister inside the area 20 minutes from time.

In the event it was United who had the final say when Andy Cole grabbed the clinching goal two minutes from time.

Robson was not so much annoyed about his own barren return to his former stamping ground, but the fact that his team had frozen on the biggest stage in English club football.

He told the Evening Gazette: "We let ourselves down because we didn't play. We didn't believe that we could go there and get a result."

Even so, this was only Boro's second defeat in 14 games, and they could still look back on a terrific season so far with every reason - at the time - to assume that there was more success to follow.

Tribute to Har

BORO stalwart Harold Shepherdson, who gave more than 50 years' service to the club he loved, died on September 13, 1995.

His funeral, held in St. Cuthbert's Church at Marton, was attended by many of the greatest names in English football, past and present, including Bobby and Jack Charlton.

Shep, one of the major instigators of a new, modern style of coaching shortly after the Second World War, was England trainer for a record number of 171 games. He was involved in four World Cups, including the famous victory at Wembley in 1966.

Born in Elm Street in Middlesbrough in 1918, Harold went on to captain Middlesbrough Boys at both football and cricket.

As a footballer, he was a strong and committed centre-half who attracted the attentions of the Boro when he was playing for South Bank East End in 1932. The same year Harold signed amateur forms for the Boro, and became a full-time professional four years later.

Although he was a talented young player, Shep found that his first team chances were limited at Ayresome Park in the late 1930s because he was understudy to Boro's brilliant Scottish International centre-half Bobby Baxter. He made just 17 appearances in the First Division before the outbreak of War.

Shep was a PTI sergeant instructor during the War, and studied the anatomy and physiology side of sport. This knowledge enabled him to take up coaching.

Harold played war-time football with Northampton Town, and also for the Boro when he was home on leave. He did not stay at Ayresome Park for long after the ceasing of hostilities, and was transferred to Southend United. However a knee injury effectively ended his football career before he had kicked a ball for his new club.

In 1949, Shep was recommended for the post of Boro's assistant-trainer by the long serving Charlie Cole. His abilities on the fitness front were quickly noted and he soon progressed to become the club's senior trainer on the retirement of Cole and Tom Mayson.

He wasted no time in introducing his own ideas on to the training pitch, and became so highly regarded both locally and nationally that he was called up as trainer by England manager Walter Winterbottom in 1957. Shep went on to work in tandem with England and the Boro for many years.

In 1969 he was awarded an MBE and received a testimonial from the Football Association four years later.

During his 50 years with the Boro, Harold was caretaker manager no less than four times. When the club moved to the new Cellnet Riverside Stadium in 1995, he was still involved closely with the corporate hospitality on match days.

A tribute from the Boro read: "Harold was an excellent servant to the club and his interest and passion for the Boro was evident throughout his life. He was at the match against Southampton shortly before his death and supported the team until the end."

d Shepherdson

SHEP - a great Boro and England servant

Juninho Fever

CHAPTER SEVEN:

HEN BRYAN ROBSON made references about signing top quality players, everybody on Teesside knew exactly what he was talking about.

The £5.25 million record signing of Nick Barmby from Tottenham had brought a player to the Boro who was straight out of the top drawer. At the age of 21, Barmby was already a full England international, and an exciting player with his whole career ahead of him.

Never before had Boro managed to sign an England international of such tender years. It was the most evident sign of all that Boro had truly moved into a new era under Robson's management.

So, when it was revealed that Robbo was hot on the trail of a Brazilian superstar, the fans sat up and took notice.

It had all started during the summer, of course, when Robson and Boro's chief executive Keith Lamb made a lightning visit to South America to try to pull off a transfer coup. At the time, Robson's target was not made public, though one of the names which cropped up was a highly talented young attacking midfield international called Juninho.

As England coach, Robson was already fully aware of the level of ability of most of the Brazilian stars. He had watched from the touchlines in awe as an up and coming new team of Brazilian youngsters comprehensively took England apart in the Umbro Cup competition at Wembley.

Not surprisingly Robson had made more than a mental note of some of the players who were causing England the major problems. The possibility of seeing one of those same Brazilians one day wearing the red shirt of Boro must have been a challenging prospect for him.

However, Robson's dramatic dash to Brazil to try to pull off one of the footballing coups of the century did not pay immediate dividends. In fact Robson and Lamb returned to Teesside empty handed, and for some time it looked as though their ambitious bid to pull off a deal for one of the young superstars had ended in failure.

Clearly it cannot have been easy for the two Boro men negotiating with football officials from a different culture, specially as there was no laid down precedent because Brazilian players heading for Europe did not come to England.

Instead, they headed for the Latin countries like Italy, Spain and Portugal, particularly the latter, because Portuguese is the national language of Brazil. So any bid by an English club to sign a Brazilian star was always going to be a difficult proposition, and for an unheard of club like Boro - certainly in South America - it was going to be doubly difficult.

However, Bryan Robson was absolutely determined to bring a player to the Boro who would not only set the whole of Teesside alight, but also the rest of the Premiership. And, with half of his £10 million spending money in the bank, he was calling the shots.

Even so, as the new season moved fully into gear, most of the headlines were concentrated on Boro's fine start to the season. The media was well aware of Robson's spending power, but most of the transfer stories linked the club with a continuing interest in Celtic midfielder John Collins.

That's why it came completely out of the blue when the Evening Gazette announced to the world at the beginning of October that Robson and Lamb were back in Brazil.

The deal which had been put on ice during the summer was up and running again. And the Gazette left no doubts in the minds of the fans when it revealed that Robson's target was in fact Juninho, who had not only masterminded England's Umbro Cup defeat, but had also scored one of the goals.

Naturally Robson and Lamb would not have returned all the way to South America unless they really believed there was a genuine chance of completing a deal for Juninho, who was the star player for the Sao Paulo club.

However, even if Sao Paulo agreed to sell, would one of the world's most highly regarded players consider moving to England, and to Middlesbrough in particular?

The Teesside footballing public, not used to this kind of idolised player being linked with the club, could only wait and wonder. But the realisation that there was a genuine chance that Robbo might actually pull off this remarkable coup set the initial seeds of Juninho Fever into life.

After years of apparent mediocrity, Boro were at last making a bold move to join the big league with a signing of stunning quality, and everybody on Teesside wanted a slice of the action.

The possibility of Boro getting their man increased when it was revealed in the Brazilian media that Juninho actually fancied the idea of playing football in England.

Senor Castilho, a Brazilian journalist who became the Evening Gazette's man in Sao Paulo, said: "Juninho was on a TV show and he said he wanted to leave Sao Paulo to play in England. I think he will get his wish. If Bryan Robson can convince Juninho that Middlesbrough is a good idea, then he will go there."

He added: "Sao Paulo will be willing to sell if Robson meets the asking price. The club are currently carrying out a huge rebuilding programme and need to sell players to raise the cash.

"And Juninho would be a very good signing for Middlesbrough. He is only small and he won't bash his way through your English defences. But he is a very good player with the ball."

Despite the optimism, the talks in Sao Paulo were clearly starting to drag on, and Robson and Lamb were forced to extend their stay in order to reach an outcome. It was obvious that the Brazilians had no intentions of simply handing over Juninho on a plate.

At the same time, there were strong reports from Brazil that Juninho had made up his mind that he wanted to link up with the Boro. He already knew a great deal about Bryan Robson and his England international background, and fancied the opportunity to play for his English club.

In fact Boro were not quite an unknown quantity to Juninho because he had seen the club in action on English football videos.

Everything was starting to point to Boro signing the Brazilian even if it looked as though he was not coming cheap.

Finally, on the morning of Saturday, October 7, came the marvellous news. Boro had got their man. Boro and Sao Paulo had agreed a transfer fee, and Juninho had signed on the dotted line.

The news was relayed exclusively to the Evening Gazette by Boro chairman Steve Gibson, who was on holiday in Portugal at the time - though not, apparently, with a view to brushing up on his Portuguese!

The Gazette splashed the story to the Teesside public in their main edition that night, and made contact with both Robson and Lamb in their Sao Paulo hotel, giving full details of exactly how the deal was pulled off in the Sports Gazette that evening. The print was increased in size and naturally the 'Pink' was in great demand.

It emerged that Boro had agreed to pay a Brazilian record fee of seven and a half million dollars for Juninho. Taking into account the rate of exchange at the time, it represented around £4.75 million. It was a higher fee than had been anticipated by the media, and indicated fully that the Brazilian officials had struck a very hard bargain.

However, a delighted Robson told the Gazette: "It's a great day for the club because Juninho is a world class player. We lost out on him about a month ago but I didn't give up hope and that's why we returned to Brazil to sign him.

"People were saying that we weren't a big enough club to take on a player like Juninho but we have proved them wrong."

He added: "I am looking to improve the team all the time and there's no doubt that Juninho will make a big difference to the players at the club. He's got terrific qualities."

There had been strong reports in England while the negotiations were taking place that Arsenal were also keen to sign Juninho. However Robson revealed that Boro were the only club to open negotiations with Sao Paulo and had the field to themselves.

However other Continental clubs, such as Inter Milan, Porto and Sampdoria were said to be very interested in Juninho, and he might have had the opportunity to move elsewhere should he have decided that he didn't fancy joining the Boro,

Keith Lamb was also relieved that the negotiations had been ultimately successful. He said: "The talks have gone on longer than I would have liked but the contract is in my pocket and in the end we have been successful.

"We have signed probably the most exciting footballer in the world. He has just won the Brazilian Footballer of the Year Award and is the star of the national side. And, at the age of 22, he is just starting his career."

Lamb added: "It's a testimony of the football club's ambition and Bryan Robson's persuasion, and the standing Bryan holds in the world footballing community, that we have secured this deal.

JUNINHO is coming! Boro fans celebrate to the Samba beat at the Cellnet Riverside Stadium. Pictured, left to right, are Michael King, Kirsten O'Brien, Stephen Vickers and every Boro fan's favourite lion, Roary.

Juninho Fever

"To be honest, Juninho wasn't difficult to convince. He was a dream to deal with and always indicated to us that he was keen to join us. But the fact that Bryan Robson was conducting the negotiations was significant.

"The problem which we did have was in our negotiations with Sao Paulo. Understandably they were reluctant to sell their brightest star and it's a big blow to them that they are losing him."

Lamb stressed that Boro had been forced to increase their original offer during the course of the negotiations in order to complete the deal. Yet, at £4.75 million, Boro had forked out less money for a world rated player like Juninho than they did to bring £5.25 million striker Nick Barmby to Middlesbrough from Spurs.

Lamb added: "We had hoped to tie up the deal more quickly but Sao Paulo were not keen to sell at first and we had to keep negotiating until we reached an offer which was acceptable.

"In the end we have paid a similar fee to that which we paid for Barmby. Juninho is a similar age to Barmby and he is also an international but the great thing is that he already has had a lot more experience than Barmby."

While Robson and Lamb wasted no time in flying back to England once the deal had been completed, Juninho stayed behind in Sao Paulo to tie up his personal arrangements.

In any case there was no particular rush to fly Juninho in to Teesside because Boro had to apply for a work permit from the Department of Employment, in addition to awaiting international clearance from the Brazilian FA.

No problems were envisaged over the issuing of the work permit because it was believed that Juninho met with the criteria which were laid down for foreign nationals wanting to work in this country.

However there was still plenty of paperwork which needed to be completed and exchanged with the various bodies involved. So the club estimated that it could take three weeks before Juninho was officially cleared to make his Boro debut in the Premiership.

Even so, Juninho Fever took off on Teesside as soon as it was revealed that the transfer deal had been completed. On the Monday morning, there were huge queues at the Cellnet Riverside Stadium from fans wanting season ticket application forms.

Boro had already sold just under 18,000 season tickets, which was a club record. In total, they had around 21,500 seats which could be made available to season ticket holders. These excluded the family enclosure and the seats provided for visiting supporters.

Club spokesman Dave Allan revealed that Juninho was behind the new rush for season tickets. He said: "Juninho Mania is under way. In fact it started on Saturday morning, before official confirmation was received that we had signed him.

"I would recommend that any supporters who want to watch the team regularly should buy a season ticket because, if they don't, they risk disappointment."

So, what would the new season ticket holders get for their money? Most fans had seen Juninho's terrific free kick against England in the Umbro Cup on TV, and also knew about his ability to make speedy defence splitting runs into the penalty area.

However, considering that the talented Brazilian was only 5ft 5in tall and weighed less than ten stones, some supporters questioned whether he would have the physical attributes to cope with the rigours of English football.

There was also the possibility that Juninho might struggle to reproduce his best form in the middle of the winter, when temperatures were hovering around zero and freezing rain and sleet was blowing across the pitch. In Sao Paulo, Juninho had been used to displaying his skills with the sun on his back.

Bryan Robson had no doubts that Juninho would cope on all counts. He insisted: "People are wrong about the Brazilians. They are tough people, both mentally and physically. Juninho is used to rough stuff in Brazil and he can handle it.

"And the cold won't be a problem. We'll keep him well wrapped up in training and he can warm himself up on a Saturday afternoon. In any case, our winters aren't as cold as they were a few years ago."

While it was obvious that the English conditions would be a new experience for Juninho, it was known that he was a born survivor. He had always been small for his age, and as a result had learned to take the physical knocks as he grew up on the streets of Sao Paulo, where he played alongside pals who were taller and more heavily built.

It was this struggle to survive against stronger opponents which helped Juninho develop his ball skills and close control. He also possessed electric pace, which could leave the bigger and less mobile players trailing in his wake.

This pace and inner strength did not go unnoticed, and it was his uncanny talents which led to local club Ituano offering Juninho a professional contract in 1990.

The first thing the Ituano officials did was to devise a special diet and body-building programme to build him up.

Juninho was placed on a carbohydrate diet, which had been used successfully in the past to develop the frame of his own boyhood hero, the Brazilian international Zico.

Ituano looked after Juninho well, and his progress was rapid. It was not long before he was attracting the attention of Sao Paulo officials. Naturally it was a dream come true for Juninho when Sao Paulo eventually moved in to sign him.

Even the huge step up in class failed to halt Juninho's dramatic progress. At the age of 21, the Brazilian FA called him into the full international side. It completed a phenomenal rise up the football ladder for the talented young star.

There was simply no stopping Juninho by this stage and, eight months after his international debut, he was being linked with a move to Europe. He knew that such a move could bring financial security for him and his family, and so he was naturally very interested to keep in touch with all developments.

However, despite the alleged interest by a host of clubs, Bryan Robson was the only European manager to make a personal visit to Sao Paulo to try to complete the signing. Not only did Robbo move quickly to make sure that he was ahead of the field, but the personal touch from his visit convinced Juninho that a move to the Boro was the right one to make at this stage of his career.

WELCOME to Enlgand... Juninho is greeted by Boro chief executive Keith Lamb after landing at Teesside Airport.

Juninho said: "Mr. Robson was the only manager from Europe to come to Brazil to talk to me in person. From the beginning I liked him as a person. I saw it in his face. I saw what kind of man he was. A man my father and I could trust with our lives."

To support his case, Robson showed Juninho several videos of the Boro in action, so that he could see for himself the team's style of play and the individual abilities.

Juninho said: "Bryan showed me lots of films about the city, the club, the players and the way they play. I decided then that I wanted to become a Middlesbrough player."

The diminuative Brazilian was happy to commit himself to the club on a long term basis and signed a four year contract which would run until the summer of 1999.

Now the scene was set for Juninho, accompanied by his father Oswaldo Giroldo Senior, to make his first visit to Teesside. They were to fly in on Monday, October 16, and be introduced to the fans at the Cellnet Riverside Stadium the following day.

Soon afterwards, they would return to Brazil to sort out their affairs, while awaiting the work permit and international clearance which would enable Juninho to start playing in this country.

Boro's ecstatic supporters could hardly wait for his arrival. In four days, Boro handed out season ticket application forms to 2,000 fans and quickly realised that they were heading for a season ticket sell-out. In addition, many more fans were going to be disappointed.

So Boro sat down and looked at ways in which they could accommodate everybody. The result was that they announced that the system of selling tickets in the family enclosures on a match by match basis was being scrapped, and that these areas would now be offered to season ticket applicants as well.

In some respects it was a painful decision for the club to make, because they had always prided themselves in their family policy. However the demand for season tickets was too great to ignore, and in any case it made financial sense.

Having forked out a massive £4.75 million to bring Juninho to Teesside, both for the benefit of the players and the fans, Boro needed to take advantage of every opportunity to cash in on his presence.

As Juninho's impending arrival neared, Robson enthused about the benefits the Brazilian would bring to the team. He said: "Some people are saying that it is a gamble bringing a Brazilian over here because no player from that country has ever succeeded in England. My answer to that is that we have never had a really top Brazilian here.

"The previous players have been of average ability, like Mirandinha, who was playing for a poor Newcastle team at the time. But Juninho is top quality and he will succeed.

"In fact he has the potential to become the No. 1 player in the world. I will do everything possible to help him realise that potential."

It was at this stage that Robson revealed that his interest in Juninho had been partially sparked by a Boro fan living in Eaglescliffe.

Ian Wilson, a self confessed Brazilian football nut who worked as principal revenues manager for Darlington Borough Council, had written to Robbo praising the ability of Juninho and several other top young Brazilian stars. While he was pursuing Juninho, Robson had kept Ian's letter with him all the time.

Ian said: "I'm delighted that Bryan valued my letter to him. There's a lot of Brazilian football on TV if you know where to look for it, and I watch all of it. I especially like to concentrate on the young players coming through.

Juninho Fever

"When I wrote to Bryan Robson about the previous crop of young players, it was obvious that Juninho was going to be the best of them. His skills are brilliant. It is obvious that he will be a great star on Teesside."

It was at 11.10 a.m. the following Monday morning when Juninho's plane touched down at Teesside Airport. He emerged from the private jet looking tired, amid scenes resembling a Royal visit.

There were hordes of cameramen waiting to grab their own exclusive pictures. Juninho had not only grabbed the imagination of the Teesside public, but everybody in Europe. This was clearly no run of the mill foreign signing for Boro.

After a brief word with a Portuguese camera crew, Juninho was ushered into a Jaguar and sped away to a secret location on Teesside, where he would have every opportunity to sleep and recover from the long flight from Sao Paulo.

The following morning, Juninho was due to meet Boro's fans for the first time. The weather in the North-east had been bright and sunny for some time, but there was a dramatic change that day and it was cold and wet early in the morning.

However it did not prevent several thousand supporters making their way to the Cellnet Riverside Stadium for the big event. Boro had initially intended to hold a Juninho walkabout in the car park outside the stadium, but because of the weather decided to open the stadium gates and reveal Juninho to the fans inside the stadium instead.

As the big moment neared, the atmosphere was enriched by a 50-piece samba band which had been hastily put together by students from Stockton and Billingham College. They encouraged the rapidly swelling crowd to join in the fun by clapping and stamping their feet, and waving red, white and yellow balloons.

So the perfect atmosphere was created as Juninho finally emerged at 10.15 a.m. to wave to the fans from the directors' box. Then he made his way onto the pitch, where he was engulfed by cameraman.

Many fans were disappointed that the dozens of photographers were allowed to gather so closely around the Brazilian as he walked on the pitch, because he was obscured by a swirling mass of bodies. As a result there were several angry exchanges between fans and cameramen.

After his short trip on the pitch, Juninho then retired to the restaurant inside the stadium for an official press conference in front of a highly cosmopolitan crowd.

Unfortunatley Juninho could speak no English, and the translation service was not too good. So he spent much of the time talking to the Brazilian and Portuguese journalists in Portuguese, with the English press wondering what was being said.

However Juninho did say: "I am sure I can help the team, but the team will help me as well. This is not just about Juninho. It's about a whole team. Middlesbrough is already a good club to play for. I just hope that I can make it a better club. It won't be Juninho who will win games. We will do it together as a team."

On the English weather, Juninho said: "I've been warned to expect monstrous cold. But I don't think the weather in England will be that terrible. After all, it's not Siberia, is it?"

On the physical nature of the game, he added: "People keep telling me that football in England is physical but then it is physical in Brazil as well. It's the same all over the world. I don't have a problem with that."

The Boro fans remained outside in the main stand while the Press conference was taking place and were rewarded for their patience when Juninho returned to the pitch afterwards. In fact he took part in an impromptu ball juggling game with Bryan Robson, much to the delight of the supporters.

It had been a great way to meet the fans and was appreciated by everybody who turned up. However Juninho's initial stay on Teesside was very brief. He did take part in a training session at Ayresome Park with his new teammates, but was soon back on the plane to Brazil.

Boro had expected the work permit to be a formality and were duly informed on Monday, October 23, that it had been granted. If Boro could receve Juninho's international clearance quickly, they would consider blooding him in the big Premership game at Manchester United on the Saturday. Juninho was primed and ready to fly back to England as soon as clearance was received.

The club wasted no time in forwarding Juninho's work permit and a copy of his contract to the Football Association, so that they could liaise with their Brazilian counterparts and obtain the clearance papers.

Unfortunately it turned out that the paperwork took much longer than originally anticipated, and it quickly became clear that Juninho could not be in Boro's line-up at Old Trafford.

However there was every reason to believe that Juninho would receive clearance in good time to make his Boro debut in front of a sell-out crowd against Leeds United at the Cellnet Riverside Stadium on the following Saturday, November 4. So he was advised to fly back to Britain as soon as possible.

Juninho arrived back on Teesside on the Sunday, accompanied by his father Oswaldo and his mother Lucia. Once again there was a welcoming party of Boro supporters, who were delighted to see Juninho drape a Brazilian flag over his shoulders.

Despite the tiring journey, Juninho was happy to train with the Boro squad the following day. Bryan Robson told the Evening Gazette: "Juninho has had another long flight but I asked him how he felt and he said he was fine to train. It wasn't a hard session. We just got the lads' legs working again after the weekend."

Five hundred seats for the Leeds match were all that remained unsold following the huge rush for season tickets. These were put on sale to the general public the same day at the Cellnet Riverside Stadium. There were huge queues, and not surprisingly many fans were disappointed. All the tickets were snapped up in half an hour.

By the middle of the week there was growing cause for concern because Boro were still awaiting for international clearance. Juninho continued to train with the team in the hope that everything would work out well, with Bolivian striker Jaime Moreno acting as interpreter. Although Moreno spoke Spanish, the two were able to converse using a mixture of the two languages.

THE top team together. Boro boss Bryan Robson and Juninho salute the thousands of fans who turned up at the Cellnet Riverside Stadium to greet the Brazilian's arrival.

Juninho Fever

Boro maintained a stiff upper lip and maintained that the international clearance would come through, and were finally proved right on the Thursday evening. It was now all systems go.

Everybody wanted to see Juninho's debut. Boro were besieged with Press applications from all over Britain and Europe, in addition to Brazil. The club was presented with a major headache trying to accommodate all the reporters, photographers and TV crews who wanted to be there to record the big moment.

Naturally Boro did their best to satisfy the demand, especially as this opportunity offered the club vital publicity on a worldwide scale. However some news organisations did need to be refused entry because of the sheer number of applications.

The situation was hardly any different for the fans. Boro were anticipating a near 30,000 capacity crowd, but knew that they could easily have sold 50,000 seats if the stadium had been big enough.

It was no surprise when Boro announced that they had received applications for season tickets to cover the remaining 500 seats which had gone on general sale. These had come from supporters who knew that they would miss Juninho's first game for the club, but who were determined not to miss any more.

As kick off approached, there was a party atmosphere in the stands and an eager air of anticipation. Many fans had bought Brazilian international shirts and many others sported yellow and green painted faces. The roar which greeted the teams as they ran out was incredible, and all eyes were on Juninho.

Fortunately the little Brazilian did not disappoint. In fact it took him just 11 minutes to engineer the opening goal. Juninho slotted through a perfect pass to Jan Fjortoft to break forward and blast the ball past Leeds goalkeeper John Lukic.

The rest of the half belonged to Juninho. His quickness of movement, ball control, passing skills and anticipation were a joy to behold, while his presence lifted his teammates around him.

However, just when it looked as though Boro were well in control and would turn around with a one-goal advantage, Leeds struck out of the blue with the equaliser. Noel Whelan crossed from the right and, although Brian Deane did not make the best of contacts, he managed to volley the ball into the net in the last minute of the half.

Leeds, of course, were not a bad side and had not come to the Juninho debut show as lambs to the slaughter. They asserted control in the second half and, although Boro continued to work hard, Robbo's men were happy to settle for a point at the final whistle.

Juninho did tire dramatically in the final 45 minutes, which did not come as a surprise following his heavy travelling and mental exertions in handling such a high level of hysteria and expectation from the media and the supporters.

Even so, while a 1-1 draw was not the result that everybody had hoped for, Juninho's first half performance was enough to convince the fans that there was no hype involved. The Brazililian was a talented player who had a great deal to offer the club.

Bryan Robson told the Evening Gazette: "It was disappointing to give away a soft goal right at the end of the first half but overall it was not a bad performance. Juninho showed us in the first half exactly what he is capable of achieving, and I'm sure the other lads were happy to have him around.

"Juninho tired a bit in the second half but that's only to be expected. We will see the best of him once he has found his feet in England and gets to know the rest of the players."

JUNINHO holds off a determined challenge from Leeds United defenders, in his very first game for Boro.

Unfortunately Juninho did not have time to settle in on Teesside. The following day he had to return to Brazil to play for his country in an international against Argentina. Life was certainly hectic for the 22-year-old superstar.

As a result, Juninho was unavailable for Boro's Coca Cola Cup third round replay against Crystal Palace the following Wednesday.

However, he wasn't alone. Boro had suddenly been hit by a nightmare list of injuries which decimated the squad. They were left without 11 senior players for the cuptie, while a further 11 players were injured throughout the lower sides. There were more players in the treatment room than the dressing room.

The injured men included Nick Barmby, who had picked up an Achilles injury, Derek Whyte, Phil Whelan, Robbie Mustoe, Curtis Fleming, Neil Cox, John Hendrie, Graham Kavanagh and Phil Stamp.

Barmby, who had a hand in virtually every goal Boro had scored in the Premiership so far, Whyte, Cox and Mustoe had already proved themselves crucial members of the side and it was a major blow to have so many players, and their potential replacements, injured together.

Bryan Robson, who was forced to play himself against Palace, admitted to the Evening Gazette: "It's incredible. I've never known an injury situation like this in my whole career."

At the ripe old age of 38 years and 301 days, Robson became the oldest player ever to turn out in a competitive match for the club. He beat the previous record set by goalkeeper Tim Williamson, who was 38 years and 298 days when he played against Cardiff City in 1923.

The manager was joined in the Boro side by forwards Alan Moore and Jaime Moreno as the team prepared to try to finish off Palace at the

second attempt, having drawn the first meeting 2-2 at Selhurst Park.

However the major doubts did not so much concern the team, but the size of the crowd. Thousands of season ticket holders, who had booked their cuptie tickets by post, had not received them by the morning of the match. It was a recipe for disaster.

The problems stemmed in the ticket office. The overworked staff, who had been struggling to process the huge deluge of season ticket applications over the past two weeks, had not managed to get the Palace tickets in the post in time.

So, a remarkable scene greeted supporters when they arrived at the Cellnet Riverside Stadium. As the kick off approached, there were long queues at the ticket offices, as frustrated season ticket holders stood in steady rain trying to get their Palace match tickets.

The tickets had been processed and were filed into envelopes, but it was reported that they were not sorted into name order. It created an almost farcical situation as supporters desperately battled to get their tickets, and stewards were called in to assist the staff by taking handfuls of envelopes and calling out the names to the waiting fans.

In the event many fans missed the kick off, and also Craig Hignett's eighth minute opening goal. Some supporters went home in disgust without waiting for the tickets, while it was clear from the final attendance that many others had decided to miss the match in any case. The final crowd of just over 16,000 was a little disappointing, specially considering the club's new high profile.

The match itself generally belonged to Boro, once they had survived a remarkable and hectic spell of pressure shortly before the interval in which the

BORO sparkled in the Coca Cola Cup by beating Crystal Palace in the third round replay at the Cellnet Riverside Stadium. Jaime Moreno is pictured going on a run at goal.

visitors hit the bar and missed an open goal. Boro regained control after the restart and Jan Fjortoft finally settled the issue with a superb solo goal 14 minutes from time.

However Boro paid a price for the victory, because leading scorer Hignett limped off on the half hour after picking up an ankle injury from a rash challenge by Richard Shaw. It was yet another name for the injury list, and a most unwanted one because Hignett's clinical finishing had been vitally important to the side.

The following day Boro issued a public apology to the season ticket holders who had become embroiled in the ticket chaos.

The club stressed that the rush for 8,000 new season tickets in just three weeks had put an unbearable strain on the ticket office staff, but added that steps would be taken to ensure that the embarrassing situation was never again repeated.

At the same time, there was good news from Buenos Aires when it was reported that Juninho had played well in the international against Argentina, and helped Brazil win a bruising encounter by 1-0. Juninho had helped set up the winning goal and gone close to scoring himself on two occasions.

Brazil manager Mario Zagalo said: "Juninho honoured the green and gold shirt and played a vital role in what was a great win for us."

Juninho's next task was to get back on to a plane and fly back for Boro's official opening match for the Cellnet Riverside Stadium. They were entertaining Italian Serie A side Sampdoria in what was being treated as a showpiece game on Sunday, November 12. A special Boro strip had been designed for the one-off occasion.

Even so, the game had come at a very bad time for the club's coaches because of the ongoing injury crisis. There was no point in risking any of the players who were fighting their way back from injury and so it was a very weak looking Boro line-up which eventually took the field. In no way did it represent the true strength of the squad.

However Juninho entered into the spirit by playing the full 90 minutes despite having suffered from yet another long flight back to England. Manager Bryan Robson also played throughout.

The teams were:

Boro: Walsh, Liddle, Blackmore (McGargle 17, Summerbell 82), Vickers, Pearson (White 74), O'Halloran, Robson, Stamp, Moreno (Freestone 74), Juninho, Moore, Sub: Payne.

Sampdoria: Sereni, Balleri, Ferri (Zito 75), Lamonica, Pesaresi, Sacchetti, Mancini (Jacopino 53), Evani, Invernizzi (Bellucci 53), Salsano, Maniero. Sub: Marchestotti.

The game was watched by less than 10,000 fans, which was an indication that the match had not grabbed the imagination of the Teesside footballing public, despite the appearance of Juninho.

The clash also finished goalless, though nobody will ever know how. Experienced Spennymoor referee George Courtney failed to award a penalty in the tenth minute when Stefano Sacchetti blatantly handled inside the area after goalkeeper Matteo Sereni had rolled the ball out to him. Courtney initially pointed to the penalty spot, but then amazingly changed his mind and awarded a goal kick.

The referee said afterwards that he admitted making a mistake. He had disallowed the penalty in the belief that Sereni had initially taken a goal kick and that the ball had not gone out of the area, but realised his error when watching the video later.

In addition to the penalty that never was, Boro missed a great chance to settle it when Bryan Robson somehow fired wide of a gaping goal after being put through by Juninho.

Even in a friendly, the injury nightmare struck again. Clayton Blackmore limped off in the early stages with a pulled hamstring, while young midfielder Stephen McGargle was stretchered off with a bad knee injury following one of several over-zealous tackles by the Italians in the closing minutes. In fact Mr. Courtney booked five visiting players in quick succession in the final 15 minutes.

The Cellnet Riverside Stadium had another respite from Premership action when hosting England's Under-21 international against Austria on Tuesday, November 14. The match had a special appeal for Boro fans because Jamie Pollock was playing.

As a result, a half decent crowd of 13,496 turned up and provided plenty of vocal backing. Pollock was one of England's more prominent performers as the home side won an entertaining match by 2-1.

The following night, Jan Fjortoft and Chris Morris were both on full international duty. Fjortoft lined up for Norway in their crucial European Championship group five qualifier in Holland which the Norwegians needed only to draw to reach the finals in England. It was a night of similar

IT'S Juninho on the rampage again. The Brazilian is pictured in action against Sampdoria, wearing the special shirt which was commissioned for the official opening game at the Cellent Riverside Stadium. Also pictured is Spennymoor referee George Courtney.

ENGLAND expects... Boro midfielder Jamie Pollock trains with the England Under-21 squad at Ayresome Park in preparation for his international call-up against Austria at the Cellnet Riverside Stadium.

importance for Morris and the Republic of Ireland squad in Portugal.

Unfortunately the evening was one of huge disappointment for both players. Norway and the Republic were both beaten and eventually failed to qualify for the finals. It left Boro's England duo, coach Bryan Robson and striker Nick Barmby, as the only two players from the club likely to have a personal involvement in the finals.

Robson had hoped to keep his place in the Boro side for the Premiership match at Wimbledon on the Saturday, but had been suffering from a virus all week and eventually was forced to admit defeat. However he did name himself on the bench.

Juninho was in fine fettle following his recent spell of hectic travelling, and was making his London debut in a Boro shirt. Nick Barmby and Neil Cox returned after injury, while progressive teenager Phil Stamp stepped up to deputise for Robson.

Overall, it looked a strong Boro side on duty, and Robson's men were hot favourites to win because the Dons had lost their last eight games. Unfortunately it didn't work out as hoped. Boro enjoyed the bulk of the play, with Juninho and Barmby prominent in approach play, but Robbo's men had to settle for a share of the spoils in a goalless draw.

There was a flare-up in the media afterwards, when Wimbledon's midfield hard man Vinnie Jones accused Juninho of having 'dived' in attempts to win free kicks.

Jones claimed: "Juninho was diving during the match and I got a bit upset. At the end of the game I went up to him and told him he didn't do those things in the English game. He should stay on his feet and cut out the diving."

It's probable that Juninho wouldn't have had a clue what Jones was talking about, because he still had only a vague understanding of the English language. And the fact that Jones was seen to shake Juninho's hand at the end of the match indicated that most of the apparent animosity had been generated as the result of questions from the media after the game.

Robson, when pressed to reply to Jones' comments, said: "The trouble with Vinnie is that he can't get his publicity on the pitch so he had to find another way. He talks to the papers and accuses Juninho of being a cheat, just because it gets his own name in print."

Robbo then went on to praise two of his own players, Phil Stamp and Craig Liddle. He said: "I thought both lads were brilliant, particularly Stamp, because he was playing against a proven international in Oyvind Leonhardsen. Philip did exactly what I knew he could, and if he keeps his feet on the ground then the kid has a big future in the game.

"And Craig never put a foot wrong. He keeps his passing nice and simple and never tries to do anything complicated."

Both Stamp and Liddle kept their places in the line-up as Boro prepared to entertain Spurs on Tuesday, November 21. Jamie Pollock had recovered from a calf strain picked up at Wimbledon and so Bryan Robson named an unchanged team.

The match attracted a new record crowd of 29,487 to the Cellnet Riverside Stadium, despite the fact that it was a very cold evening. Unfortunately Boro seemed to freeze as well, and were beaten for the first time in their new home.

They had suffered an early blow when Pollock was stretchered off with a nasty head gash, though

Robson was on the bench again and came on as midfield replacement.

However Boro struggled to get shots on target and paid the price when they conceded the only goal of the game in the 72nd minute. The goal followed an unfortunate slip by Liddle, who lost possession to Ruel Fox. The nippy Spurs winger whipped in a cross to the far post for the unmarked Chris Armstrong to flick the ball home. There was a hint of offside, but the flag stayed down.

Afterwards, the whole Boro camp found the defeat hard to swallow because they were convinced that the goal was offside. Assistant boss Viv Anderson said: "It was blatantly obvious that Armstrong was offside. Our players said that he was at least five yards offside.

"Even Armstrong's first reaction was to look at the linesman after he had put the ball in the net. I think he couldn't believe it either when the flag stayed down. I couldn't believe it when the ref didn't disallow it. You expect officials to make the right decisions."

There was a further blow from the game because Chris Morris picked up a booking which took him past 21 penalty points. By reaching 21 points before the end of November, Morris faced a three-match ban. Bryan Robson said: "It's a blow for us, but I feel sorry for Chris because half of his bookings have been unjust."

Fortunately there was better news the following day when it was revealed in the Evening Gazette that Jamie Pollock had been cleared by the club doctor to play in the big home game against Liverpool the following Saturday. It meant that Robson was able to field an unchanged side in a match for which Boro needed no motivation.

As it turned out, they were given a dream start when Nick Barmby set up the opening goal for Neil Cox after only two minutes.

Boro went on to produce their most thrilling football of the season, with Juninho an absolute revelation with his runs from deep positions. However Robson's men could not add to their early breakthrough and paid the penalty in 63 minutes when Neil Ruddock headed in.

If Liverpool had been allowed to settle down, they might have caused Boro further problems. But Boro regained the lead within 60 seconds thanks to a terrific finish from Barmby and afterwards never looked likely to surrender their lead again.

One of the biggest contributory factors in Boro's win was the decision by Banbury referee Dermot Gallagher not to send off Gary Walsh for handballing outside his area early in the second half. Walsh, who was only booked, made a remarkable save from Ruddock's free kick which followed the offence. It was a lucky escape for Boro because they did not have a reserve keeper on the bench.

Robson still insisted that the ref had made the right decision. He told the Evening Gazette: "I didn't think Gary deserved to be sent off and it hasn't caused me to rethink my policy. I still won't put a keeper on the bench unless I feel it is right for a particular game."

The victory against Liverpool had the whole of Middlesbrough buzzing. There was more good news the following week when Robson announced that top scorer Craig Hignett had agreed a new three-year contract with the club.

Hignett's was a real rags to riches story, having initially been made available for transfer during the summer. At the time Craig, full of self belief in his ability to be a success with Boro in the Premiership, had begged Robson to allow him to stay on a reduced contract. Since then he had worked very hard to prove himself. He was the team's best player in pre-season and went on to make a big impact in the first few months of the season, scoring seven goals.

The result was that Robson was happy to award Hignett a revised and improved deal. The manager said "Craig was given a spell on a reduced wage to prove himself and he had done so. He's back in the form he was showing at the start of last season. Craig had glandular fever for part of last season and it had a big effect on him. Now, it is all behind him, and he has earned his new deal."

A delighted Hignett said: "When I was transfer listed, I told Bryan that I wanted to stay and fight for my place. The boss told me I would get my reward if I did well, and he has kept his word.

"I wanted to stay here because it is an exciting time at Boro, with the Premier League and the new stadium. It was a gamble but it has paid off. When the manager said it was time to talk about a new deal I was made up."

CRAIG LIDDLE - proved himself a jack of all trades by playing in a number of positions in the Premiership, performing well in all of them and providing valuable cover when the injuries started to take effect.

HOW about that then! Neil Cox celebrates his second minute opener against Liverpool with Juninho.

IT'S Liverpool under pressure as Jason McAteer and Mark Wright struggle to cope with one of Juninho's runs in the memorable match at the Cellnet Riverside Stadium.

Juninho Fever

Hignett was back in the Boro squad, after recovering from an ankle injury, for the team's third home game in nine days. This time Boro took a break from the Premiership when entertaining First Division Birmingham City in the fourth round of the Coca Cola Cup.

Robson once again named an unchanged side, so Hignett had to settle for a place on the bench. However he did see a bit of second half action, but had no opportunities to break the deadlock as Boro were held to a goalless draw.

Man of the match Juninho enjoyed a magnificent first half and hit the underside of the Birmingham crossbar from a free kick just before the interval. But City hit back after the restart and Boro were grateful for some excellent work by their defence and also a bit of help from the woodwork, which denied the gangly Kevin Francis a goal midway through the second period.

weeks, despite suffering from a virus which had swept the dressing room. Nigel Pearson, Jamie Pollock and Jan Fjortoft had all been affected, while Alan Moore was currently laid low by the illness.

However Pearson and Pollock were both fit to line up for Boro's next game at Queen's Park Rangers on Saturday, December 2, while Fjortoft had to settle for a place on the bench. Fjortoft's place in the starting line up went to the Bolivian Jaime Moreno, who had recently put together a string of fine performances for the reserves.

In the event Boro did not make too much impression in attack, though they gained a 1-1 draw which contained most of its action in a hectic opening 15 minutes.

Simon Barker missed a penalty for Rangers after Pearson was rather unjustly accused of handball, while Boro were then awarded a penalty of their own when Barker fouled Phil Stamp.

JAMIE POLLOCK, sporting a protector after suffering a nasty head gash against Spurs, is pictured in action against Birmingham City in the fourth round of the Coca Cola Cup at the Cellnet Riverside Stadium. The match ended goalless.

There was some consolation for the Boro, because the club received record gross receipts of £290,000 from the 28,031 crowd. This beat the previous best of £200,351 from the Coca Cola Cup tie against Newcastle United in October, 1992.

After the game, Robson revealed to the Evening Gazette that he intended to pull Juninho out of a friendly international between Brazil and Colombia in two weeks' time, so that he could play for Boro in the replay against Birmingham.

Robson insisted: "Juninho is playing for us in the cup. It's a massive game for us and so he won't be going to Brazil. We need him and I'll have a chat with him, pointing out that Brazil's game is only a friendly match."

The manager also announced that several Boro players had been playing on, over the past few

Nick Barmby's spot kick was saved but Chris Morris popped up to slide home the rebound despite claims from Rangers that Morris had been inside the area when the penalty was taken.

Boro's lead lasted just eight minutes before Rangers levelled when a header from Alan McDonald was judged to have crossed the line. On this occasion Robson's men complained to no avail.

Another player in the thick of the action that weekend was Paul Wilkinson. Boro's transfer listed striker, having completed a month's loan at Oldham Athletic, was now starting another one with his former club Watford. Wilko wasted no time in settling back into the swing by creating one of the goals in Watford's 2-1 win at Millwall.

Nick Barmby received a boost the following week when he was named in the England squad for the friendly match against Portugal at Wembley. Barmby had missed England's previous game against Switzerland because of hamstring trouble, but had proved his fitness in the Premiership over the past couple of weeks and fully merited his return to the international scene.

Barmby's first task was to do his bit for Boro in a potentially difficult match at home to Manchester City, who had improved beyond recognition from the struggling side which Boro had beaten by 1-0 at Maine Road in September. In fact revitalised City were unbeaten in their last five games, conceding just one goal, and earning manager Alan Ball the manager of the month award.

Boro were strengthened by the return of Scottish international Derek Whyte, who had successfully come through a midweek reserve game after recovering from a stomach operation. Whyte had

The visitors led early in the game through a remarkable solo goal from the talented Georgian midfielder Georgi Kinkladze, but Boro then hit back strongly and scored some great goals of their own.

Nick Barmby warmed up for his England call-up by scoring on either side of the interval and man of the match Phil Stamp grabbed a sensational individual goal. The icing on the cake came from Juninho's first goal for the club, when he reacted like lightning to poke home the loose ball after City keeper Eike Immel had fumbled a 25-yarder from Stamp.

The victory pushed Boro into fourth place in the Premiership with Robson saying: "If someone had said at the start of the season that we would have been joint third in early December then I would have been delighted with that. The one thing we have got here is a very good team spirit, which is important to us."

NICK BARMBY gets into the thick of the action by challenging Manchester City duo Niall Quinn and Keith Curle for possession. Barmby went onto score twice as Boro won 4-1.

not played in the Premiership since the middle of October.

He returned to the heart of the Boro defence with Craig Liddle, who was proving himself a very useful utility player, moving out to left back in place of Chris Morris, who was starting his three-match ban for passing 21 penalty points.

Jan Fjortoft was also back in action to lead the attack in place of Jaime Moreno, while John Hendrie, yet to start a match this season following a groin strain, was on the bench.

The game turned out to be a thriller. A terrific game of open football was won 4-1 by Boro, though City played their part and, with better finishing, might even have grabbed a share of the spoils.

Boro could certainly regard themselves as one of the top sides in the Premiership. They were particularly hard to beat, mainly because of their superb defensive qualities, and could give anybody a hard game. The only problem was that goals were proving a bit hard to come by on their travels.

In midweek, Barmby successfully came through England's 1-1 draw with Portugal, while Chris Morris also returned unscathed after being part of the Republic of Ireland squad which lost the crucial European Championship decider against Holland.

However Bryan Robson still had to face up to team problems for the difficult game away to Champions Blackburn Rovers because Jamie Pollock was ruled out with a knee injury.

It was a particularly bad time to lose one of the team's most influential players. Bryan Robson had

CHRISTMAS is coming, and Boro launched their annual children's festive appeal with a donation of dozens of cuddly toys from McDonalds. Pictured from left to right at the back are Viv Anderson, Bob Connick from McDonalds, Bryan Robson, Roary, Santa Derek Whyte and Karen Workman from McDonalds. In the foreground are Robbie Mustoe and Geraldine Ableson from McDonalds.

hoped to play himself but was not fully recovered from a calf injury so Craig Liddle was pushed forward into midfield, and Curtis Fleming was handed a dramatic recall to Premiership action at left-back.

Fleming had finally recovered from a hip injury which had kept him sidelined for much of the previous ten months and was eventually solved by an operation. He had proved his fitness in two reserve games, but faced a daunting prospect on his return by marking England and former Boro winger Stuart Ripley.

Curtis worked very hard to try to quickly pick up the pace of the Premiership again but it was a difficult afternoon not only for the Boro defence, but also the team as a whole. They did defend very well, and limited Rovers to a single goal from Alan Shearer just before the interval. But Blackburn fully deserved the three points.

There was a further blow for Boro in the dying seconds when Derek Whyte was sent off by referee Paul Danson for a second bookable offence. Both yellow cards were produced for fouls by Whyte on Shearer, though the second one was rather innocuous.

Boro, disappointed to lose the game, were incensed by the red card decision. The frustrations boiled over in the players' tunnel afterwards with Bryan Robson, Neil Cox and Nigel Pearson all involved in a heated discussion with Mr. Danson.

As a result of things which were said by the Boro trio, the referee reported the incident to the FA, and all three men were promptly charged with bringing the game into disrepute.

Blackburn also suffered their problems during the match. England left-back Graham Le Saux broke his fibula, dislocated his ankle and ruptured his tendon in a horrendous fall while making a challenge on

Juninho. It was a freak accident, and no blame was attached in any direction. But everybody was cut up by the incident, and Boro responded by sending a basket of fruit to Le Saux in hospital.

Le Saux's injury came at the same time as Boro lost a member of their own squad when top scorer Craig Hignett went into hospital for a hernia operation. It was a blow for Hignett, following so soon after being sidelined by an ankle injury.

With one big game out of the way, Boro now had another one to look forward to. They were due to visit St. Andrews for their Coca Cola Cup fourth round replay against Birmingham City.

Boro were very confident that they could win the cuptie at the second attempt and received a huge boost when Jamie Pollock returned to training following his knee injury and pronounced himself ready to face the Midlanders. Pollock resumed in midfield in place of Craig Liddle, who had done very well in a run of nine games in the side, despite regularly switching positions.

However bad news followed the good when Nick Barmby was forced to drop out on the morning of the cuptie after suffering a recurrence of his Achilles tendon injury. It was only the second match that the England striker had missed all this season, and he had proved to be a crucial member of the side.

The absence of Barmby created an opportunity for John Hendrie to return to the starting line up for the first time since the pre-season programme. The Scot, who was top scorer in Bryan Robson's first season in charge, had been missed during his injury.

Birmingham had been hit by a couple of inches of snow overnight, and match officials had worked feverishly to ensure that the cuptie could go ahead. However it was a very cold St. Andrews which greeted the travelling Boro fans, and the streets around the stadium were in a dangerous and extremely icy state.

Boro never seemed to warm up to their task, and the match was over as a contest after 18 minutes. Two out-of-character errors by Jamie Pollock, who gave the ball away to Steve Claridge on both occasions, led to Kevin Francis producing two amazing finishes to put Boro on the rack.

Bryan Robson's men never looked capable of getting back into the game, though it might have been a different story if referee Mike Pierce had awarded a penalty when Jan Fjortoft was clearly brought down by Birmingham goalkeeper Ian Bennett after only four minutes.

Robbo's team had not enjoyed the best of luck as far as having crucial penalties awarded in their favour was concerned, though they did not play well on the night and nobody could take anything away from the First Division side.

Even so, the cup KO blow left Boro in a state of depression because they had been knocked out of a competition they believed they could do well in by a side from a lower division.

At the time the defeat was regarded merely as a hiccup, but failure to beat Birmingham went much deeper than that. It was a sign that Boro were failing to maintain the high standards which they had set throughout the first three months of the season.

The outcome was that Boro were about to pay a very high price over the following three months.

The Bleak Mid Winter

CHAPTER EIGHT:

CHRISTMAS was drawing near and the weather was deteriorating. But Bryan Robson had every reason to be a happy man.

Boro had made a big impression on their return to the Premiership and were a top six side. In fact the manager's claims that the team was good enough to do well in the top flight had been fully vindicated in the first four months of the season.

It was a great time to be a Boro fan, because the team was a match for any other in the league. The major strength was in defence, where Boro were very difficult to breach. Boro's five-man defence had caused problems for the best of attacks, and clean sheets were regularly par for the course.

They had achieved this success without one of their regular defenders, Curtis Fleming, who had missed most of the action with a hip injury. Boro had also comfortably covered for other injuries, with Phil Whelan and new discovery Craig Liddle both coming in on occasions without affecting the consistency.

An unfortunate groin injury to goalkeeper Alan Miller early in the season had given an opportunity to Gary Walsh, and the former Manchester United keeper had taken his opportunity with both hands. He had proved a good shot stopper, with command of his area, and had generated confidence for players and fans alike.

Not that Boro's success was due solely to their defenders. They were very mobile as a team, with record signing Nick Barmby having transformed the club's attacking capabilities with his defence splitting play and clinical finishing.

Teesside and Boro had then threatened to take off when Brazilian superstar Juninho joined the fray in early November. The fans had responded to this major coup by snapping up all the available season tickets, and now the Cellnet Riverside Stadium was assured of a near 30,000 capacity crowd every game.

In their wildest dreams, no Boro fan could have envisaged this incredible situation only 12 months earlier. All they had wanted at the start of the season was to see Boro preserve their newly won Premiership status. Yet here was the team riding high near the top of the league with a genuine chance of qualifying for Europe.

The quality of Boro's football had been breathtaking at times. Robson had developed the passing system to the point where it had become a fine art, with Barmby, Juninho, Craig Hignett and Jan Fjortoft having developed a terrific understanding.

Remarkably, this success had been achieved without the team operating with orthodox wide players. The onus was on full-backs Neil Cox and Chris Morris to get forward at every opportunity, and both players had enjoyed fine starts to the season. But it was not possible for the duo to push out when Boro were under pressure.

Even so, Boro's apparent lack of width had not so much been a hindrance, but a bonus. Most opposing teams had struggled to cope with Boro's compact style of play, because it was unusual for a side to concentrate on playing straight through the middle.

It hadn't been smooth running all of the time. Boro had suffered one or two problems in early November when they were hit by a horrendous run of injuries, which forced Robson to field a few severely weakened sides. It was an indication that the squad did not possess real quality in depth.

However, once the injured players returned, Boro were quickly back on the rails. The only general worry was that Boro had not scored as many goals as would have been hoped, though this dearth up front had been amply compensated by the number of clean sheets at the other end of the field.

Boro's main threat up front at the start of the season was Hignett, who was top scorer with seven goals. These goals had come in his first 15 appearances. However Hignett was now recovering from a hernia operation, after earlier being sidelined with an ankle injury.

To make matters worse, influential attacker Barmby was suffering from an Achilles injury. With Jan Fjortoft struggling a little to maintain his previous prolific scoring form, there was concern up front, because this was the one department where Boro seemed to have the weakest cover.

On the plus side, John Hendrie, who was the club's top scorer in Robson's first season in charge, was on his way back from a groin strain and looking to establish himself again.

Overall, there was a mood of optimism as Boro approached their festive programme. And why not? They had not seen anything to frighten them so far in the Premiership.

Traditionally, Boro tended to do badly at Christmas. It was a time when the fans expected them to start to slide down the table. However this was a new team with a new attitude, and hopes were high that Boro could come through their hectic programme without too many problems - provided they could steer clear of injuries.

Boro opened with a home game against West Ham United on Saturday, December 23, and welcomed Bryan Robson back into the fray after recovering from his calf strain. The Boro boss slotted into his usual role in the middle of the park in place

BRYAN ROBSON'S last Premiership appearance in a Boro shirt. The Boro boss is pictured in action in the 4-2 victory at home to West Ham United just before Christmas.

of Phil Stamp, while Chris Morris was also back after suspension and replaced Curtis Fleming at left-back.

Boro were keen to make a good start to their Christmas programme and could hardly have done better. They sent the fans home happy on a bitterly cold afternoon by beating the Hammers by 4-2 in an exciting, open game of football.

The match was effectively won at half-time when Boro raced into a 3-0 lead with goals from Jan Fjortoft, Neil Cox and Chris Morris. That's how it stayed until the final ten minutes when John Hendrie marked his full Premiership debut at the Cellnet Riverside Stadium with Boro's fourth goal, which was sandwiched in between strikes from Tony Cottee and Julian Dicks for the visitors.

Boro had very little time to gather their senses before they were back in action. They trained on Christmas Day in preparation for the trip to Everton on Boxing Day. It was a big game for Boro, because they would go second top if they won.

The Blues had been going through a difficult spell, and so this was a good time for Boro to meet them. Robson was unable to cope with two games in four days, so he dropped out, with Craig Liddle taking his place in midfield. The manager also rested Chris Morris, and so Curtis Fleming resumed at left-back.

In the event, a game which looked so promising for Boro turned out to be a disaster. Boro not only suffered a humiliating 4-0 defeat, but they picked up new injuries.

Boro were chasing the game from the moment when Craig Short headed Everton in front after 11 minutes. They might have had a chance of salvaging

something in the second half had not Graham Stuart ended their hopes with Everton's second goal on the stroke of half-time. Boro looked a well beaten side in the second half and Stuart and former Bryan Robson target Andrei Kanchelskis grabbed further goals.

It was the first time all season that the Boro defence had looked suspect, though the biggest problem was off the field. Derek Whyte limped off with a calf strain, and then Chris Morris, who had replaced Whyte as substitute, picked up a thigh injury. Suddenly, two key men were out of action as the club entered the most testing run of games in the whole season.

Bryan Robson told the Evening Gazette: "The second goal was the important one from Everton's point of view because we were chasing the game in the second half. Obviously it's very disappointing to lose by four goals but the worst thing is that we have picked up new injuries and that's the last thing we need at this stage of the season."

It's amazing how quickly fortunes can change virtually overnight in football. It can be a cruel game for fans, players and coaches alike. Boro suddenly found themselves building up to Saturday's trip to Nottingham Forest without five of the players who had started the season in the first match against Chelsea.

Whyte and Morris joined Nick Barmby, Craig Hignett and Robbie Mustoe on the sidelines. A further problem was that Neil Cox had been booked at Everton and faced a two-match ban.

The problems were exacerbated on the morning of the Forest match when Jan Fjortoft was forced to drop out of the reckoning with a groin strain. It left

CELEBRATIONS all round after Chris Morris, with arms raised, had scored Boro's third goal against West Ham United. Jan Fjortoft congratulates Boro boss Bryan Robson, as Juninho moves in to join the party.

Boro without any of their orthodox front runners, who had shared most of the team's Premiership goals between them.

Robson had to juggle his players around in the best way he could and settled on a 5-3-2 formation. Craig Liddle reverted to defence in place of Whyte, Clayton Blackmore and Alan Moore joined Jamie Pollock in midfield and Juninho was promoted into an attacking role alongside John Hendrie.

In the event Boro found themselves chasing the game yet again when they conceded a disputed penalty in the ninth minute. Curtis Fleming was judged to have fouled Steve Stone and Stuart Pearce rammed home the spot kick.

Boro worked hard, and did not let themselves down. They might even have grabbed a point, but Hendrie hit the base of the left hand post from a great solo effort. However, other chances for Robson's men were few and far between.

The games were coming thick and fast and it was both a frustrated and tired Boro squad which battled to gather its senses together for another Premiership game just 48 hours later when Aston Villa visited the Cellnet Riverside Stadium on New Year's Day.

Bryan Robson was limited in the changes he could make without harming the effectiveness of the squad, though Phil Stamp and Jaime Moreno came in for Blackmore and Moore. Villa, on the other hand, went into the match both fit and fresh, because two of their Christmas games had been postponed.

The difference in fitness was evident from the start, and Villa were well on top in the first half.

They led 2-0 at the interval through two great finishes from Alan Wright and Tommy Johnson. Boro somehow dug very deep after the restart to control the possession, but they could not force themselves back into the game.

Assistant boss Viv Anderson said: "The lads put their hearts into the match but there was some fatigue. I thought we started off well, but Villa scored from two great strikes and made it difficult for us. Overall we created few chances, but the lads couldn't have worked any harder in the second half."

Suddenly Boro had suffered three Premiership defeats off the belt, and were no longer looking strong and solid. They had conceded seven goals without scoring in reply. It was only natural that the key men up front were being badly missed, but there was a general lack of spark about the side.

Fortunately they were offered a break from the rigours of the league as they prepared for an FA Cup third round tie against Notts County at Meadow Lane on January 6. County were going well in the Second Division and were in the hunt for promotion. So the fixture presented a tricky test for Boro in their current form and was a potential Cup upset.

The team received a boost in the build up to the match when Nick Barmby had a cortisone injection to ease his inflamed Achilles tendon and was pronounced ready to return.

There was further good news when Bryan Robson returned to training following his sciatica, while Phil Whelan proved his fitness in Boro reserves' goalless draw at York City, after recovering from a broken jaw.

DETERMINATION in the face of Boro skipper Nigel Pearson as he challenges Savo Milosevic for possession in the battle against Aston Villa on New Year's Day

Paul Wilkinson played in the same reserve game following his month's loan at Watford. The Hornets seemed keen to complete a permanent transfer to take Wilko back to Vicarage Road for his second spell on the payroll, but they were not prepared to pay Boro's £250,000 asking price. If Watford had been able to afford the cash, then Wilkinson would probably have moved on.

In the event, Robson sprang a huge surprise when Wilkinson was named in the Boro starting line up at Notts County. It was the first time for 11 months that the 31-year-old striker had started a game for the club. It had seemed likely for some time that he would not figure in a first team match again.

Robson had placed Wilkinson on the transfer list in the summer, but there were no takers and the player had eventually gone out on loan spells at Oldham and Watford. Now he was thrown back into the melting pot and given the opportunity to restake his claim.

Robson and Barmby passed late fitness tests and the Boro line-up had its strongest look since before Christmas. The team was: Walsh, Liddle, Fleming, Vickers, Pearson, Whelan, Barmby, Pollock, Wilkinson, Juninho, Robson. Subs: Stamp, Moreno, Miller.

However Boro were still without John Hendrie, who had suffered another frustrating groin strain against Villa, and Neil Cox, who was suspended. Liddle switched to right-back for Cox, while Phil Whelan came into the heart of the defence.

All the team's Premiership problems were forgotten as the new line-up blew away the cobwebs by cruising to a 2-1 victory. Boro controlled the game virtually throughout and the best player on the pitch, by a mile, was Robson.

The player manager was back to his vintage best, winning every tackle and never wasting a pass. It was a remarkable example to the other 21 players from a man approaching his 39th birthday.

The Bleak Mid Winter

Jamie Pollock fired Boro ahead early in the second half and Barmby, who caused the County defence huge problems with his darting runs, added a second goal. Paul Rogers reduced the arrears in the 53rd minute, but otherwise Boro were never threatened.

Wilkinson was another to enjoy an excellent game, after such a long spell away from the side. Robson told the Evening Gazette: "Paul did really well for us and played his part in winning the game. Watford said they were interested in signing him but they didn't come back to me. As long as he is a Middlesbrough player, he will be considered for selection."

As always, there was a negative side to the victory. Curtis Fleming was stretchered off in the first half with a knee injury and faced several weeks on the sidelines. It was a kick in the teeth for the plucky Irish defender, who had been working so hard to try to re-establish himself following his ten months lay off through a hip injury.

Fleming was immediately rushed to hospital for an exploratory operation, but fortunately the damage was nothing worse than routine medial ligament damage. It could be corrected with rest and treatment, and the defender was ruled out for six weeks.

The following week, there were reports in national newspapers alleging that Juninho was unhappy on Teesside. The team had not done too well since Juninho's arrival, and there were claims that the Brazilian was not enjoying his football in England.

However Juninho insisted: "It's nonsense to suggest that I'm pining for Brazil. I've got all my family here with me and we have always been close. I want to make Middlesbrough a great team and I'm sure we can do well when injuries clear up."

Even so, Juninho was obviously absorbing a certain amount of personal pressure. He had arrived on Teesside as a super hero, and must have felt that he was expected to carry the team on his shoulders.

Yet, despite his talents, Juninho could not be expected to single handedly halt Boro's gradual slide when the injuries came. He had produced some virtuoso performances at home, but no one man could solve all the problems. And, after being a winner all his career, it must have been alien to Juninho to find himself in a losing run.

However, after recovering from the Juninho scare, Boro fans found themselves facing an even bigger threat to the team's progress. On January 10, England manager Terry Venables announced that he was quitting the international arena following the European Championships in the summer.

Venables was relinquishing his post to concentrate on several elongated legal battles which he faced in the High Court and which were due to start at the end of the year.

The news was a blow not only to the Football Association, but England fans everywhere. However the news hit hardest on Teesside, specially when the national media immediately made Robson the favourite to take over the England hot seat. The prospect of losing Robson, after he had just started the task of transforming the club, was hard to bear for the fans.

But it was impossible to deny that Robson possessed excellent credentials for the England job. He was already the national coach and joined up with the squad for training before every international. As a result, Robbo worked very closely with Venables, and had a huge input into team selection and tactics.

Clearly it was a widely held belief that Robson was being groomed for the England job. He was learning his club managerial trade with the Boro, while at the same time operating as first team coach for England. The England post was part-time, but if he was to complete the natural progression and take over the helm of the international side as Venables' replacement, then undoubtedly he would then go full-time and quit club football.

There were other candidates, of course, like Kevin Keegan, who had led Newcastle United on a Championship charge. There was Glenn Hoddle, who was believed to have support within the corridors of Lancaster Gate, and there was Gerry Francis. But the bookmakers were clear cut in their beliefs, and wasted no time in making Robson favourite to replace Venables.

The threat to the Boro was further increased when FA chief executive Graham Kelly revealed that he wanted a new appointment to be made "sooner rather than later".

To make matters worse, the national press were already gathering their collective support behind Robson. They also seemed keen to see a quick appointment.

The only dissenting voices were coming from Teesside. Everybody in and around Middlesbrough was desperate to see Robson stay on with the Boro and complete the job which he had already started. The Evening Gazette received countless phone calls and letters all pleading with the manager not to leave.

One thing was certain. The national clamour of "Robson For England" was so strong that it was clear there needed to be immediate action from one quarter or another. To much relief on Teesside, the action came from Robson himself when he announced publicly that he intended to stay put. He would be honouring the remaining 18 months of his original three-year contract with Boro.

Robson told the Evening Gazette: "As far as I am concerned I expect to see the three years through with Boro. I have 18 months of that contract still to run and I will not be moving while I am under contract."

He added: "I am enjoying the job with Boro but I also enjoy the job with England and I am looking forward to the European Championships. But I am still an apprentice as far as being a manager is concerned."

At the same time, Robson had a meeting with Boro chairman Steve Gibson to give official assurances that he had no intentions of quitting the Boro while the job was only half done.

It must have been as big a relief for the directors as it was for the supporters. Boro were only a short way along the road towards realising their ambitions of becoming a big club again, and had already backed their aims with a major cash investment. It was useful for the board to know that they were not about to lose their catalyst.

JAMIE POLLOCK is on the rampage as he prepares to take on Arsenal defender Gavin McGowan at the Cellnet Riverside Stadium.

ENGLAND teammates clash as Nick Barmby battles with Arsenal's David Platt for possession.

THAT'S the way to do it! Phil Stamp celebrates after scoring a magnificent goal against Arsenal.

While the fears receded, there was no evidence that Robson was ever officially offered Venables' job. However the Boro boss did have talks with FA officials during the course of his England duties, and it's likely that he reiterated what he had told reporters, that he would like to carry on as normal while he was learning his trade. It must have contributed greatly towards nipping any potential England job offer in the bud.

Even so, most Boro fans were responsible enough to accept that Robson would probably one day leave the club, and that the odds were that he could leave Teesside to take over the England helm.

In the meantime, it was good to know that this departure was not imminent, though it was to be some time before all the speculation finally died away.

England apart, Robson already had enough to think about at the Boro. The team needed to halt a run of three consecutive Premiership defeats at home to Arsenal, both to restore morale and to try to regain a top six placing.

Unfortunately Robson was unable to make a physical contribution towards this task. His sciatica had flared up again, and he was back on the sidelines. Neil Cox, Curtis Fleming, Derek Whyte, Robbie Mustoe and Craig Hignett were also unavailable for a variety of reasons.

Clayton Blackmore replaced Robson in midfield, while Craig Liddle switched from right to left-back for the injured Fleming, Phil Stamp came in at right-back and Jan Fjortoft, having recovered from his groin strain, returned to the attack for Paul Wilkinson.

Boro made yet another slow start and found themselves trailing after just seven minutes to a Paul Merson goal. They struggled throughout much of the first half but equalised shortly before the interval when a cheeky backheel from Fjortoft put in Juninho to score from close range.

Boro began the second half with all guns blazing and when Juninho put man of the match Stamp in to give Boro the lead, it looked all over a home win. Unfortunately the Gunners had other ideas, and two goals in four minutes from David Platt and Glenn Helder turned the match on its head. The team was heading for another defeat.

In the final minute there was a further blow when Alan Moore, who had come on as a first half substitute for Jamie Pollock, was shown the red card for an elbow on Gavin McGowan. Pollock faced two matches on the sidelines with a knee injury, while Moore earned a three-match ban for his sending off.

Robson told the Evening Gazette: "We made a slow start but we should have gone on to win the game after Stamp had put us ahead. We were playing a lot of good football at that stage. But then two defensive mistakes cost us the game and that's something we need to look at.

"Obviously it's a blow to lose Jamie because one of the things we need most is experience in midfield. But the injuries just seem to be going on and on."

One answer was to go out and bring in new blood to try to fill some of the holes. But Boro did not have the cash to make a big transfer splash. Most of their spending money for the season had gone on bringing Nick Barmby and Juninho to the Cellnet Riverside Stadium, and Boro were reported to be in the process of making the second and final payment on both transfers.

No doubt Robson could have scoured the lower leagues for one or two cheap signings, but he believed that anything else than signing top quality players was a backward step.

Another alternative was to make a loan signing or two, though there was a huge stumbling block in that Premiership clubs were not allowed to make loans to each other. So it restricted Robson to looking at out of favour players from the First Division or Scotland, which didn't offer a lot of promise.

In fact Robson stressed: "I don't want to bring in a player who isn't any better than those I have already got in my squad."

Unfortunately the situation was getting worse. Juninho had picked up a knee injury against Arsenal and, when it failed to respond to treatment, he was ruled out of the Premiership clash with Southampton at The Dell on Saturday, January 20. Ironically, Robson's other major signing, Nick Barmby, was also a doubt with a knee injury leading up to the Saints game, though he recovered in time to retain his place in the side.

Fortunately Boro were boosted by the return of full-backs Neil Cox, after suspension, and Chris Morris, after injury. Stamp moved into midfield for Pollock, and Moore came in for Juninho.

There was also a recall up front for Paul Wilkinson, who reformed the partnership with Barmby which had worked so well at Notts County. Jan Fjortoft had to settle for a place on the bench.

It was an important game for Boro, because Southampton were struggling near the foot of the table and the match offered a genuine opportunity to stop the rot. Boro looked solid in the first half and Wilkinson made his mark by playing a one-two with Barmby for the England striker to fire Robson's men ahead before the interval.

But the Saints replied with a telling second half barrage and Boro cracked twice in eight minutes as goals from Neil Shipperley and Richard Hall earned the home side a 2-1 victory.

Once again there was a new injury problem for Boro to contend with as Phil Stamp limped off in the first half with a calf strain, his place going to Irish lad Keith O'Halloran. Boro also suffered a second successive sending off when Phil Whelan was shown the second of two yellow cards for fouls, followed by a red one.

Whelan received strong criticism from Bryan Robson afterwards, though Boro as a whole had struggled throughout the second half and had collapsed quickly under pressure from a relegation threatened side. Clearly, they were no longer the strong and solid defensive unit they had been at the start of the season. Confidence was slipping, and the fans were wondering where the next win was going to come from.

As a result of the poor run, Boro had dropped to 12th position in the Premiership. They were at the bottom of the leading block of clubs, having taken 33 points from 24 games. Fifth placed Aston Villa had 39 points from 22 games.

For the first time in the season, Boro found themselves looking over their shoulders. They now had the worst current form record in the Premiership and desperately needed a couple of

IT'S all happiness and joy as Juninho celebrates with the fans after scoring against the Gunners.

wins, even if they were still in a relatively safe position. Thirteenth placed Sheffield Wednesday were seven points behind, while third bottom Manchester City were a further six points away with 20 points from 23 games.

One thing which might still spark that revival was a bit of new blood, and Bryan Robson raised hopes the following week when he revealed that he had made an inquiry about Brazilian World Cup Final medal winner Branco, who could play in defence or midfield.

The 31-year-old was a free agent in his home country, having spent part of his career in Portugal and a highly successful spell in Italy with Genoa. Clearly Branco had a terrific pedigree, and possessed experience, which was a commodity Boro were lacking.

The prospect of Bryan Robson signing another Brazilian would bring a "soul mate" for Juninho to Teesside. There was no doubt that Robson fancied the idea of having two Brazilians in his side, and it was certainly possible because Branco was a free agent and was available to join any club at any time.

Naturally Boro faced having to fork out a signing on fee and high wages if they were to sign Branco, but the lack of a transfer fee made the deal particularly attractive.

Boro's injury situation was getting worse rather than better and so Robson wasted no time in hardening up his interest in Branco. There was still a genuine doubt that the Brazilian might not qualify for a work permit because he hadn't played international football for the past 18 months. But it was a risk worth taking as far as Robson was concerned and he took initial steps towards bringing the Brazilian over to England for contract talks.

While the discussions continued with Branco by telephone, it was a frustrated and injury racked Boro squad which started its preparations for the next game - the FA Cup fourth round tie at home to Wimbledon.

Jamie Pollock, Phil Stamp, Juninho and Bryan Robson were among those who were definitely ruled out of the match, and Robson could have been excused for wishing that the game could be postponed as Saturday approached. But the Cellnet Riverside pitch was protected by the futuristic plastic pitch cover which had been installed early in the season.

The cover, which was designed by Iain MacLeod, consisted of a series of plastic sheets which were held together by Velcro. The sheets were fastened to the ground just in front of the stands, and were inflated down the centre of the pitch by pumping air into a long sausage shaped central balloon.

The cover offered protection from snow, frost and rain, and could be inflated high enough for groundsman David Rigg to work underneath it on the pitch.

There was no threat to the grass because light filtered through to the playing surface, while the air temperature inside could be regulated by blowing in hot air. As a result, Rigg was able to reproduce the same high quality playing surface week in and week out, without having to worry about the weather.

So, in the knowledge that the pitch would be in perfect condition, the Cuptie was pronounced 'Definitely On' on the Friday lunchtime, despite the fact that snow had fallen in Teesside during the week. Ground staff prepared the way for the game to go ahead by spending much of Friday scraping the snow off the pitch cover.

However, just as Boro began to psyche themselves up for a match they didn't really want, while the injuries raged, they were given a helping hand from the gods.

There was another heavy fall of snow on the Saturday morning, which was blown several feet into the Cellnet Riverside stands by a strong wind. There was no time for the ground staff to clear the snow from the stands, and the new layer of snow on the pitch cover, in time for the Cuptie to kick off on time.

In addition, the snow lying around the stadium created a potential hazard to both cars and pedestrians. So, bearing in mind the obvious problems, and taking into account advice from the police, Boro announced that the match was off.

There were few tears shed. Even the fans cannot have fancied the idea of sitting watching the match in sub-zero temperatures. However there was every reason to feel sympathy for the Wimbledon squad, who had already arrived in the North-east in the belief that the tie was going ahead as planned.

Boro would have struggled to win the tie under the circumstances and were probably happy about the postponement. They were given a second boost the following day when they flew out to Tenerife for a five-day training trip in the sunshine.

Assistant manager Viv Anderson led a 20-strong party which included Juninho, John Hendrie, Derek Whyte and Jamie Pollock, all of whom were having treatment for injuries.

However physio Bob Ward also travelled with the party and worked out with the injured men in Tenerife, while the rest of the squad got on with their regular training. The only player left behind in Teesside from the first team squad was Phil Stamp, whose calf strain was being looked after by assistant physio Gary Henderson at Ayresome Park.

The other notable absentee was Bryan Robson, who had jetted out to Milan with coach John Pickering. The official announcement was that Robbo was exploring the training techniques of the big Italian clubs, in particular at Parma.

But Robson was already setting his sights on next season and wanted to run the rule over potential targets, in addition to discussing the future of transer fees with Italian coaches following the ruling in the Bosman case.

One game which Robson took in was Inter Milan against Parma, which led to the Italian media connecting him with a strong interest in Inter's Brazilian left-back Roberto Carlos. Two days later the Italian newspaper Corriere dello Sport insisted that Robson had made an £8 million bid for Lazio's Croatian striker Alen Boksic, which had been turned down. Whatever the truth of the matter, it was obvious that Robson was thinking big. Very big.

Robson told the Evening Gazette from his Italian hotel: "I watched the Inter-Parma game and was able to put down some feelers for the future. It's all about making inquiries at this stage. Of course I am interested in players like Boksic and Roberto Carlos. I am interested in all good players.

"But all I am doing is putting down tentative inquiries, to see which players might become available, and try to discover what financial packages might be involved.

"When we are in a position to strengthen the side, we need to have done our homework and know who might be available, and whether we can afford them."

While Robson was away in Milan, there was a further threat to his future with Boro. The FA's five-man committee, who had been charged with the task of finding a successor to Terry Venables, met at Lancaster Gate. According to the tabloid press, Robson remained their No. 1 target as the next England manager.

There was a general belief that the committee was looking to make a quick appointment, and so it was feared that an approach might be made to Boro chairman Steve Gibson for permission to speak to Robson. In the event, the committee met, but reported that they would be delaying their decision.

Boro players Nigel Pearson and Neil Cox were also fined £500 each and warned over their involvement in the same incident, which took place outside the referee's dressing room door. It followed Mr. Danson's decision to send off Boro defender Derek Whyte in the last minute for an alleged second bookable offence.

Before returning to England, Robson informed the Evening Gazette from Milan that three of the club's top young players, Phil Stamp, Craig Liddle and Ben Roberts, had all agreed new three and a half year contracts.

Boro were not only responding to the terrific potential shown by the trio, but also making sure that the lads were secured to the club over a long period in the wake of the Bosman case.

Robson said: "Stamp and Liddle have done very well since they came into the first team and it's only right that we reward them. They have proved that they can hold their own in the Premiership, while Liddle has played in five different positions.

BORO had the perfect answer to protecting the pitch during the harshness of the winter. This revolutionary pitch cover, which can be inflated with warm air, was designed by Iain MacLeod.

Robson was non-plussed that the meeting had taken place. He told the Evening Gazette: "Nothing has changed. I intend to see out the rest of my contract with Middlesbrough, and I have tried to make it clear to everybody."

Ironically, while the FA allegedly fancied Robson as the next England manager, they also delivered him with a rap over his knuckles. The Boro boss was fined £750 and warned over his future conduct after being found guilty on a disrepute charge over "foul and abusive" remarks made to Leicester referee Paul Danson after Boro's 1-0 defeat at Blackburn Rovers on December 16.

"Ben Roberts is also very highly rated by the coaches at this club. We believe he has a bright future ahead of him."

Any hopes that Boro's injury situation might have improved during the week in Tenerife were quickly extinguished when the team returned to Ayresome Park. There were no new injuries, but the squad had to prepare for the live TV game at Chelsea on the Sunday afternoon, February 4, without Phil Whelan as well as the previously injured crew. Whelan was serving a one-match ban following his dismissal at Southampton for two bookable offences.

There was one welcome new face in the starting line up. Craig Hignett, who had come on in the last ten minutes at The Dell after recovering from a hernia operation, as fully fit again. Bryan Robson also brought Keith O'Halloran and Craig Liddle into a congested five-man midfield, playing behind returning striker Jan Fjortoft.

It meant that Boro went into the match at Stamford Bridge with a flat back four. It was a gamble which didn't work. Boro were a shambles and were crushed 5-0 by a Chelsea team who were playing at the very peak of their form.

Boro were torn to shreds and were five-down after only 54 minutes. The scoreline could have been even more embarrassing, but Chelsea seemed to take their feet off the accelerator with the three points already guaranteed.

A bad defeat had come hand in hand with a bad performance. They really had been swept aside, and at times had looked out of their depth. However Robson remained philosophical afterwards, saying: "When we are missing four or five players we will struggle."

There was better news the following day when Brazilian international Branco flew into Teesside Airport. He was accompanied by his wife Stella. Waiting to meet him was Juninho's father Oswaldo, plus Tyne Tees TV cameras and the Evening Gazette.

Branco said: "I'm very happy to be here and I hope to have the same success with Middlesbrough that I have had throughout my career. I am looking forward to playing alongside Juninho, because he is such a great player."

The following day, Branco joined in his first Boro training session. Unfortunately Ayresome Park was frozen over, so the first team squad had to train on the all weather pitch at Holme House Prison. It was an unusual introduction to English football for Branco, but by all accounts the Brazilian made an early impact and Robson revealed that he had been impressed with his contribution.

After leaving the prison, Branco joined up with Robson at the Cellnet Riverside Stadium for contract talks. By all accounts the talks went smoothly, and a deal was quickly hammered out.

However Branco was then put through stringent medicals, and the fact that the results of some tests were not available until the Thursday morning meant that Boro were unable to announce his signing at the rearranged FA Cup fourth round tie at home to Wimbledon on Wednesday, February 7. Branco and his wife still watched the match from the directors' box.

Branco must have been left in no doubt that he could do a job for the team after watching Boro held to a goalless draw.

Bryan Robson's men had been strengthened by the return of Jamie Pollock and Juninho after injury, and Phil Whelan after suspension, and had Paul Wilkinson back up front for Jan Fjortoft, who was on international duty with Norway in Spain.

Unfortunately the team as a whole was very nervous at the start, following their battering at Chelsea, and had to work very hard to stay in the tie in the first half. They finally got it together after the restart, but were unable to find a way through for the winning goal.

Robson admitted: "The lads were a bit edgy in the first half but they battled well enough in the second half and I thought we started to look like our old selves.

"Jamie Pollock made a huge difference to us. He has a presence on the pitch and gives confidence to the players around him."

The following day it was revealed that Branco had passed his medicals, and Boro immediately applied for a work permit. There were strong doubts in some quarters that the Brazilian might not qualify, but Robson insisted: "Branco is a proven international player. I'll be very disappointed if we don't get a work permit."

Boro had restored some much needed morale in the second half against Wimbledon, which had come at just the right time as they prepared for their biggest game of the season at home to title chasing North-east rivals Newcastle United.

The Magpies were sweeping all before them and were clear at the top of the Premiership. But Boro had an excellent record at home to Newcastle, and were not without a chance. In fact the Magpies had not won a league game on Teesside for 32 years.

Robson was planning to take an unchanged line up into the derby match, but made a change shortly before the kick off when he discovered that Phil Stamp had made a sudden recovery from his calf strain. The 20-year-old had the engines to get around the pitch and returned in place of Keith O'Halloran, who had done well considering he had been pitched into a difficult situation.

The injury hoodoo returned when Stamp lasted just 45 minutes before he was forced to retire with a recurrence of his injury. However, by that time, Boro were one-up courtesy of an own goal from John Beresford, following a fine run and cross by Juninho.

Boro then proceeded to batter Newcastle at the beginning of the second half but could not grab the killer goal. They paid the penalty in the last 16 minutes, when the Magpies were revived by the introduction of substitute Faustino Asprilla.

The Columbian, signed from Parma for £7.5 million only 48 hours earlier, came off the bench to set up the equaliser for Steve Watson after only seven minutes on the pitch. As Boro suddenly wavered, a rare error by goalkeeper Gary Walsh gifted the Magpies a second goal on a plate for Les Ferdinand.

Victory was snatched away from Robson's men at the death, and it was a very weary and frustrated Boro side which trudged off the pitch at the final whistle. It was their seventh Premiership defeat in a row and they seemed to possess no answers to how to stop the run.

Bryan Robson told the Evening Gazette: "The lads couldn't have tried any harder to win the game, but we missed some great chances and you can't afford to do that against a team like Newcastle.

"Newcastle proved that, by hitting back to win the game, but then we have got to look back at two defensive mistakes which cost us the points. We must learn from them and make sure they don't happen again."

Despite the derby defeat, Boro were clearly in a positive frame of mind by the time they set off for the FA Cup fourth round replay against Wimbledon at Selhurst Park. The players believed that winning this match at the second attempt was well within their capabilities.

HELLO and goodbye... Nick Barmby breezes between Steve Watson and Warren Barton in the big derby clash against Newcastle United at the Cellnet Riverside Stadium.

JUNINHO battles for possession with Robert Lee in the home derby against the Magpies.

The Bleak Mid Winter

They travelled without Phil Stamp, who was ruled out for three weeks. so Keith O'Halloran was back in the starting line-up.

Boro were quickly into gear from the start of the Cuptie and dominated the first half. They should have had the match sewn up at half-time, but Wimbledon goalkeeper Neil Sullivan made great saves from Nick Barmby and Chris Morris.

At half-time it seemed only a matter of time before Boro would break through. But they went off the boil after the restart and the Dons grabbed what proved to be the winning goal through Dean Holdsworth in the 74th minute.

Boro still had a chance to snatch an equaliser in the last minute when substitute Craig Hignett set up Barmby, but the England striker's shot came back off the crossbar. So it was Wimbledon who prepared to travel to Huddersfield Town in the fifth round.

It was yet another game that Boro should have won, but didn't, which begged the question that the team might have lost the ability to win matches. There were a few hurdles to cross if Boro were to get back to where they were at the start of the season, but they kept falling over.

Robson told the Evening Gazette: "Overall I thought we deserved something out of the game but we didn't put away our chances. Things are not going right for us. We dominated for 60 minutes but suddenly our passing started to let us down and Wimbledon got back into it."

Boro had nothing left to concentrate on but the league, with the ever increasing threat that they might be dragged into a battle for survival. And they had to face up to the next three games without Juninho. Immediately following the Cup defeat he flew out from Heathrow to join up with the Brazil squad for the South American qualifying tournament for the Olympics, which was being held in Argentina. Jaime Moreno had already flown out to link up with Bolivia for the same competition.

Even so, Boro had a gilt edged chance to finally record their first Premiership win of 1996 when they entertained struggling Bolton Wanderers at the Cellnet Riverside Stadium on Saturday, February 17. Bolton, who were managed by former Boro boss Colin Todd, were promoted along with Boro the previous season, but had found it tough in the top flight. In fact they were well adrift at the foot of the table without an away win to their credit.

So it was an important game for Boro, both to get a much needed win on the board, and to restore confidence. It also offered the team the opportunity to avoid having to share an unwanted record. They had lost seven league games in a row, which was just one short of the club record of eight losing games in 1954.

Bryan Robson, well aware of the desperate need to start scoring goals again, restored his previously successful three-pronged attack into action. Jan Fjortoft returned in place of Paul Wilkinson and Craig Hignett came in for Juninho, to play alongside Nick Barmby.

However, the match which Boro could hardly afford to lose became a total disaster. Noel Blake maintained his fine goalscoring record against Boro by scoring an early goal for the visitors, and Boro found themselves chasing another home game.

They still battled hard to take control and were rewarded with the equaliser when Jamie Pollock guided the ball home from close range after playing a one-two with Fjortoft.

The scene was set for Boro to go on and win the game, but Robbo's men were chasing it again when

JAMIE POLLOCK runs in to challenge Newcastle United full-back Warren Barton at the Cellnet Riverside Stadium.

ACTION from Boro's humiliating 4-1 defeat at home by bottom dogs Bolton Wanderers. Pictured left to right are former Boro defender Jimmy Phillips, NIck Barmby and Keith O'Halloran.

former Boro defender Simon Coleman, playing his first match for 11 months following a broken leg, headed Bolton back in front shortly before the interval.

Once again Boro created openings to get back on level terms, but they fell apart in the second half when Fabian De Freitas scored a third goal for Bolton. Heads went down, and Bolton strolled through the rest of the game, scoring a fourth goal through David Lee.

It was a humiliating and embarrassing defeat, which left the players totally in the doldrums. The fans could hardly believe what they had seen. If Chelsea was rock bottom, then Boro had now broken through the rock.

Bryan Robson was clearly as shellshocked as his players. He still remained defiant that the team would turn things around, saying: "We let ourselves down badly with bad defending. We can't expect to defend like that and get anything out of the game. But we've got to keep working at it until we get it right.

"I still don't see it as a relegation battle. One win will make all the difference to us and we must continue to work hard until we get it."

Robson was a lot more confident than the media. Boro were pilloried in the press over the weekend, and grave doubts were expressed about their ability to avoid being sucked into the relegation mire.

Boro were still stuck on 33 points, nine points clear of third bottom Coventry City. They had been on 33 points since before Christmas, and the only win in the previous two months had come at Notts County in the third round of the FA Cup.

Ironically, Boro's next match was to be played against Coventry, at Highfield Road. It was another crucial game. Unfortunately Bryan Robson faced further problems in selecting his side. In addition to missing Juninho and Jaime Moreno, who were in South America, Boro were without Nigel Pearson, Craig Liddle and Chris Morris, all of whom were starting two-match bans.

Pearson was doubly sidelined, because he was suffering from pleurisy. He had been taken ill

HEADS I win! Nigel Pearson gets up high to win an aerial battle against Bolton Wanderers.

during the first half against Bolton and replaced at the interval by Derek Whyte, and had been told to rest at home. Fortunately Whyte was able to gain 45 valuable minutes' play after returning from injury, and would start the game at Coventry.

Robson, still looking for a bit of inspiration to liven up the dressing room, was working hard to try to push through a work permit for the Brazilian international Branco. He had enlisted the support of the Brazilian FA and the Brazil team manager Mario Zagalo, both of whom had provided information about Branco's international career - and given details revealing why he had not been selected for recent Brazil matches. This was because Brazil had deliberately been fielding under-23 sides at full level.

The Boro boss had passed all of this information on to the Department of Employment, who were still processing Boro's application for a work permit. Robson had hoped to have Branco in his squad to travel to Coventry, but there was no news from the D of E by the end of the week.

Robson had been planning to play himself at Coventry, but in the end had to admit defeat as he struggled to shake off his sciatica. In the event, four players did return from injury, with Curtis Fleming, Derek Whyte, Graham Kavanagh and Robbie Mustoe all taking their places in the starting line-up at Highfield Road.

Mustoe's return was particularly well received. The gritty midfielder had been sidelined since early November with a knee injury, and Boro had not played consistently well since. Whyte had also been sorely missed, having been sidelined with a calf injury since Boxing Day, which was the start of the team's major problems.

Fleming had been out of action for seven weeks with a knee injury and welcomed the chance to start to build up his match fitness again. But Kavanagh would be the happiest man of them all. The 22-year-old midfielder had missed most of the season with a frustrating injury on the ball of his foot near to his big toe, which had taken much longer than anticipated to heal.

OPEN for business: Bryan Robson cuts the tape to launch the start of the official guided tours of the Cellnet Riverside Stadium, along with players Chris Morris, Steve Vickers and Jamie Pollock. Pictured left are tour guides Heather Machon and Carl Best.

Even so, with so many players back in action, and obviously in need of match practice, Boro fans could not be too optimistic of the team's chances at Highfield Road. In addition, the Sky Blues were boosted by a double midweek signing.

Coventry boss Ron Atkinson had paid Aberdeen £1.7 million for attacking midfielder Eoin Jess, and a further £1.4 million to Birmingham City for defender Liam Daish. Both players were expected to lift the home side, who started strong favourites.

In the event, it was Boro who were the better side, and the run of Premiership defeats at last came to an end. Boro still could not win the game, and had to settle for a goalless draw. But they were defensively stronger than they had been for months and recorded their first clean sheet in the Premiership since November 18.

The midfield trio of Mustoe, Kavanagh and Jamie Pollock worked particularly hard, with Kavanagh completing a fairytale comeback by earning the Evening Gazette's man of the match nomination.

Bryan Robson admitted: "I'm relieved to get off 33 points at last, and I was pleased with the way in which the lads worked so hard. I've always believed that we would start to turn the corner when the injured players started to return, and hopefully this is the first step towards us starting to climb the table again."

Samba Time Again

CHAPTER NINE:

BRYAN ROBSON had been successful in his first 18 months in football management. But, by the end of February,1996, the Boro player-manager was starting to experience the down side of the job.

In fact, Robson's men had picked up just one point from their last nine Premiership games and were sliding apparently helplessly down the table.

A season which had promised so much at the half-way stage was now in serious danger of collapse. In fact there was a danger that the team might even be dragged into the relegation battle.

It was a situation which had been totally inconceivable at Christmas, when not only were Boro comfortably placed in the top six, but were also well in the running for a place in Europe.

In the first few months of the season, Boro had been ultra confident, defensively stingy and a major threat to any opposition as a result of their quick breaking. But a desperate run of injuries, which started on Boxing Day, had reached epidemic proportions and shorn the side of most of its team qualities and self belief.

Boro were sitting pretty on 33 points at Christmas, but they did not move off this total until grabbing a goalless draw at Coventry City on February 24. In those two months Boro had slipped to the bottom of the 12 leading Premiership clubs, and were now in danger of being caught by the strugglers beneath them.

Robson had maintained all along that things would improve dramatically when the injured players returned, but the games were slipping by. Boro desperately needed a win to boost the dressing room, but it was difficult to see where it was going to come from.

The spirit was still remarkably high among the players. They also felt that one victory would start to reverse the trend. But they had lost the ability to win games.

At the same time it was vital that improvement came quickly, because Boro faced a difficult run-in to their Premership programme and were currently in the middle of a run of games which might have been expected to produce plenty of points earlier in the season.

Fortunately the injured players were starting to filter back and did promise to bring improvement to the team, but they still needed time to readjust to the pace of Premiership football and time was a commodity in which Boro were lacking.

To make matters worse, a run of unwanted suspensions was adding to Robson's problems just as he was beginning to anticipate having a full squad available again.

The fans were becoming disgruntled by both performances and results and there was increasing pressure on the manager to produce the vital spark which would bring the team to life again.

Robson's search for that spark had taken him on the Brazilian trail again and he had agreed terms with Branco, who had won a World Cup Final winner's medal with Brazil in 1994. Branco, who could play at left back or in midfield, had a wealth of experience which he could bring to the Boro.

However, the task of successfully applying for a work permit for Branco was not an easy task. By all accounts, the Brazilian did not meet the requirements laid down by the Department of Employment because he had not been playing regularly in recent Brazil internationals.

The D of E insisted that foreign nationals should have played in at least 75 per cent of their countries' recent games over the previous two years, which would normally have excluded Branco.

Boro were arguing that Branco had been omitted from Brazil's recent games because his country had been deliberately fielding under-23 players in recent internationals. In fact all the regular full international players had been omitted for the same purpose, while at the same time still being regarded in Brazil as current first teamers.

To this extent, Robson had received letters from the Brazilian FA and national team manager Mario Zagalo to support his claims and these had been passed on to the D of E.

So it was quite a relief for the Boro boss when the D of E finally announced on February 27 that Branco had indeed been granted a work permit. The news was relayed to Branco without delay, and he made plans to fly out from South America the same day. As a result, Boro now had two big Brazilian stars on their pay-roll, with Branco providing a cultural partner for Juninho.

Robson told the Evening Gazette: "Obviously I am delighted with the news. I always believed that Branco qualified for a work permit and that he should get one quickly. We have already made plans to get him over here and he will probably train with us on Thursday."

Branco, who was signed on a free transfer, had not played a competitive game since December 17 and was bound to be well short of general fitness, in addition to a lack of match fitness.

Robson told the Evening Gazette: "Branco has not been playing competitive games and we need to take that into account. But we still want him in our squad against Everton on Saturday because it will give everybody a boost."

WELCOME to the frozen north! Branco braces himself against a biting wind as he alights at Teesside Airport for the first time.

HEY, I speak the same language! Branco and Juninho are pictured following training at Holme House Prison at Stockton.

THE meeting of the legends… Branco and Boro boss Bryan Robson meet before a training session at Ayresome Park.

Despite the Brazilian's obvious lack of fitness, Robson was left with no option but to bring him straight into the squad. The Boro boss was no less than eight players short for the visit of Everton. It was not getting any easier.

Five of the missing players were banned. Defensive trio Nigel Pearson, Craig Liddle and Chris Morris were all completing their two match-bans by sitting out of the game. Jamie Pollock and Phil Whelan were starting their two-match bans, the latter two both being suspended under the totting up procedure.

In addition Juninho and Jaime Moreno were still in Argentina, where they were involved in the South American section of the Olympics football qualifying tournament with Brazil and Bolivia respectively.

In their final group games, Brazil had qualified for the second phase of the tournament following a goalless draw with Uruguay. Bolivia beat Paraguay 4-1 in their final match, but were still eliminated.

To make matters worse at home, Steve Vickers had suffered strained knee ligaments and so was the fifth defender to be ruled out of a match which Boro desperately wanted to win.

Branco, who had arrived back in England with his wife Stella and ten months old son Stefano, was ready to help fill the breach. He told the Evening Gazette: "I am very happy to be here and I'm looking forward to playing for Middlesbrough. I hope I can make some difference but don't expect me to perform magic right away. I just want to do well for myself and for the club."

The Brazilian did train with Boro in two sessions on Thursday and Friday, when it was clear that his fitness level was lower than had been hoped. He was not yet ready for 90 minutes of Premiership football, so he was named on the bench as Boro looked for their first league win in ten starts against Joe Royle's Everton.

In the build up to the game, there had seemed a possibility that assistant manager Viv Anderson might be pitched into the fray to solve the defensive problem.

However Robson opted instead to give 21-year-old Michael Barron his Premiership debut. Barron had been a stalwart for the reserve side all season and deserved his chance. He came in alongside Derek Whyte in the heart of the defence as Robson surprisingly opted to play a flat back four in a 4-4-2 formation.

Curtis Fleming was back at left-back in place of the suspended Morris, while Craig Hignett and Alan Moore returned to the starting line-up alongside Graham Kavanagh and Robbie Mustoe in the middle of the park.

Any hopes that this much revamped Boro side might be good enough to halt the progress of one of the Premiership form teams quickly disappeared. Everton were too strong from the start and had the points in the bag at the interval through goals from Tony Grant and a penalty by Andy Hinchcliffe.

Boro did revive their fortunes in the second half, mainly because Everton were happy to sit back on their lead. The home crowd was brought to life ten minutes from time when Branco finally made his

THE Branco power in action as the Brazilian tries a shot at the Everton goal on his Boro debut, watched by former Boro target Andrei Kanchelskis.

apperance, but the Brazilian susbstitute had little opportunity to show what he could do in such a short space of time.

However Branco did hit one cracking 40 yarder, which was only inches wide of the target, and it turned out to be a bigger talking point in the pubs and clubs that evening than the fact that Boro had lost another Premiership match.

At the same time, Branco's Brazilian colleague was hitting top form in Argentina. Juninho grabbed a goal in each half and was named man of the match as Brazil beat Uruguay 3-1 in Buenos Aires to make certain of their place in the Olympic Games in Atlanta.

Juninho was due to link up with Boro again at the end of the week, but Branco had a midweek date with Boro reserves as he started his quest for match fitness. The 31-year-old was named to start the match against Leicester City reserves at the Cellnet Riverside Stadium.

Branco told the Evening Gazette: "I was only 60 or 70 per cent fit when I arrived at Middlesbrough. You must remember that it is holiday time in Brazil. There is no competitive football at the moment.

"But I will work hard to improve with every training session and I am looking forward to the reserve game."

A lot more people were also looking forward to the reserve game. In fact a remarkable crowd of 15,143 turned up to see Branco's full debut in a Boro shirt. It was the biggest crowd for a reserve match in Boro's history.

The roads around the Cellnet Riverside Stadium were lit up by a sea of car headlights as the fans flocked to the match. Nobody could have anticipated such a crowd, and the kick off had to be delayed for 15 minutes to allow the fans to get inside the stadium.

Entrance was available through the East Stand turnstiles, but this stand filled up very quickly and the fans were allowed behind both goals. By the time the match kicked off, the North and South Stands were virtually filled as well. Only the West Stand was empty.

Only two years earlier this would have been considered a good crowd for a first geam game at Ayresome Park. It was an indication of the huge groundswell of potential support on Teesside.

Unfortunately, despite so much anticipation in the stadium, Branco had very little opportunity to shine. Boro had gone into the match with a very young side and Leicester, who fielded an experienced team which assistant manager Viv Anderson claimed "was good enough to win the First Division title", won 2-0.

Even so, it was very much a surprise result because Boro reserves were 12 points clear at the top of the Pontins League Second Division before the match and had been sweeping all before them.

Branco admitted: "I thought the supporters were absolutely magnificent. I never expected so many to turn up. All I ask is that they give me time to settle in and I will fulfil everything that they are hoping for. The whole purpose of my appearance was to trot around and play for 90 minutes. But I can promise the fans that the best is yet to come."

While many of the regular fans were there simply to witness Branco's first full game in a Boro shirt, one man not watching was Bryan Robson. The Boro boss had made a lightning trip to the Continent to run the rule over a potential summer target.

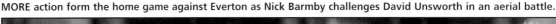

MORE action form the home game against Everton as Nick Barmby challenges David Unsworth in an aerial battle.

Robson would not reveal the name of his target but stressed in the Evening Gazette that he was determined to do his homework well in advance of next season. He wanted to be in a position to sign some top quality players at the start of the season, without being dragged into a free for all in July and August.

The Boro boss had experienced major problems the previous summer, when it was not until ten days before the season was due to start that he finally made his transfer breakthrough by snapping up record signing Nick Barmby from Spurs.

It was obvious even at this stage that Robson seemed to be concentrating his efforts on the Continent, specially as it was likely that transfer fees might be scrapped completely for out of contract European stars in the wake of the Bosman Case.

No names had been revealed to the media, so the guessing game had started. There was a national report that Robson might be planning to bring back Dean Saunders from Turkish side Galatasaray. On the home front, the Boro boss was strongly linked with Coventry City striker Dion Dublin. But Robson dismissed the stories as speculation.

Meanwhile Boro were building up to their next Premiership match at West Ham United on Saturday, March 9, believing that they were on the verge of starting to turn the corner.

The players had always maintained that they were good enough to finish the season strongly once the squad was back to full strength. Fortunately several players were back in the running for the trip to Upton Park, and hopes were high of a point or three now that Boro could field a more representative side.

Nigel Pearson, Craig Liddle and Chris Morris were all available again following suspension. However there was one setback when Steve Vickers, who was virtually free from a knee injury, picked up a calf strain in training which ruled him out for a further two weeks.

Then Bryan Robson's team plans were further interrupted when problems over flights prevented Juninho from linking up with the squad until two hours before the kick off.

Juninho had flown back from Argentina, where he had helped Brazil to qualify for the Olympics. But the Brazilian star was in no fit state to play 90 minutes of Premiership football following such a long and arduous flight, so he was put on the bench, where he formed an illustrious trio alongside Branco and John Hendrie.

Pearson returned to the heart of the Boro defence for Michael Barron, while Robson decided to solve his continuing dearth of experienced central defenders by moving Neil Cox from right-back to centre-back, alongside Pearson. Chris Morris resumed at right-back, while Alan Moore dropped out to accommodate the extra defender.

There was plenty of anticipation for Boro's travelling fans leading up to the kick off, but their hopes were shattered after just 70 seconds when goalkeeper Gary Walsh made a hash of trying to clear a backpass from Cox, and Iain Dowie was gifted a goal for the Hammers.

It was a bodyblow, and Boro were rocky for the rest of the first half. They did start to recover after the restart and were just threatening to take control, when they were dealt another hammer stroke.

Birmingham referee Michael Reed awarded West Ham a dubious penalty when a loose ball bobbled up and hit Cox on his right arm. Boro protested in vain and Julian Dicks put away the spot kick.

Juninho, Branco and Hendrie all came off the bench to enjoy a taste of the action in the second half, but the game was already slipping away from Boro.

Bryan Robson told the Evening Gazette: "You can't expect to give goals away in the first 70 seconds and then go on to win the game. We did start to put our game together in the second half, but we missed a couple of half chances and never looked like getting back into it when the ref gave West Ham that penalty. I've seen them given, I've seen them not given, though no way does anybody in our team feel that it was a penalty."

Branco was back on duty for Boro reserves the following Wednesday when he lined up at the Cellnet Riverside Stadium against York City reserves. However there was no 15,000 crowd on this occasion, though club officials were delighted to see just under 5,000 fans turn up to watch the match.

Phil Stamp, who had just recovered from a bout of German measles, scored one of the goals in his comeback game as Boro won 4-0. Phil Whelan, who was returning after suspension, also netted.

Boro had planned to play Jamie Pollock in the game for a bit of match fitness, but he had to drop out because of flu. Graham Kavanagh was another flu victim, though both players recovered in time for the weekend's crucial game at home to Nottingham Forest.

This match seemed to offer Boro their best chance yet of ending their dismal run of 11 Premiership games without a win. Forest were being forced to go into the game with an injury-hit side and it was a bit of a nuisance game for the Midlanders, coming as it did sandwiched in between two big cupties.

Forest had just lost an FA Cup sixth round tie to Aston Villa in midweek and were now looking ahead to the crucial UEFA Cup second leg tie against Bayern Munich next Tuesday. The Boro game was bang in the middle, and Forest were without several of their regulars.

Boro were boosted by the return of Pollock and Juninho in midfield, where they were accompanied by Branco for the first time at the start of a match.

Bryan Robson once again opted for a 4-4-2 formation, with Neil Cox reverting to right-back for Chris Morris and John Hendrie winning the vote up front in favour of Jan Fjortoft. Graham Kavanagh and Craig Hignett with the other players to drop out.

However, any hopes of a bright and breezy Boro display quickly evaporated. Most of the players were lacking in match fitness, and confidence as well.

However they did manage to grind out a 1-1 draw and, in terms of what had gone before, it had to be classed as a relatively good result. Even so, it was hardly an entertaining match for the fans, with both sides managing four shots between them over the 90 minutes.

BRANCO played in a few reserve games to get match fit. He is pictured in action against York City reserves at the Cellnet Riverside Stadium.

On-loan winger Chris Allen fired Forest ahead early in the second half but Robbie Mustoe, who had been a revelation for Boro since his return from injury, grabbed the equaliser within 60 seconds after John Hendrie had headed on a cross from Nick Barmby.

Bryan Robson said: "I was happy with the way in which the lads worked hard. When you have been going through a difficult spell, you can't just turn the corner overnight. But this game was a step in the right direction.

"Robbie's goal made a big difference to us. If we had been chasing the game, Forest might have made it hard for us. But the goal came at the perfect time, immediately after Forest had scored."

Mustoe, who had just signed a new four-year contract, had now played four games since returning from injury and was helping to bring stability to the side. With Pollock and Juninho also returning, Boro were starting to look like their old selves again. However Steve Vickers was still sidelined with knee and calf injuries.

There was little time for Boro to relax after their draw with Forest, because they were off to Aston Villa on the Tuesday, March 19, to play a rearranged match. It had been brought forward from the weekend because Villa were due to meet Leeds United in the Coca Cola Cup Final at Wembley.

Once again Boro were presented with a golden opportunity to record a win. Villa were shorn of several players through injury and suspension, while it was only natural that their players would have one eye on the cup final just five days away.

With so many players missing, Villa boss Brian Little handed three teenagers their full debuts in the Premiership. One of them was Lee Hendrie, who was the cousin of Boro's John. The two Hendries lined up against each other for the first time in a competitive match as Bryan Robson opted for an unchanged side, which meant that he was playing 4-4-2 away from home on a rare occasion.

Unfortunately another game which provided Boro with great hope produced just one point. Boro always looked the side which most wanted to win, but they were unable to find the back of the net and had to settle for a goalless draw.

It was two points lost rather than one gained, but at least it was another step forward in the team's rehabilitation. The only real worry was that Boro were still struggling to find the back of the net despite creating occasional chances.

There was a new injury scare for Robson in the match when Juninho limped off in the first half with a dead leg, with Craig Hignett coming on to take his place. However Juninho made a rapid recovery and was able to fly out the following day to link up with the Brazil squad for their friendly match against Chile.

Branco also came off at half-time against Villa and Robson told the Evening Gazette: "I think the games have caught up with Branco. He has worked very hard to find his fitness but was starting to show a bit of tiredness and so I brought on Graham Kavanagh in the second half for a fresh pair of legs."

Despite the dropped points, Robson was happy with the team performance at Villa. He said: "We needed one of the chances around Villa's box to go in and then we would have gone on to win the game. But all away points are useful and the overall team display was better. The players are gaining self belief again and now all they need is a break."

Boro had edged on to 36 points, which gave them a healthy 11 point cushion over third bottom Southampton, though the Saints had no less than four games in hand.

BORO had high hopes of finally grabbing their first win of 1996 in the Premiership when entertaining Nottingham Forest, but had to settle for a 1-1 draw. Here Juninho goes on a run at goal.

ROBBIE MUSTOE, pictured in a midfield tussle against Nottingham Forest, made a huge impact when he returned from injury. He also netted Boro's equaliser against Forest.

Samba Time Again

Unfortunately Boro were once again looking ahead to continuing their recovery programme without the influential Jamie Pollock, who had picked up a booking at Villa which took him past 33 penalty points and earned a two match ban. He would miss both Easter games, against Sheffield Wednesday and Spurs.

The following week the squad welcomed back goalkeeper Ben Roberts following his three-months loan stint with Second Division Wycombe Wanderers. By all accounts the keeper had done well at Wycombe and had naturally benefitted from the experience of playing regular league football.

Boro immediately wasted no time in fixing up Roberts with another loan spell and arranged for him to go to Third Division Preston North End. However the keeper picked up a hip injury in training with Boro, and the arrangement had to be scrapped.

Boro were left without a match at the weekend following the moving of the Villa game. So the first team took part in a fund raising friendly against Billingham Synthonia at Central Avenue on the Thursday. It was a cold night, but a decent crowd turned up.

Most of the available Boro first team squad played at least half the game, with Bryan Robson's men winning 7-1. Craig Hignett, Chris Freestone and Phil Stamp all scored twice with Jan Fjortoft netting the other. Paul Wratten, Synners' Middlesbrough born midfielder, scored for the home side.

Robson missed the match, having gone back to the Continent on another fact finding mission. It was an ongoing process for the Boro boss, who was compiling a useful dossier on the big name players who might become available in the summer.

Robson told the Evening Gazette: "I've put another foot in the door, which is something I've been doing for a few months now. I'm looking to bring in two or three top quality players in the summer. I want to be in a position to move quickly as soon as this season is over."

With the transfer deadline approaching, Robson stressed that there would be no new faces on Teesside before the end of the season. The manager was leaving it to the current first team squad to get the show back on the rails.

In any case, Boro had already spent all their available cash on players during the season, with Nick Barmby and Juninho having cost a combined total of £10 million. There was no more cash in the kitty. Robson's money for his planned summer spending was due to come largely from season ticket sales.

However, although there were no incoming players before the transfer deadline, Robson arranged for young midfielder Keith O'Halloran to spend a month on loan with Scunthorpe United. The Irish lad had made four first team starts for Boro this season, and would benefit from more league football in the Third Division.

Paul Wilkinson, who had worked hard for Boro when drafted into the first team in January and February, was also on his way. At first it looked as though he would be going on loan to Portsmouth. But this deal fell through and eventually Wilkinson linked up with former Boro boss Lennie Lawrence at Luton Town.

There was disappointing news for Boro during the week when it was revealed that a hold up with the release of the land at Eston Leisure Centre meant that the club was very unlikely to be able to move into their planned new training headquarters for the start of the next season. There was no major problem, just the routine paperwork and the passing of plans, but it meant that Boro would not be moving in at the beginning of July.

Boro had spent the whole of their Premiership season training on the pitch at Ayresome Park and the old stadium had turned out to be a perfect headquarters. However workmen were already starting to strip down Ayresome ready for closure, and so Boro had only a few weeks left at their cultural home. The stadium had been bought by Wimpey Homes and was due to be bulldozed for housing.

The problem facing Robson was that there was going to be a long spell between Boro leaving Ayresome and eventually moving to Eston, where they would be left without any training facilities.

Now Robson was in a position of having to look for temporary training facilities later in the summer as Boro waited for the green light for work to start on their proposed state of the art £2 million headquarters at Eston.

It was an international week in both Europe and South America, and Boro had a handful of players involved. Juninho masterminded Brazil's 8-2 crushing defeat of Ghana, while Jan Fjortoft helped Norway win in Northern Ireland, and also hit a post in the process.

Nick Barmby was a member of Boro's squad in the 1-0 friendly win against Bulgaria and Bryan Robson was the coach, while Chris Morris was with the Irish squad for the match against Russia in Dublin. Seventeen-year-old YTS player Steven Baker also enjoyed a debut for the Republic of Ireland under-21s against Russia.

All the players reported fit from their international escapades, though Juninho did not arrive back in England until the Friday afternoon and was obviously suffering tiredness from the effects of the long flight back from Brazil.

So Robson decided to drop the Brazilian star to the bench for the derby test against Leeds United at Elland Road on Saturday, March 30. Graham Kavanagh was called back into the fray in midfield. The Boro boss also decided to revert to the five-man defence, which meant Branco dropping to the bench and Phil Whelan coming in.

Once again, this was another fine opportunity for Boro to get off the mark in the Premiership for 1996 and end their run of 13 league games without a win.

Leeds had been well beaten by 3-0 by Aston Villa in the Coca Cola Cup Final the previous weekend and had been heavily criticised in the media for their poor team performance. Manager Howard Wilkinson had come under heavy fire from the Leeds fans for an alleged negative approach in the match, while even Carlton Palmer had criticised the commitment of his own teammates.

It must have combined to leave the Leeds dressing room somewhat in disarray, and presented Boro with the ideal platform from which to go on and win the game.

That's exactly what happened, and there was fun and laughter on a Saturday night in Teesside for the first time in months as Boro finally secured a Premiership win. Bryan Robson's men were solid and committed throughout and won 1-0. The feeling of relief was immense, specially as it meant that Boro's continuing presence in the Premiership was now virtually assured.

The all-important goal came from the penalty spot from Graham Kavanagh after only four minutes. Phil Whelan knocked the ball forward to Nick Barmby, who was barged down from behind by Lucas Radebe as he raced into the box and Harrow referee David Elleray immediately pointed to the spot.

Kavanagh, who had just come back into the side, seemed an unlikely choice of penalty taker following his lack of recent senior experience. But the Irishman showed terrific maturity and bravery to step forward and slot the ball wide of Leeds goalkeeper John Lukic and give Boro a valuable early lead.

The only time that Boro's lead was threatened also came from the penalty spot. Neil Cox was judged to have fouled Brian Deane just after the restart, but this time Gary McAllister put Leeds' penalty into the crowd.

Otherwise it was a canter for Boro, though they missed good chances to increase their lead against replacement rookie keeper Radebe, who played the whole of the second half between the sticks after Lukic had left the field with a head injury.

Bryan Robson told the Evening Gazette: "That win has given the lads all their confidence back, and now they should enjoy themselves in the remaining games. I want to finish as high as possible in the Premiership and that is the challenge I am setting the lads."

Boro were still not statistically certain to hold on to their place in the Premiership, but only an unmitigated disaster could now drag them into the relegation zone. At last the players could settle down and play without pressure as they battled to try to refind their early season form.

The only setback from the win at Leeds was that Scottish defender Derek Whyte had reached 21 penalty points following a booking in the second half, and would miss the game at home to Wimbledon in two weeks' time.

There had been a scare just before the final whistle when Curtis Fleming and Phil Whelan clashed heads and needed stitches in nasty gashes, but both were fit to resume training on the Monday, despite Whelan sporting a magnificent shiner.

The same day, Bryan Robson revealed that he intended to take out his player's registration again the following season. The Boro boss stressed that he had no intentions of playing regularly, but wanted to stay fit and available in case he was needed in an emergency.

If Robson was to play in Boro's second season in the Premiership, he could become the first 40-year-old ever to play in competitive action for the club.

Boro kept busy by playing a behind closed doors friendly game at Ayresome Park on Tuesday, April 2, against touring Norwegian side Tromso. The visitors were building up towards the start of their new season and were staying in the North-east.

It was a useful match for the Boro, specially as Robson could take advantage of the situation by keeping his squad match fit, bearing in mind that there was no midweek reserve game.

BRYAN ROBSON had no worries about pitching in the youngsters if they are good enough,, and 16-year-old Andrew Campbell made his Premiership debut as a second half substitute against Sheffield Wednesday. Campbell, who became the third youngest player ever to represent the club, is pictured alongside Des Walker and Steve Nicol.

Samba Time Again

In particular, central defender Steve Vickers was able to get in a good blow-out after recovering from injury. Branco also played the full 90 minutes and hit the crossbar with a piledriver.

Unfortunately the result didn't go Boro's way with Tromso winning 3-1, thanks to a hat-trick from Sigurd Rushveldt, who had been connected with a possible £600,000 move to Teesside in Bryan Robson's first season in charge. Boro's reply came from Jaime Moreno.

The match was played at a highly competitive pace, with a qualified referee and linesman. No doubt this match will create a headache for the football statisticians when they argue which was the last ever match to be played at Ayresome Park.

The match was a personal disappointment for Chris Morris, who picked up a thigh injury in the first half which put him on the sidelines. Another injured player was Phil Stamp, whose injury plagued season continued when he suffered an ankle ligament injury in training.

Vickers was back in action for Boro's clash with Sheffield Wednesday at the Cellnet Riverside Stadium on Good Friday, which was being shown live on TV.

With Boro virtually safe from the threat of relegation, Robson took advantage by making unenforced changes. Jan Fjortoft was back to form a new striking partnership up front with Chris Freestone, who had been in prolific scoring form for the reserves all season.

Freestone had scored 24 goals in the Pontins League and had played a big part in Gordon McQueen's men edging nearer towards promotion. The 24-year-old, who had been signed from Arnold Town the previous season, fully deserved his chance in the Premiership.

Brazilian duo Juninho and Branco also resumed for Boro, with Curtis Fleming switching to right-back in place of Neil Cox, who was rested. Nick Barmby and John Hendrie were missing due to minor knocks, while Jamie Pollock was starting a two-match suspension and Phil Whelan was dropped to the bench.

The biggest surprise of all came in Robson's choice of substitutes. He called up 16-year-old striker Andrew Campbell, who had been pulled out of Boro Juniors' Easter trip to Italy to play in the Enzo Ferrari tournament. Middlesbrough-born Campbell had played regularly for Boro's youth team all season, but was still a first year YTS player and had played only a handful of times for the reserves.

It was a pleasant sunny night, but the first half against Wednesday was a bit of an anti-climax and ended goalless. After the restart, Boro suddenly moved into gear to produce their best 45 minutes of football since Christmas.

They went on to win comfortably by 3-1, with Jan Fjortoft returning to the goals trail with a clinical brace, while Freestone had the delight of marking his senior debut in the Premiership with the third goal after Derek Whyte had headed on a Juninho corner.

In the final six minutes, with Boro assured of victory, Robson called Campbell off the bench for his first team debut. The young striker not only became the youngest player ever to represent Boro in the Premiership, but it was reported that he was the youngest to play in the competition for any club.

Campbell, who showed a couple of nice touches in his short spell on the pitch, followed in the footsteps of fellow 16-year-olds Sam Lawrie and Stephen Bell to play first team football for Boro. However both Lawrie and Bell were younger than Campbell.

Bryan Robson told the Evening Gazette: "I wanted to give some of the lads a chance to show what they could do, now that the pressure is off the team, and I thought that Freestone and Campbell both did well for us.

"We gave the ball away a bit too often in the first half but I was pleased with our second half performance. Juninho caused Wednesday big problems when the game opened up. I was delighted that we gave the fans something to shout about at last."

Robson revealed in the Evening Gazette the following day that Boro were planning a trip to China. The club intended to play three matches in China as part of a pre-season tour in July.

The match against the Owls had produced the almost obligatory injury with midfielder Graham Kavanagh going for X-rays after limping off with a shin injury. Fortunately the X-rays showed that there was no break, though Kavanagh's shin was badly bruised and he was ruled out of the trip to Tottenham on Easter Monday.

MARK SUMMERBELL – the Durham teenager came on for his debut against Spurs at White Hart Lane and had a terrific game.

Steve Vickers also picked up a minor calf strain and missed the game at White Hart Lane as a precaution, though worse was to follow when goalkeeper Gary Walsh and Jan Fjortoft both picked up a virus over the weekend and were unable to play.

The absence of Walsh meant that Alan Miller was called up for his first senior game since August. Neil Cox resumed at right-back, Phil Whelan returned in place of Vickers, and Craig Hignett and Alan Moore were recalled to the midfield.

Any fears that the changes might disrupt the side quickly disappeared as Boro went on to produce their best all-round performance so far in 1996. They were solid under pressure in the first half, with skipper Nigel Pearson outstanding, and then broke out to control the play throughout the second period.

Unfortunately Boro had to settle for a share of the spoils in a 1-1 draw. Chris Armstrong put Spurs ahead against the run of play six minutes from time, but Phil Whelan scored his first senior goal for four years to equalise 60 seconds later.

There was yet another injury. Boro lost Robbie Mustoe six minutes before the interval with strained ankle ligaments. His absence gave Bryan Robson the chance to blood 19-year-old Mark Summerbell, who had been named on the Boro bench for the first time.

Summerbell, who had broken through from the youth team to the reserve side this season, looked a slight figure as he took to the field. But any fears that he might be unable to hold up the midfield quickly disappeared.

In fact the Durham lad showed no signs of nerves or inexperience and he went on to become one of the more dominant players on the pitch and might even have grabbed a couple of second half goals.

Another player who did really well was Miller, who showed terrific confidence from the start. Naturally this confidence was quickly relayed to the rest of the side. It was hard to believe that he had not played a senior game for more than seven months.

Bryan Robson told the Evening Gazette: "I thought our lads were the better side. They did really well to come straight back after Spurs had taken the lead against the run of play. It was a blow to lose Robbie, but Mark Summerbell came on and did a great job for us."

The first team's success was repeated by Boro's youth team, who travelled to Marinello in Italy to win the prestigious Enzo Ferrari Trophy, beating Italian national youth champions Juventus in the final on penalties. David Geddis's lads were the only non-Italian side to reach any of the four age group finals.

As the youth team returned from Italy, Bryan Robson was on his way to Portugal to run the rule over a potential summer signing. Robbo took in the Porto-Sporting Lisbon clash to watch Porto's Brazilian-born midfielder Emerson, who was available for transfer.

Emerson, who was valued at £4 million, held a Portuguese passport, and therefore would present no problems over qualifying for a work permit.

After returning to Teesside, Robson was not prepared to go into too many details about the

PHIL WHELAN – the big defender improved considerably during the season and scored his first goal for the club at Spurs.

strength of his interest in Emerson, saying: "I went to watch the match because I had been alerted that there were five top quality players in action in the two sides who would be available in the summer."

Robson was also being strongly linked with an interest in his former Manchester United teammate Paul Ince, who was said to be unhappy at Inter Milan. However, within a matter of days, Italian sources claimed that Ince had changed his mind and was on the verge of signing a new contract with the Italian club. Robson was also linked with a keen interest in Juventus' colourful striker Gianluca Vialli, who was reported to be looking for a move.

However the manager's most immediate task was to prepare his team for the Premiership clash with Wimbledon at the Cellnet Riverside Stadium on Saturday, April 13. Boro had so far failed to beat the Dons in three previous meetings this season, and Robson was particularly determined to grab a victory.

The Boro boss was boosted by the return from injury of England striker Nick Barmby while Jamie Pollock was back after suspension. Steve Vickers also resumed in defence, and Graham Kavanagh bounced back in midfield after making a quick recovery from his shin injury against Sheffield Wednesday just eight days earlier.

Derek Whyte was serving a one-match ban and Robbie Mustoe was sidelined for two or three

ALAN MOORE had a great game against Wimbledon at the Cellnet Riverside Stadium and earned his first full Republic of Ireland cap as a result. Moore is pictured with the Dons' Vinnie Jones and teammate Graham Kavanagh.

weeks, though Alan Miller and Alan Moore deservedly retained their places in the line-up.

Boro went into the game with plenty of optimism, but once again found it difficult to perform against the hard working Dons and their five-match unbeaten run came to an end in a 2-1 defeat.

Robbie Earle grabbed an early goal for the visitors but Boro battled back to equalise thanks to Curtis Fleming's first goal for the club. The Irish defender had battled back to reach peak form again and his debut goal in front of more than 29,000 fans was one of the most popularly received events of the season.

Fleming broke his goal scoring duck in his 151st game for the club when scoring with a right footed drive.

However Boro were unable to build on Fleming's goal and went off the boil in the second half. As a result it was no surprise when Efan Ekoku grabbed the winner for the Dons.

Robson had experimented by playing Barmby and Juninho as a twin strikeforce, and the idea never looked like paying any dividends as Boro created few chances.

The Boro boss was still angry afterwards, telling the Evening Gazette: "Our performance was annoying. We had a 30,000 crowd and they deserved more. If we had lost 4-3 in an entertaining game I wouldn't have minded so much. But our passing and movement was poor, and we played in only a 20 minute spell in the first half."

Robson had left Branco on the bench throughout the game and there was speculation over the weekend that the Brazilian's stay on Teesside might be cut short, with him moving on either to Japan or the new professional league in the United States.

However Robson dismissed the speculation. He explained his reasons for not playing Branco by saying: "When Branco arrived here, he had done very little training for the previous two months.

"It meant that his fitness level was a long way behind the rest of the players. So, really, we are looking at next season. With the benefit of a full pre-season's training, Branco will do well for us".

There was a huge boost for the club on the Tuesday when five Boro players were named in international squads. It produced a big breakthrough for Curtis Fleming and Alan Moore, both of whom were included in the full Republic of Ireland squad for the first time. The Irish were due to meet the Czech Republic in Prague.

Both players had been watched by new Irish boss Mick McCarthy playing for Boro against Wimbledon on the Saturday. McCarthy could hardly have picked a better time to run the rule over the duo because Fleming and Moore were the best two Boro players on the pitch.

Moore was a constant tormentor of the Dons with his strong runs from midfield, while Fleming picked the match to score his very first goal in senior football, in addition to enjoying an absolute cracker of a game.

There was more international selection that week, with Nick Barmby retaining his place in the England squad for the match against Croatia at Wembley, and Jan Fjortoft selected in the Norwegian squad to meet France.

Derek Whyte failed to win a place in the Scottish squad against Denmark, but was named captain of the Scottish B team which was due to meet their Danish counterparts. It gave Whyte a chance of boosting his claims for a place in the full international squad for the European Championships in the summer.

There was more good news for the club the following night when Boro reserves clinched promotion to the first division of the Pontins League. Gordon McQueen's men had led the division all season and made sure of their place in the top echelon of reserve team football by beating Rotherham United by 1-0 in front of 2,500 fans at the Cellnet Riverside Stadium. It was no surprise that the all important goal came from the reserves' man of the season Chris Freestone.

McQueen told the Evening Gazette: "Everybody who has played for the team this season has shown a great attitude and I feel particularly pleased for the players who have formed the backbone of the side. Micky Barron, Alan White, Chris Freestone and Mark Summerbell have played in virtually every game".

Thursday, April 18, turned out to be Boro's very last day at Ayresome Park. They had trained on the once hallowed turf all season, and used the stadium's full facilities, including the gym, dressing rooms and physio's department.

However the stadium was due to be handed over to the new owners, Wimpey Homes, for redevelopment as housing and so, after that last day's training was completed, the players and coaching staff left the 93 years old stadium, never to return.

Boro switched their training headquarters to the Cellnet Riverside Stadium for the rest of the season, though there were no plans to train on the playing surface at the new stadium.

The Riverside was used by the squad as a base for changing and showering, with the players doing much of their training on the Holme House prison pitch at Stockton.

Boro had been hoping to move into their new training headquarters at Eston Leisure Centre for the start of pre-season work in July, but this was becoming increasingly unlikely. So the players faced training at temporary headquarters at the start of their second season in the Premiership.

The medical room at the Cellnet Riverside Stadium was also being used to treat the injured players until the new state of the art facilities, which were planned at Eston, were opened.

The current set of injured players included the luckless Paul Wilkinson, who had broken a big toe while on loan with First Division Luton Town, which had effectively ended his season.

Boro had just two games left to play, at Liverpool on April 27, and at home to Manchester United eight days later. The mere thought of the United match was already generating plenty of adrenalin. In fact it was a game which the whole of Teesside - and Manchester - wanted to see.

However spare tickets were at a premium. Boro's seats were already in the hands of season ticket holders, while United fans had quickly snapped up the Old Trafford club's allocation of 2,600.

Even so, many more fans were disappointed at missing out specially as it quickly became clear that United would clinch the Championship if they could avoid defeat at the Cellnet Riverside Stadium. So the club was besieged by fans desperate for tickets, and the Evening Gazette also received a regular flow of calls. Unfortunately there was no way that either organisation could help.

The entrepreneurs on Teesside quickly realised that there was a huge market for tickets for the big game, and there were reports by the middle of April that tickets were changing hands for anything ranging from £50 to £200.

A moment to savour for Curtis Fleming after scoring his first Boro goal in his 151st appearance. Pictured celebrating Fleming's goal against Wimbledon are, left to right, Phil Whelan, Fleming, Nick Barmby, Graham Kavanagh and Juninho.

Samba Time Again

The Boro, angry that the non-transferable season tickets were reported to be being sold on by regular Boro fans, took immediate steps to stamp down on the problem.

The club announced that any fans who were found to have sold their seats would be banned from holding season tickets next season. In addition, Boro officials stressed that the touting of tickets was illegal and culprits could face police prosecution.

Despite these statements from the Boro, Cleveland Police were anticipating potential problems both inside and outside the Cellnet Riverside Stadium when the game was to take place on Sunday, May 5. So a massive operation was already being planned to keep touts and non-ticket holders away from the stadium.

Following a quiet and football-free weekend, there was a big announcement from the Boro

vital to bring in new blood to ensure that he could improve the quality of the squad during the summer, while it was clear that Boro's admission prices were still likely to be among the cheapest in the Premiership.

Robson told the Evening Gazette: "The more season ticket holders we have, the more money I will have to spend in the transfer market. It is imperative that we move quickly for top stars before other clubs make their move. Early commitment by the fans will also ensure that they will be at the Cellnet Riverside Stadium when the revolution comes".

The revolution to which Robbo was referring was the signing of three or four players which would revolutionise the Boro first team squad and give them the opportunity to become hard to beat and consistent, and hopefully good enough to make a big impact in the Premiership.

A sad day in the life of Ayresome Park as most of its assets are auctioned off. The auction, which was held in the gymnasium, attracted both representatives from smaller clubs and fans alike.

on the Monday. The club revealed their new ticket prices for next season, which involved big increases.

Prices in general were going up by 26.7 per cent, which was well in front of inflation. These prices applied to seats which were renewed before May 31, while any fans renewing after this date would face increases of 33 per cent.

The dearest seats in the Upper West Stand were to cost £342 before May 31 and £361 afterwards. These same seats had cost £270 in the inaugural season at the Cellnet Riverside Stadium. Season tickets in the North Stand were to increase from £180 to £225, with a further leap to £237.50 after May 31.

Naturally these increases had not been backed by any changes in facilities for the fans. However Bryan Robson stressed that the additional income was

Immediate reaction to the price increases was mixed, though there were indications that Boro fans would be keen to renew. The club was stressing that any ticket holders who did not renew risked missing out on potential improved fortunes ahead for the club.

Boro also took steps to replace fans who did not intend to renew by starting a reserve list of supporters who would have first opportunity to fill any vacancies. They opened a telephone hotline and had 1,500 calls within a matter of days from potential new season ticket holders.

This reserve list served a double purpose, because Boro needed to gauge the strength of their support in order to make a quick decision whether to fill in the two corners of the stadium. This project would create up to 5,000 extra seats, but would also cost somewhere in the region of £5 million, and Boro needed to know whether the venture would be financially viable.

Boro were ready to start the work in the summer if there was a huge demand from new fans for season tickets. On the other hand, if the demand was not there, then the project would be put on hold.

While much of the talk was about the future of the Cellnet Riverside Stadium, it was the end of the road for Ayresome Park. The stadium was given its final send off on Tuesday, April 23, when an official auction was held to sell off any remaining part of the ground which would attract buyers.

Fittingly, it was a damp and depressing day for the auction, which was a particularly sad event for the fans. The auction lasted for much of the day and the goods which were sold off included the floodlights, stand seats and turnstiles. Non league clubs bought most of the items for installation at their own grounds.

European Championships squad any harm at all, which was good news for the Boro defender.

The following day Alan Moore won his first full cap when he was named in the Republic of Ireland starting line-up for the match against the Czech Republic in Prague. He made his debut in an orthodox striking role alongside Niall Quinn.

Forty five minutes later Curtis Fleming became Boro's second new cap of the evening when he was brought on at half-time for the injured Denis Irwin. So it was a big night for both Moore and Fleming, and the Boro, but not so good for the Irish team in general because they lost 2-0.

The following day there was an official announcement from the Boro by chairman Steve Gibson, who revealed that Willie Maddren, one of the club's most loyal servants, was to be given a benefit year by the club. Maddren had publicly announced a couple of weeks earlier that he was suffering from Motor Neurone Disease.

THE end of the road for Ayresome Park as the gates are locked for the final time.

Many Boro fans also turned up to bid for some of the lots, though they tended to concentrate on buying wooden signs and other small pieces of memorabilia. The North Stand clock was bought by Dave Stokes to hang in the Ayresome Park pub in Albert Road.

Even former Boro goal ace Bernie Slaven got in on the act by buying a section of the Holgate End fencing, from where he used to salute the fans after scoring one of his many goals at the stadium.

The same day Derek Whyte skippered Scotland B in Denmark, though it was not a good night for the Boro defender, or the Scots, because they lost 3-0. However Scotland manager Craig Brown pointed out afterwards that his side had been hastily thrown together and that none of the players on view had done their prospects of winning a place in the

Willie, whose playing career had been cut short at the age of 27 by a crippling knee injury, had long been regarded as one of the Boro's best ever uncapped players.

He had also returned to the club as a coach, and later as manager, and had proved himself a great talent spotter by uncovering players of the calibre of Gary Pallister, Steve Pears and Bernie Slaven for the Boro.

Gibson said: "We decided straight away as a club that we wanted to help Willie. He made a contribution of quality during his career with us. We owe him a debt."

There was no shortage of takers for places on Maddren's benefit year committee, which immediately started making plans to organise a bumper match for the player at the Cellnet Riverside Stadium.

Looking to the Future

CHAPTER TEN:

BRYAN ROBSON cheered Boro fans on April 25 with the wonderful news that he had committed his future to the club.

The Boro boss revealed in the Evening Gazette that he had put pen to paper on a two-year contract extension which would keep him at the Cellnet Riverside Stadium until 1999 at least.

Robbo's announcement removed all the doubts and fears which had surfaced on Teesside since he was initially linked with the England hot seat, once Terry Venables had voiced his intentions to stand down as coach after the European Championships.

Soon after Venables had made his announcement, Robson promised Boro's supporters that he had no intentions of accepting the top job with England if he was offered it. But many fans remained worried that the Football Association might eventually approach the Boro boss with an offer he couldn't refuse.

Now, Robson's decision to sign Boro's new contract extension allayed all the fears. He had just led Boro to their highest league placing for 15 years and it was seen as crucial by the fans that he stayed with the club to carry on the task of trying to bring back the good times.

When the former England international captain arrived on Teesside in the summer of 1994, the Boro were a mid-table First Division side which was suffering from falling attendances and unfulfilled ambitions. The Boro had long since been regarded as one of the non-achievers, occasionally flirting with the big time but then quickly falling away through lack of investment.

Robson's arrival had come hand in hand with a genuine offer of hard cash to spend from chairman Steve Gibson. Robbo's mere presence on Teesside generated a new wave of optimism and he swept the club back into the Premiership at the first attempt.

In fact Boro won the First Division Championship as a result of an attractive passing style of football, and the fans came flooding back in their droves.

Boro's return to the Premiership came hand in hand with a move to their modern £16 million new stadium at Middlesbrough Dock and suddenly Boro had the feel of a big club again.

Robson was given £10 million to spend to consolidate Boro's place in the Premiership and he spent it wisely, bringing in 21-year-old full England international striker Nick Barmby, and the immensely talented Brazilian superstar Juninho. Boro fans had never been given such luxury in their lives.

Boro did settle into the hurly burly of life in the Premiership, though a disastrous run of injuries and a loss of confidence contributed to the team finishing in 12th position when it had been hoped that they would finish much higher.

The season was witnessed by near capacity crowds at the Cellnet Riverside Stadium. The average attendance of more than 29,000 was the highest on Teesside for 45 years. The good times were well and truly back at the Boro.

Not that everything was always hunky dory. Robson has clearly made mistakes along the way, both in terms of one or two signings and occasionally with tactics. But this is Robson's first managerial post and it is bound to be a learning process.

However, the indications are that Robson has learned very quickly, and he has never wavered in his determination to try to restore Boro among the top echelon of English football.

In any case, on the day of his appointment in May, 1994, every Boro fan in the country would have happily settled for 12th position in the Premiership at the end of Robson's second season at the helm.

There would seem to be no obvious reason why, with the continued backing and support of the boardroom, Robson can't continue to take Boro to new heights over the next three seasons and build a platform for a much longer period of success.

Clearly Robson is looking forward to the challenge. He told the Evening Gazette: "I'm absolutely delighted to extend my contract. Since I joined the club, chairman Steve Gibson has always backed my decisions 100 per cent, while making the money available for me to go out and compete with other top clubs for the world's best players.

"However the deciding factor which really swayed me was the way the people of Teesside have backed the team and turned up in their droves week in and week out.

"I always knew Boro were well supported but until this season I would never have believed Boro could attract crowds of 30,000 for every home match. I can't thank the fans enough for their support."

Assistant manager Viv Anderson also signed a two-year extension to his contract, which guaranteed that the highly successful managerial partnership would continue.

Anderson was happy to let Robson take the spotlight, but the Boro boss would be the first to admit that he owed a lot to his former England and Manchester United colleague. On the occasions when Robson was away on international duty coaching the England squad, Anderson took over the reins and maintained the smooth running of the club.

With the contract extensions duly signed, club chairman Steve Gibson was one of the happiest men on Teesside. It was Gibson who was instrumental in bringing Robson to Boro in the first place, and he had backed his judgement in supporting the manager and meeting his demands and needs.

Gibson said: "We are very pleased with the job that Bryan has done and we are delighted that he wants to stay to help us achieve our ambitions of being very successful in the future.

"I was aware of the stories linking Bryan with the England job but they were always stronger outside the club than in it.

"I only once spoke to Bryan about the England job. He said his future was here. That was good enough for me. He has always been true to his word and once he had given it we left the speculating to others."

The fans were already being bombarded with club appeals to renew their season tickets quickly. But the reasons were three-pronged. Boro wanted cash to enter the transfer market, they needed to give themselves as much time as possible to try to ensure another sell-out, and they also wanted to discover if there was a heavy enough demand for seats to deliver a mandate for the club to fill in the corners at the Cellnet Riverside Stadium, thus creating another 5,000 seats.

While the club officials and fans were delighted that Robson was definitely staying on, the news was greeted with similar enthusiasm by the players.

Skipper Nigel Pearson said: "It's great news for the club and the players that Bryan has extended his contract. It puts everybody's minds at rest, especially as many people had it at the back of their minds that he might not be here in the not too distant future.

THE magic moment for Boro fans as Bryan Robson puts pen to paper on his contract extension, watched by chairman Steve Gibson.

Within minutes of signing the extended contract, Robson was already making his plans for the future. He said: "I want to bring in more quality players for the start of next season to ensure supporters can see a winning, exciting Boro team in the Premiership."

The Boro boss needed plenty of financial backing if he was to attract and afford the calibre of player he was seeking. So he took a personal interest in trying to ensure that Boro's season ticket sales for the 1996-97 season matched those of the club's first year back in the top flight.

He added: "Boro fans can play their part in helping me to bring in the type of players I am looking for by renewing their season tickets before the May 31 deadline which has been set, or by adding their names to the waiting list. I can promise them that their money will be spent on team strengthening and even better facilities."

"Basically it's good for the continued progress of the club that Bryan stays. We have come a long way in two years but then our results in the second half of the season showed that we still have a long way to go."

He added: "The target for this club has got to be to get some silverware on the table. And the fact that Bryan has pledged himself to the club makes the time scale more realistic."

While everybody was starting to look forward to the new season with great anticipation, Boro still had two games to play to complete their first season back in the Premiership. Both were tough tests. They were to visit Liverpool on April 27 and then entertain Champions elect Manchester United on May 5.

Beforehand, the Boro reserves had a Championship date of their own. They entertained nearest rivals Sunderland reserves and secured the Pontins League second division title with a 2-0 win.

Both goals were scored by Bolivian international Jaime Moreno, who was being watched from the stands by Aberdeen manager Roy Aitken. Moreno had enjoyed an excellent season with the reserves, but had gained few first team opportunities, and it was clear that Robson was ready to allow the 22-year-old to move on.

Robson told the Evening Gazette: "I have had a chat with Jaime and he understands the situation. At this stage of his career he needs regular first team football.

"I still have every faith in his ability but I can't wait for him to develop to his full potential."

One player who was pushing very hard for a first team breakthrough was free-scoring striker Chris Freestone, who had accepted a new two-year contract. The former Arnold Town player had scored 26 goals in the season, including one on his Premiership debut against Sheffield Wednesday on Good Friday.

However, neither Moreno nor Freestone featured in the Boro squad as they set off for their last away game of the season at Liverpool. The team was also without one of its regulars because Curtis Fleming suffered a knee injury in training just 24 hours before the game and had to drop out.

Branco stepped in to fill the breach at left-back while Derek Whyte also returned to the heart of the defence after suspension and replaced Phil Whelan.

Midfield duo Alan Moore and Graham Kavanagh dropped out to allow for the return of Phil Stamp, while Robson also handed a full debut to YTS player Andy Campbell, who had celebrated his 17th birthday just nine days earlier.

Campbell, who made his Premiership debut for Boro as a 16-year-old substitute against Sheffield Wednesday, was drafted in to lead the Boro attack, facing a daunting prospect against Liverpool defenders of the calibre of Neil Ruddock and John Scales.

Boro did not even have an away shirt packed in their kitbag with Campbell's name and number printed on the back. In fact they did not even have a blank shirt. So quick thinking physio Bob Ward went outside the stadium to collar the first Boro fan he could find wearing the blue and black away shirt.

The first fan Bob bumped into was Graham Walker, from Harvey Court in Dormanstown, Graham wasn't so sure about giving up his shirt at first, specially as he had borrowed it from workmate Mick Riddiough and was intending to return it to his pal after the game.

However, when Graham was led into the Boro dressing room and offered Bryan Robson's shirt in exchange, it was an offer he could hardly refuse. So Campbell took to the field wearing Graham's blank shirt, after Boro had initially obtained permission from referee Roger Dilkes to field a player wearing no name or number.

In the event the 17-year-old did not have much opportunity to get the shirt dirty because Boro spent much of the match on the defensive on a hot afternoon.

Their task of trying to grab something from the game was made all the more difficult early in the second half when Nigel Pearson, who had been the best Boro player on view, was led off the field to have 11 stitches inserted in a gash just above his right eye. Pearson had collided with the right hand post in attempting to make a clearance. Whelan came on as substitute and Boro continued to defend feverishly. However they were finally cracked open in 70 minutes when Stan Collymore netted after he had been left in the clear following an unfortunate deflection through their back line.

Even so, Boro finished the match very strongly and were most unfortunate not to grab a late equaliser when Neil Cox hit the inside of the right hand post.

Assistant boss Viv Anderson was pleased with the way Boro had worked hard to try to get something out of the game. He told the Evening Gazette: "We had a game plan. If you go to Liverpool gung ho you will concede six or seven. But we stuck to our plan and it almost paid dividends for us.

"We had three or four chances after Liverpool had scored and overall I thought we did pretty well. When you think that Liverpool score goals for fun and we had several young players in our side, it puts everything into perspective.

On the Monday evening, Cellnet staged their Boro Player of the Year awards dinner at the Cellnet Riverside Stadium. The invited audience of club officials, players, business people and media representatives were treated to an exclusive dinner and video review of Boro's season.

Steve Vickers, who had played consistently well in his first season in Premiership football, was crowned Cellnet player of the year. The Boro central defender had come out tops in a three-way poll which was voted for by the club's supporters, so it was a well received and popular decision. The trophy was presented by Paul Leonard, Cellnet's head of marketing communications.

Vickers had performed particularly well when the team was struggling during its bad run early in the year. He said: "I'm very pleased to receive the award. But I think that a lot of the credit should go to the players around me."

Jan Fjortoft won the Cellnet goal of the season award for his strike against Leeds United in November, which included an assist from Juninho in his first game for Boro.

Boro's 2-0 victory against Blackburn Rovers in September was judged team performance of the season, while Gary Walsh's magnificent stop from Neil Shipperley at Southampton was considered save of the season and Neil Cox won the best goal celebration for his Monty Python take-off following his strike against West Ham in December.

The following day, on Tuesday, April 30, Boro's first new signing of the summer was announced, though not by the club. Danish newspapers claimed that the 22-year-old striker Mikkel Beck, who played for Fortuna Cologne in Germany, had signed a four year contract with the Boro. Beck was Denmark's current attack leader, having scored three goals in eight internationals.

An eminent Danish journalist told the Evening Gazette: "Mikkel is a very good player. He has developed into a strong and powerful striker during his three years with Fortuna Cologne.

"He is a very good header and he's very quick. He is very left-footed, but that is not a problem to him."

BORO fan Graham Walker, who swapped his shirt for Bryan Robson's shirt at Liverpool. It was worn by 17-year-old Andy Campbell, making his full Premiership debut.

Beck was officially out of contract this summer and Boro had signed him believing that they would not have to pay a fee to the German club, under the terms of the Bosman Case ruling. However, the Cologne side threw a spanner into the works by insisting that they had a year's option on Beck, and were therefore demanding a fee.

It was a difficult situation because the ruling of the Bosman Case had so far not been officially tested in the law courts. It was a matter for the legal eagles, so Boro were in no position to make any public comment until a solution had been found.

Within 24 hours of the Beck story breaking, a London based sports agency announced that Boro had completed a second signing. This time they were reported to have agreed to pay Portuguese champions Porto a fee of £4 million for the 23-year-old Brazilian born midfield star Emerson.

Bryan Robson had been impressed with Emerson's aggressive style of play and passing skills when he flew to Portugal to watch him in action, and had been quick to push through a deal. One of the bonuses of this signing was that Emerson possessed a Portuguese passport, and so Boro did not need to apply for a work permit.

However, once again, Boro were unable to make any official comment on the revelation. There were still matters to be sorted out at the Porto end and Boro would have to wait until the Portuguese season had finished before they could bring Emerson over to England.

However, despite the hiccups, the double swoop was good news for the Boro fans. It was an indication that Bryan Robson had been true to his word when he stressed that he was determined to bring in top quality players during the summer. And

the fact that Robson had targetted up to four new signings was even better news.

There was a further boost for Boro, on the international front, when central defender Derek Whyte was named in the Scotland squad for a two-match tour to the United States at the end of May.

Whyte could have been excused for believing that his chances of being involved in the European Championships had disappeared when he played for the Scotland B team in a recent international in Denmark. But the U.S. call-up left the Boro man in no doubt that the door to the Scottish squad was still open.

Meanwhile the build-up was continuing to Boro's mouth watering final game of the season at home to Manchester United. The clamour for tickets for this game was virtually without parallel. Boro's games at home to United traditionally attracted huge crowds, but this match was extra special because Alex Ferguson's men would clinch the Premiership title if they were to win or draw against Boro.

The clamour for seats meant that those fans already with tickets were put under pressure to sell them. There were media reports that Manchester United fans were willing to pay vastly inflated prices for tickets, which might tempt Boro season ticket holders to sell.

The last thing Boro officials wanted to see was Manchester United fans sitting in Boro areas of the ground, so the club were quick to try to prevent tickets changing hands by announcing that any fans who sold their tickets would not be allowed to renew their season tickets for the next season.

It was a serious threat, but there were still reports coming into the Evening Gazette that tickets were changing hands for anything between £50 and £200 in the week leading up to the match.

Looking to the Future

While it was a big match on Teesside, it was a crucial match as far as football fans on Tyneside were concerned. If Boro could beat Manchester United, and neighbours Newcastle United defeated Spurs at St. James's Park, then the Magpies would win the Championship.

So Boro boss Bryan Robson was very much the pig in the middle. Newcastle fans were looking for him to do them a favour by beating his old club. Manchester United fans were hoping to benefit from an old pals act.

However Robson had no intentions of doing any other club any favours. This was a high profile match, being televised around the world, and Robson wanted the Boro to win it for themselves and for the fans on Teesside.

The Boro boss wanted to see his players finish the season in style and take a big scalp at the same time. The destination of the Championship was the last thing on Robson's mind as he worked out a game plan to try to win the match.

Robson told the Evening Gazette: "In many ways I just can't win because Newcastle and Manchester United are looking closely at our game for the right result. It's a catch 22 situation for me but it's certainly not pressure. All the pressure is on Kevin Keegan and Alex Ferguson, the two managers involved in the title battle.

"All we have to think about is going out to try to win a big game. It's a great challenge for our players."

Boro officials were determined to make United's visit a party day, regardless of the result. A series of pre-match events were organised, including face painting, balloons and flags for the young fans. The Teesside Pipe Band played inside the stadium, while stiltwalkers paraded around the pitch along with Roary and the Manchester United mascot, Fred the Red.

Boro skipper Nigel Pearson had recovered sufficiently from his gashed eye to keep his place in the side, though Robson sprang a pre-match surprise by bringing back Gary Walsh in goal for Alan Miller, who had been Boro's man of the match the previous week at Liverpool.

Walsh had played most of the season in goal for Boro, and Robson revealed that he wanted to give the keeper the chance to play in one of the big end of season games, having earlier lost his place because of injury. It gave Walsh the chance to play against his former club, having joined Boro from Manchester United the previous August.

Jan Fjortoft was also back to lead the attack in place of teenager Andy Campbell, while Robbie Mustoe had made a rapid recovery from his ankle injury and resumed in place of Phil Stamp. The teams on duty were:

Boro: Walsh, Cox, Branco, Vickers, Pearson, Whyte, Barmby, Pollock, Fjortoft, Juninho, Mustoe. Subs: Moore, Stamp, Whelan.

Manchester United: Schmeichel, Irwin, P. Neville, May, Pallister, Keane, Butt, Beckham, Scholes, Cantona, Giggs. Subs: Cole, Bruce, G. Neville.

The match kicked off amid a terrific atmosphere, with the United fans singing virtually throughout the whole 90 minutes. The visitors were given the perfect start when slack marking by Boro allowed David May to head in a Ryan Giggs corner after only 15 minutes, which ensured that the United fans stayed in full voice.

Boro had their chances to get back into it before the interval but could not take them. Eight minutes after the restart Andy Cole came off the bench to

THE one that got away. Neil Cox outjumps Phil Neville but sends this header wide of the target in the opening minutes of the final game against Manchester United. If this one had gone in it might have been a different result.

STOP me if you can… Juninho goes past Manchester United defender Denis Irwin.

JAN FJORTOFT was unhappy with his final tally of just eight goals. He is pictured keeping Manchester United's David May at bay.

ROBBIE MUSTOE made a quick recovery from an ankle injury to return against Manchester United. He is pictured in action against David May.

score United's second goal with his first kick, again from a Giggs corner, and the title was on its way back to Old Trafford. Giggs put the icing on the cake for the visitors with a third goal ten minutes from time.

After the final whistle, Boro emerged from the dressing room to make a lap of honour. It was a way of saying thank-you to the fans for their magnificent support during the whole season.

Boro were followed by United, who received the Championship trophy on the pitch, along with their medals. The occasion was warmly received by the inquisitive Boro fans, who gave the United players a standing ovation when they did a lap of honour. It was a marvellous reaction from the home fans, who had seen their own team well beaten.

As expected, many ticketless fans had turned up at the Cellnet Riverside Stadium in the hope of somehow getting in. In fact there were still hundreds swarming outside the stadium when the match kicked off at four o'clock.

However there was a huge police presence out in force and they gradually dispersed the ticketless fans. Inside the stadium there were three or four incidents in the stands when United fans were found to be sitting in Boro areas, but these incidents fortunately were isolated and were dealt with by the team of stewards.

Everybody had been heavily pumped up with adrenalin all afternoon, though Bryan Robson was still extremely frustrated at the final whistle that Boro had not run United a lot closer.

He told the Evening Gazette: "I was disappointed because I felt that we played ever so well for 70 minutes. But we didn't keep going until the final whistle. In the last 15 minutes we were giving the ball away all the time.

"We were the better team for a long period in the first half but we gave a couple of bad goals away and paid a high price. We did show people that we had no intentions of lying down for United but I would have preferred a better show. If we had put away our first half chances it might have been a different story."

It had been a more successful weekend for Boro Juniors, whose 2-0 victory at Bradford City ensured them of their third Northern Intermediate League title in three seasons.

David Geddis's lads had gone into the match needing only a point to pip nearest rivals Leeds United for the crown, but made doubly sure by winning the match. Kris Trevor put Boro ahead in the first half and Andy Campbell added a last minute clincher.

On Tuesday, May 7, Bryan Robson announced his retained list. There were no surprises. Paul Wilkinson and Jaime Moreno were available for transfer at a fee, but this was already known. Young pros. Wesley Byrne, Richard Ward and Ross Skingsley were handed free transfers.

Robson revealed that he also intended having further talks with Jamie Pollock, who was out of contract during the summer. Pollock and the manager had apparently held initial talks over the offer of a new deal, though the midfielder had so far not put pen to paper. The 22-year-old from Norton was in no rush and was exercising his right to consider all options.

However reserve team skipper Mickey Barron had signed a new one year deal and teenage left-back Craig Harrison, the only second year YTS player to be offered a pro contract, had signed for two years.

The same day, Boro right-back Neil Cox went into hospital for a hernia operation. Robson said: "Neil has been carrying the injury for about four weeks but we thought we would wait until the season was over. It's just a routine op and he will be back with everybody else for the start of pre-season."

Twenty year old Phil Stamp was another player facing a minor operation before the end of the month. The highly promising midfielder was due to have some troublesome scar tissue scraped away from his ankle. The operation forced him to drop out of the stand-by squad for the England Under-21s for their annual summer tournament in Toulon.

Robson had intended to extend the players' season by another week, to cut down the amount of time they would be away from the club during the summer. So an extra game was fixed up against St. Patricks' Athletic in Dublin on the Thursday night. Boro were due to fly out on the Thursday morning and spend four days in light training in the Emerald Isle.

However the Irish club was very keen to see Juninho among the Boro line up, but the Brazilian star had picked up a knock playing against Manchester United and could not risk the injury.

Juninho was soon to fly back to Brazil to play in an international against Croatia, and also had the Olympics to look forward to. In addition to the Brazilian, several other Boro players dropped out of the trip to Ireland, and Robson was forced, reluctantly, to scrap the visit.

It meant that Boro's season was finally over for most of the squad. Naturally Juninho faced a very busy summer because he would be training with the Brazil squad before the Olympics, which were taking place in Atlanta in August.

Another player keeping busy was striker Nick Barmby, who had been named in Terry Venables' squad for England's match against Hungary at Wembley on May 18. Boro were doubly represented in the England camp because manager Bryan Robson was coach to the international team.

On Friday, May 10, sources in London revealed to the Evening Gazette that Emerson was due to fly in to Teesside within 72 hours. He was playing his final Portuguese league match for Porto on the Sunday, and would arrive at the Cellnet Riverside Stadium the following day. It was confirmation that Boro had definitely signed the £4 million Brazilian born midfielder.

The following day, Italian newspapers reported that Boro were one of several clubs very keen on Juventus striker Gianluca Vialli. The flamboyant 31-year-old Italian international was out of contract during the summer and was keen to move to Britain.

The speculation continued. Within 48 hours of the Vialli revelation, Boro were being linked with another European superstar. This time they were said to be chasing German striker Jurgen Klinsmann, who had been a teammate of Nick Barmby's at Tottenham.

However, the speculation took a back seat on Tuesday, May 14, when the Brazilian born midfielder Emerson was officially unveiled as Boro's first new signing of the summer. Boro had indeed paid £4 million to Porto for the 24-year-old.

THANKS FOR THE MEMORIES. The Boro squad, led by Bryan Robson, made a lap of honour following the final match against Manchester United.

Looking to the Future

Emerson attended a packed press conference at the Cellnet Riverside Stadium before going outside the main entrance in warm sunshine to meet the fans and sign a few autographs.

A delighted Bryan Robson told the Evening Gazette: "Emerson is a strong, intelligent player who can dictate the pace of the game. He's a good passer and can score goals, so he'll be an exciting player for us. I'm sure that the fans will take to him as soon as they see him.

"Emerson is the kind of player who can lift the crowd as well as the team. I'm delighted to have completed the deal because I know that a lot of other clubs were looking at him as well."

Robson added: "Porto manager Bobby Robson rates Emerson highly and wasn't keen to let him go, but he was the one player in Portuguese football who everybody wanted."

Emerson, whose real name is Emerson Moises Costa, had signed a three-year contract with the Boro. He still had a year of his contract with Porto to run, which is the reason why Boro had to fork out a high fee for his services.

The midfielder was making something of a sideways step on the face of things, because he could have stayed with Porto and played in the European Champions Cup in the new season. He could also have moved on to one of several major Italian clubs. Sampdoria, Inter Milan and Fiorentina were all said to be very keen.

However Emerson left no doubts that Boro were the club for him. An obvious attraction for the Brazilian was that Boro was Juninho's club. It was absolute proof that once you bring in a couple of world class players, the rest will follow of their own accord.

It emerged very quickly at the press conference that Emerson was keen to make the transition into international football. He had developed as a top quality player over the past two years but had not yet caught the eye of the Brazil selectors. Perhaps the fact that he was now playing alongside Juninho in club football would boost his international chances.

Emerson admitted: "I think that I will be able to play very well alongside Juninho. We are different types of players but we can play very well together. Hopefully my performances will be noted and I would love to play for Brazil alongside Juninho."

At the same time, Emerson made it clear that he believed that he was joining a progressive club and fully intended to continue to win trophies. He said: "There's a great project going on at Middlesbrough. The manager Bryan Robson has charisma and he has convinced me that Middlesbrough will be a force in the Premiership next season.

"I want to be a part of that project. We have to win trophies and qualify for a place in Europe. I believe that I can help Middlesbrough to play better. I think the style of English football will suit me."

Boro indicated that Emerson would be the only signing that the club would be able to reveal to the fans before Euro '96 was over. Bryan Robson had already done much of his player hunting and had placed his irons in the fire, but now he had to tone down his club affairs to link up with England. Robson had a far East tour to undertake with England and the European Championships, and would not be back at his desk at the Cellnet Riverside Stadium until July.

In any case, most of the major European clubs were expecting a very quiet time in the transfer

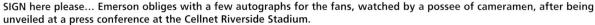

SIGN here please... Emerson obliges with a few autographs for the fans, watched by a possee of cameramen, after being unveiled at a press conference at the Cellnet Riverside Stadium.

GLAD to be here! Emerson walks out to meet the fans after completing his £4 million move from Porto.

market during June, specially as most of the top quality players were involved in Euro '96. Everybody was expecting a deluge of signings in July.

Of course, Boro had already been widely reported to have completed the signing of Mikkel Beck. However, Fortuna Cologne's apparent determination to hang on for a fee, even though the player was officially out of contract, was causing a massive problem. So Boro were not commenting on the Beck situation while legal negotiations carried on in the background.

There were different stories appearing from various sources, particularly in the Danish press. The Danes had a keen interest in the outcome of the alleged tug of war involving Beck.

The Danes claimed that German newspapers were reporting that Beck was ready to go to court to try to secure his release from Fortuna Cologne without the buying club incurring a fee.

On May 18, the Evening Gazette reported that Italian sources were linking Boro with the

bulldozed for housing, hosted an international clash between England and Scotland.

The two representative sides were actually made up of the best players from the workforce from Wimpey Homes, who were the new owners of the stadium.

Wimpey had started to strip the stands ready for the demolition job, having received outline planning permission to build up to 130 terraced and semi-detached houses on the site.

However Wimpey's staff did not want to see the stadium die without making use of the nostalgic surroundings for one last match, and so the international was arranged. For the record, the last match at Ayresome Park produced an away win, because the Scots won 1-0.

Back at the Riverside, Scottish striker John Hendrie was dismissing reports which claimed that he could soon be leaving the club for £1 million. Hendrie revealed that he was staying put and intended to fight for his place.

A sad sight as the back of the Holgate End of Ayresome Park falls into disrepair following its closure.

Argentinian striker Gabriel Batistuta, who had been playing for Fiorentina in Serie A.

Batistuta was yet another of the kind of top quality players who would be guaranteed to pack in the fans wherever Boro were in action. Batistuta joined other big names like Gianluca Vialli and Jurgen Klinsmann, who were already revealed on Bryan Robson's potential list of targets. It was becoming increasingly obvious that Robson was angling for big fish only, and it was great news for the fans.

There will be many arguments in future years over the actual last match at Ayresome Park, and many quiz participants will plum for Sunday, May 19, when the grand old stadium, which was about to be

Hendrie, who was top scorer in Bryan Robson's first year on Teesside, had been badly hit by injury during Boro's first 12 months back in the Premiership and was looking to put it all behind him and contest a place in the attack.

The popular Scot said: "I'll compete with anybody for a place and if I am not in the team I will make sure that the players who are in there are kept on their toes."

The same day Derek Whyte jetted off to the United States looking to make a fine impression with the Scottish squad and earn a place in manager Craig Brown's final 22 for Euro 96.

And there was good news for Boro fans the following day when Nick Barmby was named in

UNWANTED and broken seats litter the front of the North Terrace as workmen continue to strip Ayresome Park.

England's starting line up for the international against China in the Beijing Workers' Stadium. Barmby was about to win his sixth cap and it was the perfect opportunity to make a final impression before Terry Venables announced his Euro '96 squad.

At the same time, England's manager elect Glenn Hoddle and his proposed assistant John Gorman were meeting FA officials at Lancaster Gate. The meeting had been arranged to rubber stamp contracts for both men and devise plans for the future.

Gorman's official involvement in the England set-up was marvellous news for Boro fans because it meant that there would probably be no place for Bryan Robson after the European Championships.

Robson had operated as Terry Venables' close assistant and would obviously not stay in the international set up as deputy to Gorman. As far as Boro fans were concerned, the implications were that Robson would eventually be quitting the England coaching post to concentrate all of his energies into maintaining the Boro revolution and that wasn't a bad thing.

However Robbo had already stressed his wish to be involved with England at managerial level at some stage in the future, and it was not inconceivable that one day he would be granted his wish - but not until after his Boro contract had expired in 1999. Even then, it would depend on the England hot seat being available at that time.

For the time being, Robson was enjoying helping England to build up for their Euro '96 assault. He was a happy man as Nick Barmby went out and did the business for his country in China, scoring two goals in the 3-0 victory and being named man of the match.

The clash with China was England's last full international before the European Championships, so Barmby could hardly have selected a better time to score his first two goals for England. Not only did he stake his solid claims for a place in the final 22, but he made it virtually impossible for Terry Venables to leave him out.

In finding the back of the net, Barmby became only the fifth Boro player ever to score for England. The last Boro player to score for England was Alan Peacock, who netted twice against Wales in 1962.

Barmby said: "I was very pleased to score a couple of goals. Nobody has a divine right to be in the squad, but hopefully I put something into Terry Venables' mind. I'd love to have the chance to build on this performance."

On Friday, May 24, Boro lost out on potential target Gianluca Vialli. The Italian international opted to join Chelsea. The Juventus striker had held up the European Cup 48 hours earlier after the Italians had beaten Ajax on penalties in the final.

Vialli joined Chelsea on a three-year contract and would probably line up against Boro in the Premiership on several occasions over the ensuing

THE East Stand at Ayresome Park, stripped of its dignity and ready to be broken up.

EVERY picture tells a story. The demise of Ayresome Park is perfectly summed up by this poignant picture by Evening Gazette chief photographer Doug Moody of a line of dandelions bordering the once perfect pitch.

seasons. But any sense of frustration initially felt by the Boro fans would eventually disappear when Bryan Robson finally snapped up a big name striker of his own.

One man who would definitely be making a major impact in the Boro attack in the new season was Barmby, who was duly named in England's 22 for Euro '96. It was a big moment for the talented 22-year-old, who admitted: "I am honoured to be selected by my country for such a prestigious tournament, specially as it is being held in England this year."

It was doubly good news for Boro because Whyte was also named in the Scotland 22. Whyte had won his ninth Scottish cap playing for the Scots against the United States in New Britain, though he had unfortunately given a penalty away as the Americans won 2-1.

But Whyte's ability was not doubted, and the Boro central defender was officially welcomed back into the fold by manager Craig Brown. In some respects it was a Boro treble in the European Championships, because Mikkel Beck, reported to have signed a Boro contract by Danish sources, was in the Danish squad.

Boro duo Curtis Fleming and Alan Moore also faced a hectic start to the summer by taking part in the Republic of Ireland's run of six friendly matches, which carried on until the middle of June. Juninho, too, was busy training with Brazil and building up towards the Olympics in Atlanta.

For the rest of the Boro squad, the summer produced a welcome break from the rigours of regular training and playing, and the opportunity to holiday, relax and have a break from football.

Robson, naturally, was busy with his England coaching responsibilities, but the prospects for what he was trying to achieve with Boro in the new season would never be far from his thoughts.

Certainly he had already taken the club a long, long way in two relatively short years. The key to all this success was winning promotion at the very first attempt, because the Boro revolution could not take place while the club was marooned within the financial restraints of the First Division.

However, from the first day he joined the club, Robson was strengthening and planning for the future. The wisdom of bringing in experienced Premiership players like Neil Cox and Nigel Pearson to help bring about promotion cannot be underplayed because it meant that Boro had the right calibre of players within their ranks to help them bridge the ever increasing gap between the top two leagues.

Bolton Wanderers, for example, came up with fewer experienced men from the top flight, and found they had not got the cash to buy all the players they needed to put together a side capable of holding its own.

Cash was obviously the other key factor in the success story and the £10 million which was put at

Robson's disposal was used very wisely. The signing of Nick Barmby and Juninho gave the club players of a level of quality which they had rarely experienced in the past. Two similar signings of this calibre every summer and Boro would eventually have a tremendously talented line-up.

And, while some of the results were very disappointing in the second half of the first season back in the Premiership, Robson had not only built a platform but also introduced a policy and pattern to which Boro could adhere to bring continued success.

Obviously it could not have happened so quickly without the fans. It was the capacity crowds at the Cellnet Riverside Stadium, and the soaring commercial turnover, which paved the way for Robson to be able to match the biggest clubs in the world when offering contracts to the pick of the best players.

The only way to keep strengthening is to ensure that the stadium continues to sell out, and that the commercial openings are fully utilised. The carefully orchestrated club campaign to sell the season tickets as quickly as possible in the summer of 1996 is a sign that they are thinking along similar lines.

In addition, many new members of staff in newly created specialist positions have been taken on to develop the marketing side of the club's activities. There's a whole new machine in force which did not exist two years ago.

Such rapid progress is not without its setbacks, particularly on the playing side. One or two players, who have made a major contribution in the past, have been left behind by the dramatic surge into the big time.

By the end of last season, it was clear that not all of the current first team squad were able to perform consistently well to the required standards of the big stage. In fact some were limited in terms of playing regular Premiership football.

However the mixed levels of ability is no different to any other squad elsewhere in the country. It's important that Robson retains a big squad, to cope with all eventualities, specially considering last season's horrendous run of injuries.

One thing that Robson has been able to count on from all his players is the right attitude and plenty of commitment. It has often helped to pull the team through when the chips were down.

Even so, there are signs that the make-up of the side is gradually changing from honest hard work and endeavour, to the type of players who can perform consistently at a high quality level.

This is the breakthrough which must be made if Robson is to develop a side capable of winning trophies, which has been his ambition since the first day he arrived on Teesside.

But don't think that Robson will be just about signing top drawer players over the next three years. The manager has never lost faith in the young footballers of the North-east and will give them their chance if he feels they are good enough.

The evidence of this came last season with the remarkable promotion from the youth team of Andy Campbell, when he made his Premiership debut as a 16-year-old against Sheffield Wednesday.

Mark Summerbell was another to be given his chance, at the age of 19, and Robson is well aware of the individual talents of the rest of the Boro youngsters in the pipeline.

Certainly the mere presence of Robson at the Cellnet Riverside Stadium should be enough to convince good young players that Boro is the club to join. Even so, Robson apart, the new stadium and the arrival of Juninho have already given the club a totally new high profile.

Not that Robson is likely to pitch in the kids too early in the new season as he concentrates on taking the club forward again.

The manager's first task this summer was to make sure that the balance of the side was right for the new season. It meant that he had to solve last term's major problem, which was the way in which the goals dried up in the second half of the season.

In the event, Nick Barmby's nine goal haul was enough to make him Boro's top scorer, but Robson will undoubtedly be looking for at least two players to comfortably reach double figures this time.

One of them was bound to be Fabrizio Ravanelli, who became Boro's record signing when agreeing a staggering £7 million move from European Cup holders Juventus on July 4.

Boro's swift and successful move for the 27-year-old goal ace shocked the football world. It was yet another sign of how much the Boro had progressed in just two short years.

Not only had they signed one of the top strikers in the world for such a huge fee, but they had signed him from Italian giants Juventus, one of the biggest clubs in the world.

Ravanelli, who was known as the 'White Feather' because he was prematurely grey, was very much in a Juninho mould - one of the top players in his position in the world. And he was with the Boro!

Ravanelli's goals had helped Juventus to win the Italian Championship and the European Cup the following season. While it seemed incredible that Juventus had agreed to sell him, Ravanelli had needed little convincing to sign for Boro after meeting Bryan Robson. However Italian newspapers did report that the Italian was trebling his wages by signing on the dotted line for Boro.

A delighted Robson said: "Ravanelli is one of the best strikers in the world and is rated as the top Italian striker in Serie A.

"He has cost a lot of money, but you must be prepared to pay a lot of money to get this type of player. The main thing is that we have pulled it off for the club and for the supporters.

"We have been trying to get Ravanelli for a long time and, although Juventus would not sell him at first, they finally accepted our offer. We're very pleased to get him. Ravanelli's quality is clear to see. He is powerful and a great goalscorer."

Ravanelli was on holiday in Sardinia when Juventus accepted Boro's offer but flew in to meet Robson at Milan airport, where details of the contract were quickly agreed. The Italian then flew back to join up with his familly on the holiday isle, in preparation to starting training with Boro on July 22.

The Italian said: "I believe that this is the right time to move on. I could have stayed with Juventus and played in the Champions Cup next season, but I needed a fresh challenge.

Ayresome Park.

FROM THE END OF AN ERA, TO A NEW BEGINNING

Cellnet Riverside Stadium.

GREAT to be here! Mikkel Beck displays his total commitment to the Boro by reporting for pre-season training despite being involved in litigation with Fortuna Cologne over the terms of his contract.

"I have admired Bryan Robson since I was a boy and so obviously I was very keen to talk to him when I was informed of his interest in me.

"I was very impressed with what he had to say. Bryan Robson is an ambitious manager and Middlesbrough are an ambitious club. I want to help to make them a major club. I want to win trophies while I am with Middlesbrough."

Ravanelli has signed a four year contract with Boro with an option for a fifth year. He has an important part to play in the Boro Revolution, specially by ensuring that Boro have one of the most feared attacks in the Premiership this season.

The same week that the Evening Gazette announced the signing of Ravanelli, it was also revealed that Mikkel Beck had won a preliminary hearing at a German Court of Labour to secure his release from Fortuna Cologne under freedom of contract.

The Danish international immediately handed in his notice with the German second division club and prepared to link up with Boro. The result of the preliminary hearing would not be rubber stamped until November, but in the meantime Beck was free to start his four-year contract at the Cellnet Riverside Stadium.

The arrival of the two international strikers meant that Robson had totally revamped his attack in time for the start of the new season. Naturally there would be pressure on Ravanelli and his fellow forwards to produce the goals from the start, though they would still need plenty of help from elsewhere in the team if they were to be presented with goalscoring chances.

The ability of Brazilian duo Emerson and Juninho to blend together and make things happen will be very important to how the team performs over the season. One thing they must do is ensure that Boro spend most of the time playing in the opposition half, rather than in their own.

Naturally the expectations will be high, and once again Boro are looking at the season as potentially offering the club its first major trophy in its history. Perhaps its only right that demanding targets are set, so that the whole club has something positive to work towards.

However, most fans will be happy simply to see the team play entertaining football and take another step forward. One thing which will be appreciated is the stability and overall consistency which was missing in the first season back in the Premiership.

At the same time, every bit of success will be welcome and Boro supporters can rest assured, that in Bryan Robson, they have got one of the most determined and go-ahead managers in the country.

In addition, there is an ambition and determination from within the boardroom which has not been witnessed for many a year. When a football club has got it right at the very top, the supporters can't ask for very much more.

The great thing about the current vibes emerging from within the club is that nobody will feel that they have achieved anything until the first trophy is in the cabinet.

It means that nobody at Boro will be resting on their laurels over the next few years.

Least of all Bryan Robson.

FULL BORO RECORD
SEASON 1995-96

1995

Aug 20	Arsenal	1-1	Barmby	37,308
Aug 26	CHELSEA	2-0	Hignett, Fjortoft	28,286
Aug 30	Newcastle United	0-1		36,483
Sep 9	Bolton Wanderers	1-1	Hignett	18,376
Sep 12	SOUTHAMPTON	0-0		29,181
Sep 16	COVENTRY CITY	2-1	Vickers, Fjortoft	27,882
Sep 20	Coca Cola Cup second round, first leg			
	ROTHERHAM UNITED	2-1	Mustoe, Fjortoft	13,280
Sep 23	Manchester City	1-0	Barmby	25,865
Sep 30	BLACKBURN ROVERS	2-0	Barmby, Hignett	29,462
Oct 3	Coca Cola Cup second round, second leg			
	Rotherham United	1-0	Vickers	6,867
Oct 15	Sheffield Wednesday	1-0	Hignett pen	21,177
Oct 21	QUEEN PARK RANGERS	1-0	Hignett pen	29,293
Oct 25	Coca Cola Cup third round			
	Crystal Palace	2-2	Barmby, Hignett	11,873
Oct 28	Manchester United	0-2		36,580
Nov 4	LEEDS UNITED	1-1	Fjortoft	29,467
Nov 8	Coca Cola Cup third round replay			
	CRYSTAL PALACE	2-0	Hignett, Fjortoft	16,150
Nov 18	Wimbledon	0-0		13,780
Nov 21	TOTTENHAM HOTSPUR	0-1		29,487
Nov 25	LIVERPOOL	2-1	Cox, Barmby	29,390
Nov 29	Coca Cola Cup fourth round			
	BIRMINGHAM CITY	0-0		28,031
Dec 2	Queens Park Rangers	1-1	Morris	17,540
Dec 9	MANCHESTER CITY	4-1	Barmby 2, Stamp, Juninho	29,469
Dec 16	Blackburn Rovers	0-1		27,996
Dec 20	Coca Cola fourth round replay			
	Birmingham City	0-2		19,878
Dec 23	WEST HAM UNITED	4-2	Fjortoft, Cox, Morris, Hendrie	28,640
Dec 26	Everton	0-4		40,091
Dec 30	Nottingham Forest	0-1		27,027

1996

Jan 1	ASTON VILLA	0-2		28,535
Jan 6	FA Cup third round			
	Notts County	2-1	Pollock, Barmby	12,621
Jan 13	ARSENAL	2-3	Juninho, Stamp	29,359
Jan 20	Southampton	1-2	Barmby	15,151
Feb 4	Chelsea	0-5		21,060
Feb 7	FA Cup fourth round			
	WIMBLEDON	0-0		28,915
Feb 10	NEWCASTLE UNITED	1-2	Beresford og	30,011
Feb 13	FA Cup fourth round replay			
	Wimbledon	0-1		5,220
Feb 17	BOLTON WANDERERS	1-4	Pollock	29,354
Feb 24	Coventry City	0-0		18,810
Mar 2	EVERTON	0-2		29,807
Mar 9	West Ham United	0-2		23,850
Mar 16	NOTTINGHAM FOREST	1-1	Mustoe	29,392
Mar 19	Aston Villa	0-0		23,933
Mar 30	Leeds United	1-0	Kavanagh pen	31,778
Apr 5	SHEFFIELD WEDNESDAY	3-1	Fjortoft 2, Freestone	29,751
Apr 8	Tottenham Hotspur	1-1	Whelan	32,036
Apr 13	WIMBLEDON	1-2	Fleming	29,192
Apr 27	Liverpool	0-1		40,782
May 5	MANCHESTER UNITED	0-3		29,921

APPEARANCES

LEAGUE: Pearson 36, Cox 35, Walsh 32, Vickers 32, Barmby 32, Pollock 31, Fjortoft 27, Whyte 25, Morris 23, Hignett 22, Juninho 21, Mustoe 21, Fleming 13, Liddle 13, Hendrie 13, Moore 13, Whelan 13, Stamp 12, Branco 7, Kavanagh 7, Moreno 7, Miller 6, Blackmore 5, Freestone 3, O'Halloran 3, Robson 3, Wilkinson 3, Campbell 2, Barron 1, Summerbell 1.

FA CUP: Barmby 3, Juninho 3, Pearson 3, Pollock 3, Vickers 3, Walsh 3, Whelan 3, Wilkinson 3, Cox 2, O'Halloran 2, Morris 2, Fleming 1, Freestone 1, Hignett 1, Liddle 1, Moreno 1, Robson 1, Stamp 2.

COCA COLA CUP: Fjortoft 6, Pearson 6, Pollock 6, Vickers 6, Walsh 6, Cox 5, Barmby 4, Hignett 4, Morris 4, Moore 3, Mustoe 3, Whelan 3, Whyte 3, Hendrie 2, Juninho 2, Liddle 2, Moreno 2, Stamp 2, Blackmore 1, Fleming 1, Robson 1.

GOALS

LEAGUE: Barmby 7, Fjortoft 6, Hignett 5, Cox 2, Juninho 2, Morris 2, Stamp 2, Fleming 1, Freestone 1, Hendrie 1, Kavanagh 1, Mustoe 1, Pollock 1, Vickers 1, Whelan 1, own goal 1.

FA CUP: Barmby 1, Pollock 1.

COCA COLA CUP: Fjortoft 2, Hignett 2, Barmby 1, Mustoe 1, Vickers 1.

Some of the fans who witnessed Boro's first season at the Cellnet Riverside Stadium

A. Abbott, Connaught Ct, Nunthorpe
R. Adam, Skiddaw Ct, Nunthorpe
J. Adam, Applegarth, Coulby Newham
L. Adamson, Wheatlands, Great Ayton
T. Adamson, West Dyke Road, Redcar
K. Adamson, Fulmerton Cres, Redcar
B. Adamson, Fulmerton Cres, Redcar
K. Adamson, Fulmerton Cres, Redcar
M. Adamson, Fulmerton Cres, Redcar
K. Adamson, Croxton Close, Fairfield
M. Adamson, Croxton Close, Fairfield
V. Agar, Phillips Ave, Linthorpe
D. Agar, Millhouses Lane, Sheffield
R. Agar, Millhouses Lane, Sheffield
K. Aitchison, Old Road, Billingham
G. Alcock, Sheraton Park, Stockton
S. Alcock, Office Row, Grosmont
G. Alderson, Southwell Rd, Linthorpe
G. Alderson, Southwell Rd, Middlesbrough
M. Alderson, Crookeshill Cl, Nunthorpe
P. Alderson, Guisborough
C. Alderson, Guisborough
R. Alderson, Trefoil Wood, Marton
J. Alderton, Skripka Dr, Billingham
J. Aldus, Springhill Gr, Ingleby Barwick
C. Aldus, Springhill Gr, Ingleby Barwick
D. Aldus, Springhill Gr, Ingleby Barwick
T. Aldus, Springhill Gr, Ingleby Barwick
R. Allan, Burnmoor Cl, Redcar
J. Allan, Burnmoor Cl, Redcar
C. Allan, Burnmoor Cl, Redcar
N. Allan, Burnmoor Cl, Redcar
J. Allen, Park Ave, Teesville
J. Allen, Farndale Dr, Guisborough
C. Allen, Chapel Rd, Billingham
D. Allinson, Thornton Vale, Middlesbrough
D. Allinson, Thornton Vale, Middlesbrough
M. G. Allinson, Winston Dr, Eston
M. J. Allinson, Winston Dr, Eston
I. Allinson, Winston Dr, Eston
S. Allison, Sycamore Cres, Teesville
D. Allison, South Park Village, Glasgow
N. Allison, Prospect Pl, Skelton
G. Allport, Fulbeck Rd, Netherfields
M. Allport, Fulbeck Rd, Netherfields
M. Amos, Elm Road, Redcar
B. Amos, Elm Road, Redcar
L. Anderson, Hartburn Ave, Stockton
J. Anderson, Hartburn Ave, Stockton
A. Anderson, Hartburn Ave, Stockton
D. Anderson, Osprey Close, Norton
P. Anderson, Dinsdale Dr, Eaglescliffe
C. Anderson, Dinsdale Dr, Eaglescliffe
C. Anderson, Ruskin Ave, Acklam
M. Anderson, Ruskin Ave, Acklam
R. Anderson, Ruskin Ave, Acklam
N. Anderson, Marske Mill Lane, Saltburn
M. Anderson, Miller Close, Yarm
M. Anderson, Miller Close, Yarm
N. Anderson, Miller Close, Yarm
G. Anderson, Dunbar Dr, Eaglescliffe
C. Anderson, Guisborough
C. Andrews, Endeavour Pub, Tollesby Hall
P. Angel, Davenport Dr, Newcastle
A. M. Angel, Davenport Dr, Newcastle
A. Angel, Collingwood Chase, Brotton
I. Angel, Collingwood Chase, Brotton
H. Antill, Dorset Road, Skelton
P. Appleby, Earle Cl, Yarm
A. Applegarth, Byland Rd, Eston
L. Applegarth, Kinloch Rd, Normanby
M. Applegarth, Byland Rd, Eston
F. Appleton, Westminster Close, Eston
J. Appleton, Willowbank, Coulby Newham
B. Appleton, Willowbank, Coulby Newham
L. Appleton, Willowbank, Coulby Newham
A. Appleton, Willowbank, Coulby Newham
D. Appleton, Eagle Park, Marton
D. Appleton, Chalford Oaks, Acklam
N. Appleton, Kingston Park, Newcastle
D. Appleton Jnr, Chalford Oaks, Acklam
I. Appleyard, Manitoba Gds, Middlesbrough
S. Appleyard, Manitoba Gds, Middlesbrough
S. Archard, The Green, Kirklevington
D. Archard, The Green, Kirklevington
T. Armatage, Dinsdale Dr, Eaglescliffe
E. Armatage, Dinsdale Dr, Eaglescliffe
H. Armstrong, Sledwick Rd, Billingham
I. Armstrong, Tunstall Ave, Billingham
N. Armstrong, The Pastures, Co. Newham
K. Armstrong, The Pastures, Co. Newham
M. Armstrong, Fairfield Rd, Staithes
M. A. Aronson, Hildyard Cl, Stokesley
E. Arrowsmith, Linsley Cl, North Ormesby
C. Ascough, Redcar Rd, Marske
D. Ascough, Redcar Rd, Marske
J. Ashcroft, Helmsley Cl, Acklam
I. Ashcroft, Aberfalls Rd, Hemlington
C. Ashley, Westfield Cres, Stockton
B. Ashton, Sinderby Cl, Billingham
S. Aspery, Ennerdale Ave, Acklam
B. A. Aspery, Newton Rd, Great Ayton
M. Atkinson, Yew Tree Gr, Marton
A. Atkinson, Beningboro' Gds, Ingleby Barwick
T. Atkinson, Beningboro' Gds,Ingleby Barwick
J. Atkinson, Beningboro' Gds, Ingleby Barwick
M. Atkinson, Wigton Sands, Acklam
I. Atkinson, Yeoman St, Skelton
B. Atkinson, The Endeavour, Nunthorpe
C. Atkinson, The Endeavour, Nunthorpe
K. Atkinson, Highbury Ave, Tollesby
R. Atkinson, Aston Rd, Billingham
A. Atkinson, Aston Rd, Billingham
T. Atkinson, Aston Rd, Billingham
M. Atkinson, Woodrow Ave, Marton
J. Atkinson, Henley Road, Linthorpe
P. Atkinson, Conifer Cl, Middlesbrough
T. Atkinson, Easterside Rd, Middlesbrough
T. Atkinson, Oakhill, Coulby Newham
M. T. M. Atkinson, Gatenby Dr, Acklam
P. M. Atkinson, Gatenby Dr, Acklam
B. Atkinson, Rothwell Mews, Eston
O. Atkinson, Rothwell Mews, Eston
C. Atkinson, Wychgate, Eston
S. H. Atkinson, Mapleton Cres, Redcar
J. Attwood, Jubilee St, North. Ormesby
G. Aungiers, Gunnergate Ln, Marton
J. Aungiers, Gunnergate Ln, Marton
M. Auty, Roseberry Ave, Stokesley
S. Ayre, Ruthin Cl, Roseworth
T. Ayre, Reeth Rd, Hartburn
M. Ayre, Reeth Rd, Hartburn
A. Ayre, Reeth Rd, Hartburn
A. Ayre, Jesmond Gr, Hartburn
E. Ayre, Jesmond Gr, Hartburn
J. Ayre, Vulcan Way, Lincoln
M. Ayre, Euclid Ave, Harrogate
W. Ayres, East Scar, Redcar
C. Ayres, Eskdale Rd, Redcar

B

P. Bacon, Achilles Cl, South Bank
D. J. Baddeley, Cleveland View, Marske
L. J. Baddeley, Cleveland View, Marske
K. Bailey, Kinloch Rd, Normanby
P. Bailey, Kinloch Rd, Normanby
N. Bailey, Brisbane Gr, Hartburn
M. Bailey, Brisbane Gr, Hartburn
A. Bailey, Tranmere Ave, Middlesbrough
C. E. Bailey, Tranmere Ave, Middlesbrough
T. Bailey, York Road, Middlesbrough
A. J. Bainbridge, Tintern Ave, Billingham
B. Bainbridge, Church Lane, Eston
J. Bainbridge, Church Lane, Eston
A. Bainbridge, Severn Grove, Skelton
G. Bainbridge, Kirby Cl, Middlesbrough
S. Bainbridge, Kirby Cl, Middlesbrough
S. Baines, Maldon Rd, Middlesbrough
J. Baines, Downside Rd, Middlesbrough
J. Baitup, Tetlott Cl, Guisborough
P. Baker, Kenley Gdns, Norton
R. Baker, Palm Grove, Fairfield
J. Baker, Hemingford Gds, Yarm
M. Baker, Hemingford Gds, Yarm
S. Baker, Marmaduke Place, Norton
D. Baker, Rook Lane, Norton
J. Baker, Riverside Ct, Leeds
G. Baker, Cedarwood Slade, Stainton
J. Baker, Cedarwood Slade, Stainton
M. Ball, The Argory, Ingleby Barwick
J. Ball, The Argory, Ingleby Barwick
A. Ball, Manor Close, Low Worsall
I. T. Bambro, Penton Ct, Billington
D. Banks, Skiplam Cl, Hemlington
A. Bargewell, Woodlea, Coulby Newham
C. Bargewell, Woodlea, Coulby Newham
P. Bargewell, Woodlea, Coulby Newham
S. Bargewell, Beckenham Gr, Hemlington
S. Bargewell, Beckenham Rd, Hemlington
M. Barker, Buckingham Rd, Oxbridge
P. Barker, Yeoman Street, Redcar
D. Barker, Riversdene, Stokesley
J. Barlow, Cleadon Ave, Billingham
S. Barlow, Cleadon Ave, Billingham
J. Barlow, Cleadon Ave, Billingham
R. Barrett Jnr, Southwood, Coulby Newham
R. Barrett Snr, Southwood, Coulby Newham
A. Barrow, North Stand
A. Barrow, Fabian Road, Eston
P. Barry, Carlow St, Middlesbrough
J. Bartley, Fairfield Rd, Stokesley
C. Barton, Hartburn La, Stockton
S. Barton, Hartburn La, Stockton
K. Barwick, Endeavour Pub, Tollesby Hall
J. Bates, Canberra Rd, Marton
A. J. Bates, Canberra Rd, Marton
I. M. Bates, Canberra Rd, Marton
C. Beadnall, East Row, Eston
M. Beadnall, Hills View Rd, Eston
P. Beadnall, Gladstone St, Eston
C. Beamson, Mitford Cres, Bishopsgarth
R. Beamson, Mitford Cres, Bishopsgarth
A. Beamson, Mitford Cres, Bishopsgarth
J. Bebb, Lark Close, Tidworth
C. Beck, Glentworth House, Netherfields
K. Beckett, Westfield Ave, Redcar
P. Beckwith, Sandy La, Billingham
C. Beckwith, Sandy La, Billingham
A. Bell, Hambledon Rd, Linthorpe
T. E. Bell, Arlington Rd, Middlesbrough
J. Bell, Ayresome Park Rd, Middlesbrough
A. R. Bell, Oxbridge Ave, Stockton
G. Bell, Oxbridge Ave, Stockton
M. Bell, Oxbridge Ave, Stockton
S. Bell, Penllyn Way, Hamlington
R. Bell, Penllyn Way, Hemlington
L. Bell, Penllyn Way, Hemlington
R. Bell, Shevington Gr, Marton
B. Bell, Shevington Gr, Marton
D. Bell, Shevington Gr, Marton
R. Bell, Shevington Gr, Marton
C. J. Bell, Carlton Dr, Thornaby
J. D. Bell, Barton Cl, Thornaby
K. Bellamy, Skripka Drive, Billingham
M. Bennett, Weymouth Ave, Middlesbrough
M. Bennett, Ely Street, Middlesbrough
A. R. Bennett, Lysander Cl, Marske
M. Benson, Low Grange Ave, Billingham
M. Benson, Low Grange Ave, Billingham
H. M. Bentley, Sandsend Rd, Redcar
M. Best, Sandmoor Rd, New Marske
G. Best, Sandmoor Rd, New Marske
K. Bibby, Coast Road, Redcar
L. E. Bibby, Troutbeck Road, Redcar
C. Biewer, Endeavour Pub, Tollesby Hall
K. Binks, Appleton Road, Linthorpe
G. Bishop, Killinghall Gr, Hartburn
R. Bishop, Killinghall Gr, Hartburn
N. Bishop, Killinghall Gr, Hartburn
C. Bishop, Killinghall Gr, Hartburn
I. Bishop, Killinghall Gr, Hartburn
L. Blackburn, Runswick Avenue, Acklam
T. Blackburn, Milburn Cres, Norton
T. W. Blackburn, Milburn Cres, Norton
D. Blackley, Trenholme Road, Longlands
K. Blair, Larkspur Rd, Marton
S. Blair, Leamington Gr, Ormesby
K. S. Blair, Premier Rd, Ormesby
M. Blamire, Ravenscroft Ave, Middlesbrough
M. Bloomfield, Lauderdale Dr, Guisborough
A. Bloomfield, Lauderdale Dr, Guisborough
E. Blott, Winston Dr, Eston
I. Blott, Church Lane, Thwing
R. Blott, Church Lane, Thwing
E. Blowman, Linnet Ct, Norton
J. Blowman, Linnet Ct, Norton
G. S. Blyth, Quebec Gr, Longlands
G. Blyth, Quebec Gr, Middlesbrough
A. Boal, Boulby Rd, Redcar
C. Boal, Boulby Rd, Redcar
D. Boddy, Normanby Rd, South Bank
A. Boddy, Keswick Grove, Acklam
J. Boddy, Keswick Grove, Acklam
J. Boddy, Keswick Grove, Acklam
D. Boddy, Keswick Grove, Acklam
J. Boddy, Zetland Hotel, Saltburn
P. Boddy, Scotforth Cl, Marton
F. Bointon, Elland Ave, Easterside
T. W. Bollen, Canberra Rd, Marton
P. Bollen, Stoneyhurst Ave, Acklam
D. Boocock, Powburn Cl, Bishopsgarth
M. Boocock, Powburn Cl, Bishopsgarth
M. Booth, Stoke Gifford, Bristol
M. Booth, Wandsworth, London
P. Bosomworth, Premier Rd, Ormesby
P. Bottrill, Highgate, Eston
A. Bourne, Longfield View, Normanby
S. Bourne, Longfield View, Normanby
T. Bourne, Somerset Cres, Skelton
J. Bourner, Harrow Rd, Linthorpe
K. Boutell, Connaught Rd, Middlesbrough
P. M. Bowdler, Ings Rd, Redcar
C. I. Bowdler, Ings Rd, Redcar
C. Bowdler, Ings Rd, Redcar
S. Bower, Rosemount Rd, New Marske
J. Bower, Rosemount Rd, New Marske
D. Bower, Rosemount Rd, New Marske
G. Bowes, Cumberland St, Darlington
A. M. Bowles, Faverdale Cl, Middlesbrough
P. E. Bowles, Preen Dr, Acklam
K. Bowmaker, Birkdale Rd, New Marske
R. A. Bowmaker, Birkdale Rd, New Marske
G. Bowman, Mayfair Ave, Normanby
C. Boyd, Harwell Close, Beechwood
P. Boyd, Mosedale Road, Grangetown
D. Boyd, Branston, Lincoln
G. Boyes, Redcar Rd, Dunsdale
D. Boyes, Bramham Down, Guisborough
L. Boyes, Bramham Down, Guisborough
T. Boyle, Ashbourne Cl, Eston
D. Brabanski, Oughton Cl, Yarm
M. Brabanski, Oughton Cl, Yarm
J. Bradburn, Dalwood Ct, Hemlington
C. N. Braddock, Sandling Ct, Marton
I. Bradford, Epsom Road, Redcar
M. Bradford, Epsom Road, Redcar
S. Bradford, Epsom Road, Redcar
K. Bradley, Kirby Fleetham, Northallerton
A. J. Bradley, Beverley Rd, Redcar
M. Bradley, Beverley Rd, Redcar
C. Bradley, Hartington Ct, London
J. Bradshaw, Nimbus Cl, Marton
K. Bradshaw, Webster Cl, Stockton
S. E, Brady, Hawthorn Ave, Billingham
C. Braithwaite, Craven St, Middlesbrough
D. Braithwaite, Craven St, Middlesbrough
D. Braithwaite, Westbourne Gr, Middlesbrough
J. Braithwaite, Westbourne Gr, Middlesbrough
S. Braithwaite, Westbourne Gr, Middlesbrough
H. Braithwaite, West La, Middlesbrough
R. Braithwaite, West La, Middlesbrough
I. Braithwaite, Winchester Rd, Linthorpe
R. Braithwaite, Winchester Rd, Linthorpe
H. Braithwaite, Winchester Rd, Linthorpe
M. Bramley, Appleton Rd, Linthorpe
T. Bramley, Appleton Rd, Linthorpe
L. Bramley, Crescent Rd, Middlesbrough
L. Bramley, Crescent Rd, Middlesbrough
V. Branfoot, Hutton Ave, Hartlepool
D. Bratt, Midville Walk, Netherfields
L. Bratt, Midville Walk, Netherfields
G. D. Bray, Moorhouse Estate, Stockton
K. N. Bray, Moorhouse Estate, Stockton
E. Bray, Moorhouse Estate, Stockton
P. Bray, Moorhouse Estate, Stockton
M. Brazier, The Green, Kirklevington
M. Breckon, Emsworth Dr, Eaglescliffe
M. Breckon, Emsworth Dr, Eaglescliffe
I. Breckon, Emsworth Dr, Eaglescliffe
P. Breckon, Emsworth Dr, Eaglescliffe
D. R. Breckon, Rounton Gates, W. Rounton
S. Breckon, Rounton Gates, W. Rounton
A. Breckon, Rounton Gates, W. Rounton
A. Brereton, Ullswater Ave, Acklam
T. Brettle, The Derby, Marton
E. Brettle, The Derby, Marton
G. Brettle, The Derby, Marton
C. Brewer, Skippers Lane, Normanby
P. Brewer, Skippers Lane, Normanby
M. Bridgett, Canterbury Rd, Brotton
R. Briggs, Castleton Rd, Eston
B. Briggs, Castleton Rd, Eston
C. Brighty, Shevington Gr, Marton
H. Brighty, Wellspring Cl, Acklam
L. Brighty, Wellspring Cl, Acklam
M. S. & R. Bringloe
S. Brittain, Malvern Rd, Billingham

A. Brittain, Malvern Rd, Billingham
J. W. Broadbent, Johnson Gr, Norton
D. Broadbent, Shearwater Lane, Norton
M. Broadbent, Shearwater Lane, Norton
N. Broadbent, Shearwater Lane, Norton
B. Broadbent, Ravensworth Gr, Hartburn
P. Broadbent, Ravensworth Gr, Hartburn
T. Broadbent, Newent, Gloucestershire
T. Broadbent, Newent, Gloucestershire
P. Broadbent, Newent, Gloucestershire
A. Broadbent, Selby Rd, Leeds
G. Brockbank, St. Crispins Ct, Stockton
G. Brogden, North Park, Billingham
P. M. Brooke, Longbeck Rd, Marske
M. J. Brooke, Longbeck Rd, Marske
J. Brookes, Darlington Rd, Hartburn
J. Brookes, Orchard Rd, Fairfield
D. Brooks, Windermere Avenue, Redcar
S. Brooks, Windermere Ave, Redcar
N. Brooks, Ottawa Road, Longlands
P. Brooks, Captains Cooks Cres, Marton
C. Brooks, Captain Cooks Cres, Marton
S. Brooks, Captain Cooks Cres, Marton
J. Brooks, Captain Cooks Cres, Marton
J. Broome, Limes Cres, Marske
S. P. Brotton, Brass Castle La, Marton
R. Brown, Tern Grove, Redcar
R. Brown, Tern Grove, Redcar
N. Brown, Osborne Rd, Linthorpe
C. Brown, Osborne Rd, Linthorpe
C. Brown, Irvin Ave, Saltburn
D. Brown, Irvin Ave, Saltburn
C. Brown, Irvin Ave, Saltburn
A. Brown, Irvin Ave, Saltburn
G. Brown, Old Row, Eston
P. Brown, Parkfield Ave, Tollesby
S. R. Brown, Beaumont Rd, North Ormesby
A. Brown, High Wycome, Bucks
D. Brown, Redcar Lane, Redcar
T. Brown, Fabian Road, Eston
M. Brown, Keithlands Ave, Norton
C. Brown, Keithlands Ave, Norton
G. Brown, Letch Lane, Carlton
P. Brown, Cumberland Gr, Norton
G. Brown, Ragpath Lane, Stockton
D. A. Brown, Hatfield Ave, Yarm
A. Brown, Hatfield Ave, Yarm
C. Brown, Adstock, Bucks.
O. Brown, The Green, Kirklevington
A. Brown, Leinster Rd, Middlesbrough
S. F. Brown, Aster Cl, Marton Manor
J. Brown, Crayke Rd, Stockton
C. Brown, Church Lane, Ormesby
I. Brown, Carisbrooke Ave, Thorntree
Mr. Brownbridge, Ormesby Bank, Ormesby
C. Bruce, Eden Park Rd, Hutton Rudby
R. Bruce, Eden Park Rd, Hutton Rudby
D. Bruce, Eden Park Rd, Hutton Rudby
A. Bruce, Ayresome St, Middlesbrough
D. Brundall, Angrove Dr, Great Ayton
A. Brydon, Twyford, Berkshire
C. Buchanan, Brackenberry Cres, Redcar
C. Budd, Montrose Close, Marton
H. Budd, Montrose Close, Marton
D. Budd, Montrose Close, Marton
G. Bullock, Thomas St, North Ormesby
S. Bullock, Westcroft Rd, Grangetown
R. Bullock, Crathorne Cres, Middlesbrough
F. G. Bullock, St. Germains La, Marske
M. Bulman, Needles Close, Hedcar
G. R. Bunn, Upsall Gr, Fairfield
P. Bunnett, Blackmore Cl, Guisborough
R. Bunting, Auckland Terr, Shildon
M. Bunting, Auckland Terr, Shildon
P. A. Bunting, Auckland Terr, Shildon
J. Bunting, Auckland Terr, Shildon
E. Bunting, Auckland Terr, Shildon
R. Bunting, Auckland Terr, Shildon
M. Burke, Lavender Ct, Marske
L. M. Burke, Lavender Ct, Marske
G. Burluraux, North Terrace, Skelton
S. Burnett, Spell Close, Yarm
J. F. Burnett, Spell Close, Yarm
N. R. Burniston, Stirling Rd, Redcar
A. Burniston, Stirling Rd, Redcar
J. Burns, Guisborough Rd, Nunthorpe
C. Burns, Southhampton St, Redcar
L. Burns, Thirlmere Rd, Redcar
S. Burr, Castlereagh Rd, Stockton
S. Burr, Castlereagh Rd, Stockton
C. Burr, Castlereagh Rd, Stockton
J. Burrows, Easson St, Middlesbrough
J. J. Burrows, Easson St, Middlesbrough
J. Burt, Kilkenny Rd, Guisborough
A. Burt, Kilkenny Rd, Guisborough
A. Burton, Harrowgate Lane, Stockton
D. Busfield, Riversdene, Stokesley
C. Busfield, Riversdene, Stokesley
D. Butta, Derby Terrace, Thornaby
C. Butters, Moorcock Cl, Eston
A. Buttery, Falcon Lane, Norton
C. Buttery, Falcon Lane, Norton
S. Buttery, Falcon Lane, Norton
G. N. D. Byass, Cumberland Cres, Billingham
P. Byrne, Granwood Rd, Eston
K. Byrne, Granwood Rd, Eston
K. Byrne, Granwood Rd, Eston
G. Bytheway, Bransdale Rd, Berwick Hills
R. Bytheway, Bransdale Rd, Berwick Hills

C

D. Cairnes, Copgrove Cl, Berwick Hills
J. Cairns, Pennyman Cl, Normanby
J. R. Calder, Yarm
G. Callaghan, Offerton Dr, Hemlington
C. Callaghan, Northiam Cl, Hemlington
P. Calvert, Grove St, Stockton
D. Calvert, Grove St, Stockton
A. Calvert, Endeavour Pub, Tollesby Hall
R. Calvert, Endeavour Pub, Tollesby Hall
L. Calvert, Endeavour Pub, Tollesby Hall
W. C. Calvert, Southpark Ave, Normanby
P. C. Calvert, Southpark Ave, Normanby
L. Cammish, Arndale Way, Filey
J. Campbell, Windsor Ct, Grangetown
S. Campbell, Amesbury Cres, Hemlington
M. Cannell, Netherby Gn, Middlesbrough
C. Capocci, Endeavour Pub, Tollesby Hall
J. Cardwell, Bonny Grove, Marton
P. Cardwell, Bonny Grove, Marton
S. Cardwell, Bonny Grove, Marton
I. Carlton, Wolviston Rd, Billingham
S. Carlyon, Longford St, Middlesbrough
D. Carrigan, Cayton Dr, Tollesby
J. C. Carrigan, Moortown Rd, Saltersgill
A. Carson, Lynmouth Rd. Norton
N. Carson, Lynmouth Road, Norton
R. Carter, Southfield Rd, Middlesbrough
W. T. Carter, Barnes Wallis Way, Marske
M. M. Carter, Barnes Wallis Way, Marske
D. R. Carter, Barnes Wallis Way, Marske
R. Carter, Bingfield Ct, Billingham
D. Carter, Thornfield Rd, Middlesbrough
P. Carter, Thornfield Rd, Middlesbrough
D. Carter, Lansdown Way, Billingham
W. Carter, Hoylake Rd, Saltersgill
J. Cartwright, Hillview Terr, New Marske
M. Cartwright, Hillview Terr, New Marske
S. Cartwright, Hillview Terr, New Marske
J. Cass, Normanby Road, Normanby
N. Casson
J. Catchpole, Needles Cl, Redcar
A. Catterson, York Road, Linthorpe
J. Catterson, York Road, Linthorpe
H. Catterson, York Road, Linthorpe
C. Catterson, South Street, Eston
L. Catterson, South Street, Eston
S. Catterson, South Street, Eston
L. Catterson, South Street, Eston
J. Catterson, South Street, Eston
A. Catterson, Longbank Rd, Ormesby
A. Catterson, Longbank Rd, Ormesby
J. P. Cavanagh, Belmont Ave, South Bank
P. Cavanagh, Belmont Ave, South Bank
T. Cavanagh, Norcliffe St, North Ormesby
N. Caygill, Stokesley Cres, Billingham
C. Chambers, Heythrop Dr, Acklam
P. Chambers, Hutton Rd, Middlesbrough
P. W. Chambers, Westminster Rd, Middlesbrough
I. Chambers, Whitegate Cl, Rickmansworth
C. Chapman, Greta Road, Skelton
B. Chapman, Station Lane, Skelton
A. Chapman, Lumley St, Loftus
S. Chapman, Croxden Gr, Priestfields
S. A. Chesney, Ashbourne Cl, Eston
P. Chillmaid, Campion Gr, Marton Manor
I. Chillmaid, Campion Gr, Marton Manor
A. Chillmaid, Campion Gr, Marton Manor
P. Chillmaid, Campion Gr, Marton Manor
D. Chillmaid, Campion Gr, Marton Manor
D. Chillmaid, Mandale Road, Acklam
I. Chinnock, Fabian Road, Teesville
N. Cholmondeley, Regency Ave, Normanby
S. Christie, Billingham Rd, Norton
D. Christon, Dartmouth Gr, Redcar
T. Christon, Dartmouth Gr, Redcar
J. Clare, Low Lane, Brookfield
S. J. Clark, Lorton Rd, Redcar
L. Clark, Trimdon Ave, Acklam
M. G. Clarke, Norton Rd, Stockton
S. Clarke, Loudwater, Bucks
L. Clarke, Crestwood, Redcar
G. Clarke, Crestwood, Redcar
S. Clarke, Knaresborough Ave, Marton
A. Claxton, Fairfield Cl, Redcar
S. Clayton, Priestcrofts, Marske
A. Clayton, Chillingham Ct, Billingham
G. Cliff, Endeavour Pub, Tollesby Hall
C. Clifft, Hornbeam Walk, Stockton
D. W. Coaten, Brotton Rd, Carlin How
P. D. Coaten, Brotton Rd, Carlin How
J. Coates, Lulsgate, Thornaby
J. Cochrane, Queen Street, Redcar
M. Cockburn, Emmett Gds, Ingleby Barwick
S. Cockerill, Carlbury Ave, Acklam
M. E. Cocks, Oakley Cl, Guisborough
C. J. Cocks, Oakley Cl, Guisborough
D. Cody, Spencerfield Cres, Thorntree
I. Coghlan, South Stand
I. Colclough, Lyndale, Guisborough
L. Cole, Pine Hill, Coulby Newham
G. Cole, Pine Hill, Coulby Newham
P. Cole, Pine Hill, Coulby Newham
J. Cole, Wycherley Ave, Linthorpe
V. Cole, Wycherley Ave, Linthorpe
N. Cole, Wycherley Ave, Linthorpe
R. Cole, Wycherley Ave, Linthorpe
M. Coleby, Trimdon Ave, Acklam
P. Coleby, Trimdon Ave, Acklam
J. Coleby, Trimdon Ave, Acklam
W. Coleby, Geltsdale, Acklam
M. Coleman, Stone Stoup Fm, I. Greenhow
V. Coleman, Stone Stoup Fm, I. Greenhow
S. Coleman, Stone Stoup Fm, I. Greenhow
S. Coleman, Stone Stoup Fm, I. Greenhow
P. Coleman, Stone Stoup Fm, I. Greenhow
B. Colligan, Thornton St, North Ormesby
S. Colligan, Thornton St, North Ormesby
N. Colligan, Thornton St, North Ormesby
M. Colligan, Thornton St, North Ormesby
J. Colligan, Ormesby Rd, North Ormesby
S. Colligan, Ormesby Rd, North Ormesby
J. Colligon, Auckland Ave, Marton
C. Collins.
P. Collins, Fox Howe, Coulby Newham
T. Collins, Crestwood, Redcar
N. Collins, Hilderthorpe, Nunthorpe
S. Collins, Hilderthorpe, Nunthorpe
P. Collins, Hilderthorpe, Nunthorpe
G. Collins, Crimdon Walk, Hardwick
M. Collins, Westfield Avenue, Redcar
L. Collins, Westfield Avenue, Redcar
J. Collins, Thorndyke Road, Eston
S. Collins, Thorndyke Road, Eston
M. Collins, Yeoman St, Redcar
M. Compitus, Westwick Terr, Middlesbrough
M. C. Compitus, Westwick Terr, Middlesbrough
S. Compitus, Westwick Terr, Middlesbrough
W. Compitus, Worcester Park, Surrey
P. Cone, Whorlton, Barnard Castle
P. Conley, Endeavour Pub, Tollesby Hall
I. Conlin. Saltscar, Redcar
D. Conlin, Westfield Ave, Redcar
A. Conlin, Hastings Cl, Nunthorpe
M. Conlin, Hastings Cl, Nunthorpe
A. Conlin, Hastings Cl, Nunthorpe
J, M. J. & P. J. Conlon,
M. Connor, Wolsingham Dr, Thornaby
M. Connor, Wolsingham Dr, Thornaby
S. Connor, Wolsingham Dr, Thornaby
J. F. Connorton, Falkland Cl, Marske
P. Connorton, Premier Rd, Middlesbrough
J. Connorton, Bradhope Rd, Middlesbrough
M. Connorton, Meath St, Middlesbrough
P. Constantine, Ashwood Cl, Hartlepool
W. Constantine, Lawson Rd, Hartlepool
W. R. Constantine, Valley Dr, Yarm
P. Convery, Phoenix Park, Hemlington
P. Conway, Eider Cl, Ingleby Barwick
K. Conway, Tollesby Lane, Marton
R. Conway, Buchanan St, Stockton
E. Cook, Newmarket Rd, Redcar
C. Cook, Newmarket Rd, Redcar
J. Cook, Boosbeck Rd, Skelton Green
A. Cook, Mandale Road, Acklam
A. Cook, Monarch Grove, Marton
D. Cook, Shelley Cl, Billingham
W. F. Cook, High Leven, Yarm
D. Cook, High Leven, Yarm
M. Cook, Culcross Grove, Fairfield
C. Cook, Newmarket Road, Redcar
T. Cook, Newmarket Road, Redcar
A. Cooke, Willow Dr, Normanby
M. Cooke, Willow Dr, Normanby
A. Cooke, Willow Dr, Normanby
L. Cooke, Willow Dr, Normanby
D. Coombes, Newlands Rd, Eaglescliffe
P. Coombes, Newlands Rd, Eaglescliffe
D. R. Cooper, Beale Cl, Ingleby Barwick
A. Cooper, Tawney Road, Eston
J. Cope, The Pastures, Coulby Newham
E. Cope, The Pastures, Coulby Newham
D. Cope, The Pastures, Coulby Newham
G. J. Copeland, Woodlea, Coulby Newham
J. J. Copeland, Margill Close, Marton
J. Copeland, Margill Cl, Marton
D. Corfield, Wolsingham Drive, Acklam
P. Corker, Blenheim Ave, Marske
P. Corking, Boulby Rd, Redcar
A. D. Corner, Greatham Cl, Acklam
I. Cornfield, Hilderthorpe, Nunthorpe
C. R. Cornfield, Hilderthorpe, Nunthorpe
L. J. Cornfield, Hilderthorpe, Nunthorpe
A. Cornforth, Newlands Ave, Norton
J. Cornforth, Newlands Ave, Norton
P. Cornforth, Grantham Rd, Norton
G. Cornforth, Urlay Nk Rd, Eaglescliffe
M. Coulson, Bexley Dr, Normanby
J. Coulson, Bexley Dr, Normanby
S. Coulson, Bexley Dr, Normanby
D. Coulton, Thornfield Rd, Linthorpe
R. Cousins, Marylebone, London
J. Coverdale, Endeavour Pub, Tollesby
J. Coward, Greta St, Saltburn
D. Cowe, Preston Ct, Linlithgow
R. R. Cowell, Corporation Rd, Redcar
D. Cowell, Park Ave, Teesville
H. Cowell, Manor Green, Normanby
N. Cowley, Durham Rd, Wolviston
R. Cowperthwaite, Elwick Ave, Acklam
C. Cowperthwaite, Elwick Ave, Acklam
J. Cox, Churchill Dr, Marske
C. Cox, Churchill Dr, Marske
M. Cox, Churchill Dr, Marske
J. Cox, Churchill Dr, Marske
D. Cox, Ainsford Way, Spencerbeck
A. Coxon, Desford Gn, Pallister Park
B. Coxon, Desford Gn, Pallister Park
G. Coxon, Desford Gn, Pallister Park
J. Craven, Brampton Cl, Hemlington
I. Craven, Brampton Cl, Hemlington
C. Crawford, High St. West, Redcar
A. Crawford, High St. West, Redcar
V. Crawford, High St. West, Redcar
S. Crawford, High St. West, Redcar
D. Crawford, Pennyman Cl, Normanby
R. Crichton, Hambledon Road, Linthorpe
D. Crinion, Southdean Dr, Hemlington
P. Critchley, Flodden Way, Billingham
J. B. Crossley, Kinderton Gr, Norton
J. Crossling, Geneva Drive, Redcar
A. Crossling, Geneva Dr, Redcar
A. A. Crow, Acklam Road, Middlesbrough
G. A. Crow, Kingcroft Rd, Marton Manor
M. Csorba, Evesham Rd, Middlesbrough
C. Cullen, Orwell St, Middlesbrough
G. Culley, Guildford Rd, Normanby
K. Culley, Roman Road, Linthorpe
D. Cummins, Bassenthwaite, Acklam
C. Cummins, Bassenthwaite, Acklam
D. Cummins, Embsay Cl, Ingleby Barwick
A. Cummins, Embsay Cl, Ingleby Barwick
M. Cummins, Lumley Road, Redcar
C. Cummins, Lumley Road, Redcar
M. Cummins, Lumley Road, Redcar
D. Cummins, Lumley Road, Redcar
K. D. Cummins, Reeth Road, Hartburn

P. D. Cummins, Reeth Road, Hartburn
A. Cunningham, Lapwing Lane, Norton
C. Cunningham, Allison St, Guisborough
N. Cunningham, Allison St, Guisborough
G. Cunningham, W. Rounton, Northallerton
C. Cunningham, W. Rounton, Northallerton
D. Currie, De Heeg, Maastricht
A. Currie, Westbourne Gr, Teesville
J. Currie, Westbourne Gr, Teesville
P. Curtis, Ickworth Ct, Ingleby Barwick
A. Curtis, Ickworth Ct, Ingleby Barwick
C. Cuthbert, Yeoman St, Redcar
S. Cuthbert, Yeoman St, Redcar
H. Cuthbert, Yeoman St, Redcar
G. Cuthbert, Yeoman St, Redcar
T. Czifra, Amesbury Cres, Hemlington

D

B. Daggett, Park Ave. North Ormesby Village
L. Daggett, Park Ave. North Ormesby Village
L. Daggett, Park Ave. North Ormesby Village
C. Dale, Churchill Dr, Marske
M. Dale, Braid Cres, Billingham
L. Dale, Hazelmere Cl, Billingham
D. Danby, Hartsbourne Cres, New Marske
S. Danby, Hartsbourne Cres, New Marske
J. Darbey, Grange Dr, Stokesley
A. B. Darbey, Grange Dr, Stokesley
G. J. Darbey, Grange Dr, Stokesley
L. M. Darbey, Grange Dr, Stokesley
A. Darbyshire, St. Helens Cl, Marton on Swale
K. Darbyshire, St. Helens Cl, Marton on Swale
S. Darbyshire, St. Helens Cl, Marton on Swale
N. A. Darbyshire, Wycliffe Ave, Romanby
R. Darcy, Saltburn Rd, Brotton
D. Darcy, Saltburn Rd, Brotton
B. Darcy, Saltburn Rd, Brotton
D. Darragh, Hutton Cl, Thornaby
A. Davey, Greenfield Rd, Eaglescliffe
R. Davey, Windsor Cres, Nunthorpe
A. Davey Jnr, Windsor Cres, Nunthorpe
A. Davey Snr, Windsor Cres, Nunthorpe
C. Davidson, Burnside Ct, Hartburn
A. Davidson, Eastbourne Rd, Linthorpe
N. Davidson, Eastbourne Rd, Linthorpe
M. G. Davie, Marton Dr, Billingham
G. Davies, Martonside Way, Beechwood
A. Davies, Watchgate, Nunthorpe
P. Davies, Watchgate, Nunthorpe
P. J. Davies, The Greenway, Middlesbrough
R. Davies, Broadway East, Redcar
L. Davies, Fairfield Rd, Stockton
N. Davies, Fairfield Rd, Stockton
K. Davies, Stanhope Rd, Billingham
L. Davies, Stanhope Rd, Billingham
S. Davies, Northfield Rd, Marske
L. Davies, Northfield Rd, Marske
G. Davies, Penrith Rd, Park End
J. Davies, Penrith Rd, Park End
J. Davies, Cheddar Cl, Eston
S. M. Davis, Pallister Ave, Brambles Farm
F. Davison, Millbrook Ave, Brambles Farm
P. Davison, Mendip Road, Billingham
D. A. Davison, Mendip Rd, Billingham
R. Davison, Marlborough Rd, Marton
N. Davison, Marlborough Rd, Marton
R. Davison, Marlborough Rd, Marton
M. Davison, Marlborough Rd, Marton
P. Davison, Coatham Rd, Redcar
E. Davison, Foxglove Cl, Northallerton
D. Davison, The Willow Chase, Long Newton
A. Davison, Gunnerside Rd, Fairfield
S. G. Davison, Sandy Flatts Ln, Acklam
J. Dawson, Swinburns Yard, Yarm
N. Dawson, Crowland Ave, Middlesbrough
N. Dawson, Stoneyhurst Ave, Acklam
J. Dawson, High St, Great Ayton
B. K. Day, Deerness Rd, Bishop Auckland
B. Day, Gypsy Lane, Nunthorpe
I. Day, Northiam Cl, Hemlington
J. Day, Ashdown Cl, Thornaby
K. Day, Woodrush, Coulby Newham
J. Day, Woodrush, Coulby Newham
R. Day, Woodrush, Coulby Newham
R. Daykin, Brocklesby Rd, Guisborough
J. Daykin, Brocklesby Rd, Guisborough
D. De-Peiza, West Lane, Middlesbrough
S. Deakin, Addison Rd, Linthorpe
D. Deakin, Addison Rd, Linthorpe
L. Deakin, Addison Rd, Linthorpe

J. Dell, Saltwells Rd, Middlesbrough
S. Denham, St. Aidan's Cres, Billingham
S. Denham, Glendale Rd. Tollesby
M. Denham, Glendale Rd, Tollesby
P. Denning, Durham Road, Stockton
M. Denning, Durham Road, Stockton
S. Dennis, Middleton Ave, Billingham
J. Dennis, Middleton Ave, Billingham
M. Devine, Northallerton Rd, Thornaby
C. Devine, Northallerton Rd, Thornaby
K. Devine, Northallerton Rd, Thornaby
L. Devine, Northallerton Rd, Thornaby
J. Devine, Northallerton Rd, Thornaby
J. Devitt, South View Terr, North Ormesby
S. Dhand, Waterloo Rd. Middlesbrough
R. K. Dhand, Waterloo Rd, Middlesbrough
D. Dickson, Penllyn Way, Hemlington
W. Dinsdale, Anlaby Cl, Billingham
C. Dinsdale, Anlaby Cl, Billingham
T. Distasi, Jackson Dr, Stokesley
N. Distasi, Jackson Dr, Stokesley
S. Ditchburn, Wood View, Loftus
L. Ditchburn, Thackeray Gr, Linthorpe
A. Dixon, Caxton St, Linthorpe
L. Dixon, The Grove, Marton
G. Doak, Cassop Gr, Acklam
C. Dobinson, Thompsons Cl, Wolviston
G. Dobinson, Pentland Ave, Billingham
J. Dobinson, Pentland Ave, Billingham
A. Dobson, Normanby Rd, South Bank
S. Dobson, Langley Ave, Thornaby
M. Dodds, Endeavour Pub, Tollesby Hall
A. Dodgson, Cleveland Ave, Norton
S. Dodgson, Cleveland Ave. Norton.
L. Dodsworth, Millfield Rd, Fishburn
S. Doherty, Easson St, Middlesbrough
L. Doherty, Easson St, Middlesbrough
N. Donaghy, Oak Rd, Redcar
T. Donaldson, Reeth Rd, Stockton
J. Donnelly, Burniston Dr, Thornaby
M. Donnelly, Gretton Ave, Easterside
M. Donnelly, Percy St, Middlesbrough
C. A. Donnelly, Percy St, Middlesbrough
M. Donnelly, Percy St, Middlesbrough
L. Donnelly, Percy St, Middlesbrough
N. Donnelly, Brooksbank Ave, Redcar
J. Doogan, Holywell Gn, Eaglescliffe
A. Doogan, Holywell Gn, Eaglescliffe
L. Doogan, Holywell Gn, Eaglescliffe
S. Doogan, Holywell Gn, Eaglescliffe
D. Dorgan, Tees Rd, Redcar
A. Dorgan, Tees Rd, Redcar
E. Dorgan, Tees Rd, Redcar
M. Dorgan, Tees Rd, Redcar
C. Dorgan, Tees Rd, Redcar
M. Dorgan, Tees Rd, Redcar
R. W. Douglas, Basil St, North Ormesby
L. Douthwaite, Headlam Rd, Billingham
W. Douthwaite, Headlam Rd, Billingham
R. Douthwaite, Deighton Gr, Billingham
L. J. Dove, Ridley Ave, Acklam
R. Dove, Crescent Rd, Middlesbrough
D. Downey, Stoneyhurst Ave, Acklam
G. Downing, Latham Rd, Linthorpe
L. Downs, Bishops Way, Fairfield
D. Downs, Bishops Way, Fairfield
S. J. Dowson, Oakdene Ave, Hartburn
N. Drake, Linton Rd, Normanby
S. L. Dring, Sidmouth Cl, Marton
J. Driver, Grange Dr, Stokesley
A. Driver, Grange Dr, Stokesley
C. Driver, Burlam Rd, Linthorpe
C. Dryden, Evesham Rd, Middlesbrough
K. Dryden, Evesham Rd, Middlesbrough
E. Dryden, Queens Rd, Middlesbrough
S. Dryden, Tollesby Br, Coulby Newham
P. Duck, Newlands Rd, Skelton Green
R. Ducker, South Vale, Northallerton
J. W. Dudley, Broughton Rd, Billingham
A. Dudman, Upgang Lane, Whitby
J. Dudman, Upgang Lane, Whitby
D. A. Duffield, Kings Rd, North Ormesby
D. Duffield, Kings Rd, North Ormesby
S. Duffield, Kings Rd, North Ormesby
A. Duffy, Ida Rd, Berwick Hills
C. Duffy, Ida Rd, Berwick Hills
S. Duffy, Elgin Ave, Middlesbrough
J. M. Dunbar, Thirlmere Cres, Normanby
S. Dunk, Wortley, Leeds

S. Dunn, Radnor Cl, Roseworth
R. Dunnakey, Cheltenham Ave, Marton
P. Dunnakey, Cheltenham Ave, Marton
D. Dunning, Graham St, Liverton Mines
C. Dunning, Derwent Rd, Thornaby
S. Durham, Spencer Rd, Teesville
M. Durham, Bassleton Lane, Thornaby
S. Durham, Kintyre Dr, Thornaby
J. Durham, Kintyre Dr, Thornaby
L. Durham, Kintyre Dr, Thornaby
J. Durham, Kintyre Dr, Thornaby
C. Dye, Mulgrave Rd, Linthorpe
M. Dye, Mulgrave Rd, Linthorpe

E

W. Ealand, Regency Ave, Normanby
B. Ealand, Regency Ave, Normanby
P. Earnshaw, Hutton Lane, Guisborough
E. Earnshaw, Hutton Lane, Guisborough
N. Eastwood, Scalby Gr, Fairfield
A. Eastwood, Scalby Gr, Fairfield
T. Eaton, Whitehouse St, West Lane
J. Ebison, High Street, Staithes
C. Eddy, Pembroke Rd, Norton Grange
C. Edemenson, Lansdowne Rd, Yarm
M. Edemenson, Winpenny Cl, Yarm
R. Edemenson, Winpenny Cl, Yarm
T. Eden, The Fairway, Saltburn
N. Eden, The Fairway, Saltburn
B. W. Eden, Burdon Cl, Stockton
D. J. Edwards, Neasham Ave, Billingham
I. Edwards, Premier Rd, Ormesby
A. Edwards, Simonside Walk, Ormesby
G. Edwards, Barkston Cl, Billingham
P. J. Edwards, Barkston Cl, Billingham
J. Edwards, Truro Dr, Hartlepool
D. J. Egerton, Braidwood, Normanby
D. Elder, Cedar Dr, Thornaby
P. Elgey, Ashkirk Rd, Normanby
L. Ellerton, Gunnergate Ln, Marton
M. Ellerton, Rothbury Cl, Ingleby Barwick
M. Elliott, Blackthorn, Coulby Newham
K. Elliott, Meadowfield, Stokesley
T. A. Elliott, Meadowfield, Stokesley
L. Elliott, Meadowfield, Stokesley
G. Elliott, Hampton Cl, Nunthorpe
D. M. Elliott, Hampton Cl, Nunthorpe
A. Elliott-Smith, Crooks Barn Ln, Norton
R. Elliott-Smith, Crooks Barn Ln, Norton
D. Elliott-Smith, Crooks Barn Ln, Norton
E. Elliott-Smith, Crooks Barn Ln, Norton
L. Ellis, Newham Ave, Tollesby
C. Ellis, Newham Ave, Tollesby
D. Ellis, Newham Ave, Tollesby
S. Ellis, Newham Ave, Tollesby
R. Ellis, Rugby Rd, Stockton
M. Ellis, Sycamore Rd, Eaglescliffe
T. Ellis, Sycamore Rd, Eaglescliffe
L. Ellis, Numeaton Dr, Hemlington
D. Ellis, Nuneaton Dr, Hemlington
B. Ellis, Herdborough Rd, Scarborough
J. Ellis, Nuneaton Dr, Hemlington
B. Ellis, Elton Rd, Billingham
D. Ellis, Elton Rd, Billingham
A. Ellison, Hundale Cres, Redcar
C. Ellison, Wilton Bank, Saltburn
A. Ellison, Kilnwick Cl, Billingham
J. Ellison, Kilnwick Cl, Billingham
M. Ellison, Kilnwick Cl, Billingham
J. Ellison, Kilnwick Cl, Billingham
A. T. Ellison, Greystoke, Penrith
M. P. Emmerson, The Pastures, Coulby Newham
D. Emmerson, Ingleby Rd, Middlesbrough
C. Emmerson, Riversway, Marton
P. English, Halton Ct, Billingham
K. English, Gordon Rd, Redcar
P. & G. English
G. Evans, Mallard Ct, Redcar
R. Evans, High St, Swainby
M. Evans, High St, Swainby
A. Evans, Ragpath Lane, Roseworth
I. Evans, Chippenham Rd, Easterside
R. Evans, Sledmere Cl, Billingham
M. Evans, Sledmere Cl, Billingham
A. Evans, Surrey St, Middlesbrough
N. Evans, Surrey St, Middlesbrough
G. Evans, Coronation Gn, Ormesby
C. J. Evans, Coronation Gn, Ormesby
A. Evans, The Birches, Coulby Newham
J. Evans, The Birches, Coulby Newham

K. Evans, Ainsford Way, Ormesby
S. Evans, Ainsford Way, Ormesby
I. Evans, Ainsford Way, Ormesby
B. Everson, Easby Ave, Tollesby
A. Evetts, Ullswater Ave, Acklam
L. Evetts, Ullswater Ave, Acklam
C. Evetts, Ullswater Ave, Acklam

F

M. Fancourt, Newbury Rd, Brotton
M. Fancourt, Newbury Rd, Brotton
L. Fancourt, Newbury Rd, Brotton
Mr. & Mrs. Farmer, Shelley Cres, Teesville
N. Farmer, Shelley Cres, Teesville
D. Farmer, Shelley Cres, Teesville
H. Farmer, Shelley Cres, Teesville
L. Farmer, Shelley Cres, Teesville
G. A. Farrel, Monarch Gr, Marton
R. G. Farrel, Monarch Gr, Marton
J. G. Farrell, Glencoe Sq, Sunderland
A. Farrell, Ryehills Dr, Marske
J. Farrell, Regency Ave, Normanby
A. Farrell, Regency Ave, Normanby
G. Farrow, Worsall Rd, Yarm
K. Faulks, Westminster Rd, Linthorpe
J. Fawcett, Cambridge Ave, Linthorpe
H. Fawcett, Lansdowne Rd, Middlesbrough
P. Fawcett, Lansdowne Rd, Middlesbrough
B. Fawdon, Askrigg Rd, Stockton
N. Fawdon, Askrigg Rd. Stockton
S. Fawdon, Seamer Gr, Stockton
S. Fawdon, Seamer Gr, Stockton
S. Fawdon, Seamer Gr, Stockton
R. Fawdon, Seamer Gr, Stockton
J. Featherstone, Kendal Rd, Grangefield
D. Feeney, Kinloch Road, Normaby
L. Fell, Lynmouth Rd, Norton
C. Fell, Lynmouth Rd, Norton
M. Fell, Lynmouth Rd, Norton
H. Fell, Lynmouth Rd, Norton
T. H. Fenton, The Gables, Marton
C. Fenwick, Bridge Ct, Normanby
A. Fenwick, Bridge Ct, Normanby
J. Fenwick, Bridge Ct, Normanby
D. Ferguson, Carlton Ave, Billingham
M. Fern, Marsh House Ave, Billingham
D. Field, Northiam Cl, Hemlington
G. E. Field, Eden Rd, Skelton
L. J. Field, Eden Rd, Skelton
G. D. L. Field, Eden Rd, Skelton
R. A. L. Field, Eden Rd, Skelton
K. S. L. Field, Eden Rd, Skelton
B. Fielding, Westbeck Gds, Linthorpe
T. Finlay, Cranwell Dr, Wideopen
J. Finlayson, Scotney Rd, Billingham
C. Finn, Hutton Rd, Middlesbrough
P. Finn, Penrith Rd, Berwick Hills
S. Finn, Penrith Rd, Berwick Hills
C. Finn, Penrith Rd, Berwick Hills
M. Finnegan, Gribdale Rd, Pallister Park
M. Finnegan Jnr, Gribdale Rd, Pallister Park
A. Firman, Castlegate, Scarborough
N. Fishburn, Chillingham Ct, Billingham
G. Fisher, Buttermere Rd, Redcar
A. R. Fitzhugh, Haxby, York
R. J. Fitzhugh, Haxby, York
P. Fitzpatrick, Longford St, Middlesbrough
G. Flanagan, Spencer Rd, Teesville East
D. Flannigan, Derwentwater Ave, Acklam
S. Flannigan, Derwentwater Ave, Acklam
C. Flannigan, Derwentwater Ave, Acklam
R. Flannigan, Derwentwater Ave, Acklam
J. Fleming, Grange Wood, Coulby Newham
M. Fleming, Garstang Cl, Marton
M. Fleming, Garstang Cl, Marton
T. Fleming, Fairfield Ave, Ormesby
P. Fletcher, Stonedale Walk, Acklam
S. Fletcher, Stonedale Walk, Acklam
D. Fletcher, Wolsingham Dr, Thornaby
A. Fletcher, Wolsingham Dr, Thornaby
M. Fletcher, Wolsingham Dr, Thornaby
E. Flett, Oldford Cres, Acklam
S. Flett, Oldford Cres, Acklam
S. Flett, Oldford Cres, Acklam
J. Flett, Gilmonby Rd, Middlesbrough
L. Flett, Gilmonby Rd, Middlesbrough
G. Flintoff, Dunlin Cl, Norton
N. Flintoff, Dunlin Cl, Norton
C. Flitcroft, High St. Great Broughton
P. Flitcroft, High St, Great Broughton

P. Flowerdew, Broadwell Rd, Easterside
J. Floyd, Edgeworth Ct, Hemlington
C. Foley, Prestwick Ct, Eaglescliffe
R. Forbes, Belmangate, Guisborough
L. Forbes, Belmangate, Guisborough
S. Forbes, Belmangate, Guisborough
N. Ford, Harrogate Ln, Bishopsgarth
L. Ford, Ricknall Cl, Acklam
K. Ford, The Avenue, Linthorpe
K. Ford, Benson St, Norton
J. V. Forster, Thornfield Rd, Middlesbrough
B. Forster, Dorothy St, North Ormesby
A. Forster, Normanby Rd. Northallerton
C. Foster, Oldgate, Eston Under Nab
N. Foster, Brechin Dr, Thornaby
A. Foster, Tithebarn Rd, Hardwick
A. J. Foster, Wharfedale Rd, Barnsley
L. E. Foster, Wharfedale Rd, Barnsley
F. C. & C. Fothergill
C. Fountain, East Stand
A. Fountain, Hundale Cres, Redcar
J. E. Fowell, Crossfields, Coulby Newham
C. Fowell, Beckenham Gr, Hemlington
J. Fowell, Beckenham Gr, Hemlington
J. Fowell, Beckenham Gr, Hemlington
D. Fowler, Green Lane, Middlesbrough
A. Fowler, Green Lane, Middlesbrough
P. Fox, Hurst Park, Redcar
G. Fox, Gore Sands, Acklam
P. Fox, Guildford Rd, Billingham
B. Fox, Otley Rd, Harrogate, North Yorks
D. Fox, Otley Rd, Harrogate, North Yorks
M. France, Meadowgate, Eston
D. Frank, Barholm Cl, Netherfields
S. Frank, Hawthorne Cres, Marton
R. Frankland, Nightingale Rd, Eston
C. Frankland, Roseberry Rd, Norton
J. Franklin, Deepdale Way, Darlington
R. Franks, Perth Grove, Hartburn
D. Franks, Eagle Park, Marton
I. Fraser, Westbourne Gr, North Ormesby
A. Fraser, Coniston Grove, Acklam
R. Freeman, Birkdale Rd, New Marske
T. French, Hills View Rd, Eston
C. French, Hills View Rd, Eston
R. French, Hills View Rd, Eston
S. French, Old Row, Eston
D. J. French, Alston Gn, Pallister Park
P. Frost, Barnard Ct, Marton Grove
D. Fryett, Carisbrooke Ave, Thorntree
P. Fryett, Prichett Rd, Ormesby
R. Furness, Ely Cres, Brotton
D. I. Furness, Ely Cres, Brotton
S. Furness, Ely Cres, Brotton

G

S. Gallager, Linby Ave, Middlesbrough
D. Gallagher, Mayberry Gr, Linthorpe
M. Gallagher, Mayberry Gr, Linthorpe
R. Gallagher, Warton St, Lytham
T. Gallagher, Warton St, Lytham
N. Gallagher, Warton St, Lytham
W. Gallagher, Lastingham Ave, Eston
M. Gallagher, Dionysia Rd, Berwick Hills
J. Gallagher, Glenn Cres, Marton
G. Galloway, Eston View, Middlesbrough
S. Galloway, Eston View, Middlesbrough
T. Galloway, Fenner Cl, Marske
T. Galloway, Fenner Cl, Marske
D. Galloway, Fenner Cl, Marske
C. Garbutt, Hanson Ct, Redcar
T. Garbutt, Weastell St, Linthorpe
L. Garbutt, Weastell St, Linthorpe
A. Garbutt, St. Michaels Cl, Liverton Mines
S. Garbutt, St. Michaels Cl, Liverton Mines
A. Garbutt, Tees St, East Loftus
K. Garbutt, Tees St, East Loftus
L. Garbutt, Tees St, East Loftus
C. Garbutt, Tees St, East Loftus
S. Garbutt, Mowbray Rd, Norton
G. K. Gardner, Harlsey Rd, Hartburn
S. J. Gardner, Harlsey Rd, Hartburn
P. Gardner, Redcar Rd. South Bank
S. Garncarek, Leinster Rd, Middlesbrough
J. Garncarek, Leinster Rd, Middlesbrough
P. Garncarek, Leinster Rd, Middlesbrough
A. Garth, Offerton Dr, Hemlington
B. G. Garton
D. J. Gavachan, Strait Lane, Stainton
M. Gavachan, Chilton Village.
S. Gee, Herbert St. North Ormesby
N. Gibb, Park View, Yarm
M. Gibbons, Kilkenny Rd. Guisborough
A. Gibbons, Kilkenny Rd, Guisborough
R. Gibbons, Kilkenny Rd, Guisborough
G. Gibbs, Deighton Gr, Billingham
M. Gibbs, Killingworth, Newcastle
S. Gibbs, St. Crispins Ct, Stockton
N. Gibson, Langley Ave, Thornaby
T. Gibson, Coppice Rd, Marton Grove
J. Gibson, Scalby Gr, Fairfield
P. Gibson, Scalby Gr, Fairfield
M. Gidney, Woodlands Dr, Normanby
S. Gilday, West Gr, Trimdon Village
T. Giles, College Rd, Hereford
M. Gilhen, Cotswold Cres, Billingham
H. Gilhen, Cotswold Cres, Billingham
R. Gilhen, Cotswold Cres, Billingham
J. R. Gill, Cleveland Ave, Stokesley
I. Gill, Blackmore Cl, Guisborough
B. Gill, Sheraton Park, Stockton
G. J. Gill, Marshall Dr, Brotton
C. J. Gill, Marshall Dr, Brotton
H. Gill, Marshall Dr, Brotton
A. Gill, Yew Tree Ave, Redcar
N. Gill, Meadowcroft Rd, Normanby
C. Gill, Firtree Ave, Normanby
R. Gill, Easby Gr, Eston
C. A. Gilmour, The Strand, Redcar
D. A. Gilmour, The Strand, Redcar
L. A. Gilmour, The Strand, Redcar
L. C. Gilmour, The Strand, Redcar
G. Gladders, Kirkland Walk, Middlesbrough
D. Gladders, Kirkland Walk, Middlesbrough
L. Gladders, Gilmonby Rd, Park End
B. G. Gladwin, Newmarket Rd, Redcar
J. Gladwin, Newmarket Rd, Redcar
M. Glasgow, Corby Ave, Acklam
R. Glasgow, Corby Ave, Acklam
T. W. Glasper, Brooksbank Ave, Redcar
F. M. Glasper, Brooksbank Ave, Redcar
S. Glasper, Brooksbank Ave, Redcar
D. Glazebrook, Studley Rd. Linthorpe
A. Glover, Marshall Dr, Brotton
J. C. Glover, Sorrel Ct, Marton
D. J. Glover, Sorrel Ct, Marton
J. Godfrey, Sidlaw Rd, Billingham
J. Goldsborough, Warsett Rd. Marske
C. Goldsborough, Warsett Rd. Marske
T. Good, Langthorne Gr, Hartburn
E. Goodall, Orchard Rd, Linthorpe
M. Goodall, Heselden Ave, Acklam
N. Goodridge, Spencer Cl, Marske
J. Goodwin, Strome Cl, Ingleby Barwick
B. Goodwin, Strome Cl, Ingleby Barwick
S. Goodwin, Strome Cl, Ingleby Barwick
G. Goodwin, Strome Cl, Ingleby Berwick
P. Goodwin, Harworth, Doncaster.
N. Goodwin, Harworth, Doncaster
C. Goodwin, Harworth, Doncaster
B. Goodwin, Harworth, Doncaster
P. Goodwin, Wortley, Leeds
T. Goodwin, Wortley, Leeds
A. Goodwin, Wortley, Leeds
P. Gosling, High Newham Ct, Hardwick
K. R. Gott, Hollins Lane, Middlesbrough
V. Gough, Kinloch Rd, Normanby
W. Gowing, Thistle Rise, Coulby Newham
T. Gowing, Thistle Rise, Coulby Newham
D. Gowing, Cargo Fleet Ln, Middlesbrough
G. Grabham, The Greenway, Thorntree
P. Grace, Carlbury Ave, Acklam
B. Graham Snr.
B. Graham Jnr.
T. Graham.
C. Graham, Dewberry Pk, Middlesbrough
N. Graham, Meath St, Middlesbrough
M. J. Graham, Lambton Rd, Stockton
P. Grainger, Heathfield Dr, Hartlepool
A. Grainger, Rosedale Rd, Nunthorpe
G. Grant, Argyll Rd, Marton
D. Grant, Brier Hill View, Huddersfield
R. Gratton, Vicarage Terr, Coxhoe
D. Gratton, Vicarage Terr, Coxhoe
R. Gratton, Coronation Terr, Coxhoe
J. Gray, Alma Terr, York
D. Gray, Mansfield Ave, Thornaby
M. Gray, Cromwell Ave, Loftus
E. Gray, Cromwell Ave, Loftus
M. Gray, Cromwell Ave, Loftus
K. Gray, Cromwell Ave, Loftus
M. Green, Speeton Cl, Billingham
S. Green, Speeton Cl, Billingham
M. Green, Rievaulx Ave, Billingham
T. Green, Rievaulx Ave, Billingham
G. Green, Lockerbie Walk, Thornaby
E. Green, Farmbank Rd, Ormesby
T. Green, Farmbank Rd, Ormesby
M. Greene, Essex St, Middlesbrough
H. Greenmon, Blantyre Rd, Normanby
B. Greenmon, Blantyre Rd, Normanby
P. Greenmon, Blantyre Rd, Normanby
H. Greenmon, Blantyre Rd, Normanby
P. Greenwell, Station Rd, Billingham
A. Greenwell, Station Rd, Billingham
A. Gregory, Priorwood Gds, Ingleby Barwick
A. Gregory, Priorwood Gds, Ingleby Barwick
J. Grief, Shepton Cl, Thornaby
D. Grief, Shepton Cl, Thornaby
B. Grief, Trefoil Wood, Marton
P. Grief, Trefoil Wood, Marton
E. Grief, Cotherstone Dr, Brookfield
R. Grief, Woodside, Redcar
P. Griffiths, E. Harlsey, North Yorkshire
J. Griffiths, E. Harlsey, North Yorkshire
C. Griffiths, E. Harlsey, North Yorkshire
T. E. Griffiths, Eddison Way, Hemlington
D. Griffiths, Keynsham Ave, Middlesbrough
P. Griffiths, Windermere Dr, Skelton
T. Griffiths, Windermere Dr, Skelton
B. Grimes, Brettenham Ave, Easterside
J. A. Groat, Limbrick Ave, Fairfield
J. H. Groat, Whitby Rd. Robin Hoods Bay
A. Groom, Barker Rd, Thornaby
H. J. Grover, Carmel Gds, Nunthorpe
G. M. Groves, Moorcock Cl, Eston
G. Gunn, Hatfield Ave, Acklam
S. Gurle, Hampton Rd, Stockton
M. Gutcher, Epsom Rd, Redcar
L. Gutcher, Epsom Rd, Redcar
D. R. Gutteridge, Costa St. Middlesbrough
M. J. Gutteridge, Lambourne Dr, Marton

H

C. H-Middleton, Woodvale, Coulby Newham
G. Hagen, Cartmel Rd, Redcar
A. Hailstone, Tern Gr, Redcar
J. Hales, St. Austell Cl, Stainton Manor
R. J. Hales, Swainby, North Yorkshire
A. Haley, Nightingale Rd, Eston
V. Hall, Hillcrest Dr, Nunthorpe
A. Hall, Woodgarth, Eston
D. G. Hall, High St, Yarm
J. Hallett, Deepdale, Guisborough
S. Hallett, Deepdale, Guisborough
D. F. Halliday, Coast Rd, Marske
D. Hamilton, Grinkle Rd, Dormanstown
K. Hamilton, Grinkle Rd, Dormanstown
D. Hamilton, Grinkle Rd, Dormanstown
J. H. Hamilton, Dunbar Rd, Billingham
J. Hamilton, Station Rd, Norton
L. Hammersley, Osbourne Cl, Hemlington
M. Hammond, East Stand
P. Hampson, Aske Rd, Middlesbrough
J. Hampson, Aske Rd, Middlesbrough
D. Hampton, Felby Ave, Middlesbrough
D. Hanley, Challoner Rd, Yarm
S. Hanlon, Pelham St, Middlesbrough
A. Hannah, Maple St, Middlesbrough
D. Hannan, St. Austell Cl, Stainton Manor
K. Hannan, St. Austell Cl, Stainton Manor
S. Hannon, Mapleton Cres, Redcar
P. Hannon, Shorthill Croft, Beverley
J. R. Hanratty, Shevington Gr, Marton
A. J. Hanratty, Grey Towers, Nunthorpe
S. A. Hanratty, Falmouth St, Middlesbrough
K. J. Hanratty, St. Albans, Herts
F. J. Hansen, Shrewsbury Rd, Thorntree
C. Hansen, Shrewsbury Rd, Thorntree
M. Hanson, Oldbury Gr, Hemlington
P. Harcourt, Peveril Rd, Billingham
R. Harding, Southwell Rd, Linthorpe
G. W. Harding, Staindale Rd, Thornaby
F. Harding, Staindale Rd, Thornaby
G. Harding, Staindale Rd, Thornaby
D. Harding, Topcliffe Rd, Thornaby
A. Hardwick, Hickling Gr, Stockton
A. Hardwick, Hickling Gr, Stockton
M. Hardy, Church Lane, Ormesby
J. P. Hardy, Bowes Rd, Billingham
N. Harker, Stone Stoup Farm, Ingleby Greenhow
G. Harkin, Overdale Rd, Berwick Hills
D. J. Harland, Farne Ct, Ingleby Barwick
K. Harland, The Gables, Marton
J. Harrington, Devonshire Rd, Middlesbrough
K. Harris, Saxon Field, Coulby Newham
L. Harris, Saxon Field, Coulby Newham
C. Harris, Stainsby St, Thornaby
N. Harris, Branston, Lincoln
C. Harris, Branston, Lincoln
L. Harris, Branston, Lincoln
R. D. Harrison, Abberston Wk, Middlesbrough
N. Harrison, Charles St, Redcar
R. Harrison, Linden Gr, Linthorpe
S. Harrison, Hershall Dr, Middlesbrough
S. P. T. Harrison, South Rd, Norton
Harrison Family, Church Ln, Driffield
C. Harston, Sheraton Pk, Stockton
M. Harston, Sheraton Park, Stockton
C. Harston, Sheraton Park, Stockton
R. Hart, Greylands Ave, Norton
R. Hart, Greylands Ave, Norton
M. Hartas, Lumley St, Loftus
P. A. Hartas, Canterbury Rd, Brotton
C. Hartas, Canterbury Rd, Brotton
D. Hartley, Suffolk St, Stockton
L. Hartley, Suffolk St, Stockton
M. Hartley, Kempston Way, Norton
T. Hartness, Cricket Lane, Normanby
D. Harton, Ottawa Rd, Middlesbrough
D. J. Harton, Ottawa Rd, Middlesbrough
M. Harton, Ottawa Rd, Middlesbrough
C. Hatcher, East Cres, Whinney Banks
T. Hatfield, J Hatfield & Sons, Middlesbrough
J. Hatfield, Ingleby Greenhow, North Yorks
C. Hatton, Wrightson St, Norton
Mr. & Mrs. Haverson, Swadlincote, Derbys
B. Haw, Lindrick Rd, New Marske
D. J. Hawkins, Speeton Ave, Acklam Hall
J. Hawkins, Moor Park, Nunthorpe
V. Hawkins, Moor Park, Nunthorpe
S. Hawkins, Moor Park, Nunthorpe
M. Haye, Appleby Rd, Billingham
S. Hayes, Penistone Rd, Middlesbrough
M. Hayes, Broughton Ave, Easterside
M. Hayes, Broughton Ave, Easterside
L. Hayes, Broughton Ave, Easterside
M. Hayes Jnr. Broughton Ave, Easterside.
B. Hayne, Cranford Ave, Teesville
N. Head, Princes Sq, Thornaby
J. Headley, Elsdon St, Stockton
C. Heald, Greenbeck Rd, Hartburn
D. Heald, Greensbeck Rd, Hartburn
D. Hearfield, Buckingham Dr, Normanby
C. Hearn, Ludford Ave, Middlesbrough
D. Hearn, Ludford Ave, Middlesbrough
A. Hearn, Ludford Ave, Middlesbrough
M. Hearn, Tollesby Lane, Marton
V. Hearn, Tollesby Lane, Marton
K. L. Hearn, Tollesby Lane, Marton
L. M. Hearn, Tollesby Lane, Marton
W. Hearn, Forcett Cl, Acklam
M. Heath, Offerton Dr, Hemlington
K. Heath, Zetland Rd, Stockton
J. Heather, Busby Way, Yarm
J. Hebbron, Brompton St, Linthorpe
B. Hebden, Kepier Cl, Hardwick
C. Hebden, Kepier Cl, Hardwick
M. Helm, Dale St, New Marske
C. Helm, Muirfield Cl, New Marske
D. Helm, Muirfield Cl, New Marske
J. Helm, Arthur Terr, New Marske
P. Helm, Arthur Terr, New Marske
D. Helm, Picton Cres, Thornaby
S. Helm, Picton Cres, Thornaby
B. Henderson, Liverton Cres, Billingham
M. Henderson, Liverton Cres, Billingham
M. Henderson, Liverton Cres, Billingham
J. Henderson, Arndale Way, Filey
P. Henry, Ashbourne Rd, Stockton
C. Henry, Rettendon Cl, Roseworth
J. Henry, Priestfield Ave, Middlesbrough
J. Henry, Weatherhead Ave, Linthorpe
L. A. Henwood, Rawcliffe Ave, Brookfield
K. Heppenstall, Church Ln, Redmarshall
J. Heppenstall, Church Ln, Redmarshall
T. Heppenstall, Church Ln, Redmarshall
W. Herbert, Lastingham Ave, Eston

S. Herman, Simonside Gr, Ingleby Barwick
P. Herman, Simonside Gr, Ingleby Barwick
R. Heward, Whitehouse Rd, Billingham
A. Heward, Whitehouse Rd, Billingham
A. Heward, Whitehouse Rd, Billingham
K. Heward, Glaisdale Ave, Stockton
S. Hewitt, Carlow St, Middlesbrough
S. Hewitt, Carlow St, Middlesbrough
A. Hewson, Cleadon Ave, Billingham
J. Heywood, Westfield Rd, Rugby
T. Hickes, Eton Rd, Stockton
A. S. Hide, Mayfield Cl, Eaglescliffe
C. M. Hide, Mayfield Cl, Eaglescliffe
R. Hide, Mayfield Cl, Eaglescliffe
M. Hide, Briggs Ave, Normanby Grange
C. Hields, Mortain Cl, Yarm
A. Hields, Mortain Cl, Yarm
D. Higgett, Winchester Rd, Linthorpe
C. Higgett, Winchester Rd, Linthorpe
S. Hill, Court Rd, Beechwood
B. Hill, Longbank Rd, Ormesby
J. Hill, Longbank Rd, Ormesby
A. Hill, Longbank Rd, Ormesby
G. S. Hill, Enfield Chase, Guisborough
M. Hill, Enfield Chase, Guisborough
S. Hill, Enfield Chase, Guisborough
J. Hill, Enfield Chase, Guisborough
D. Hill, Clifton Ave, Eaglescliffe
J. Hill, Clifton Ave, Eaglescliffe
R. Hill, Ruskin Ave, Acklam
D. Hillerby, Coleton Gds, Ingleby Barwick
K. Hillerby, Coleton Gds, Ingleby Barwick
J. Hind, Birkdale Rd, Hartburn
W. Hingley, Bishopton Ave, Stockton
W. Hingley, Bishopton Ave, Stockton
T. Hingley, Bishopton Ave, Stockton
D. Hirlam, Norton Ave, Stockton
A. Hiscocks, Kinross Rd, Warrington
M. Hitchinson, Hollymead Dr, Guisborough
H. Hoar, Dunedin Ave, Hartburn
M. Hoare, Churchill Way, Kettering
L. Hoare, Liverton Ave, Middlesbrough
L. Hoare, Liverton Ave, Middlesbrough
K. T. Hobson, Nunnington Cl, Ingleby Barwick
S. E. M. Hobson, Nunnington Cl, Ingleby Barwick
B. Hobson, Marton Rd, Middlesbrough
P. Hobson, Rosewood Ct, Marton
S. Hobson, Martin Rd, Middlesbrough
M. Hobson, Barton Cl, Thornaby
B. Hobson, Barton Cl, Thornaby
J. Hobson, Barton Cl, Thornaby
C. Hobson, Barton Cl, Thornaby
I. Hodds, Larkspur Rd, Marton
G. Hodds, Larkspur Rd, Marton
D. Hodges, Sherwood Dr, Marske
H. Hodges, Sherwood Dr, Marske
A. Hodges, Sherwood Dr, Marske
M. Hodges, Sherwood Dr, Marske
C. Hodgson, Marykirk Rd, Thornaby
S. Hodgson, Meath Way, Guisborough
L. Hodgson, Eridge Rd, Guisborough
A. N. Hodgson, Eridge Rd, Guisborough
C. G. Hodgson, Bridge Rd, Guisborough
J. W. Hodgson, Southfield Rd, Middlesbrough
D. Hodgson, Marley Cl, Stockton
J. Hodgson, Petersfield, Hampshire
G. Hodgson, Highbury Ave, Tollesby
A. Hodgson, Redcar, Cleveland
J. Hodgson, Largs, Scotland
N. Hodgson, Madrid, Spain
P. Hodgson, Madrid, Spain
S. Hodgson, Madrid, Spain
B. Hodson, Bassenthwaite, Acklam
D. Holden, Harter Cl, Nunthorpe
R. Holland, Longbank Rd. Ormesby
J. Holland, Longbank Rd. Ormesby
M. Holley, Bush St, Linthorpe
S. Hollifield, Topcliffe Rd, Thornaby
G. Hollingsworth, Ringway, Stainsby Hill
D. Hollingsworth, Ringway, Stainsby Hill
B. K. Holloway, Felixkirk Village, Thirsk
C. Holloway, Felixkirk Village, Thirsk
M. Holloway, Bush St, Middlesbrough
M. J. Holloway, Bush St, Middlesbrough
S. Holloway, Rochester Rd, Middlesbrough
C. Holloway, Ayresome Pk Rd, Middlesbrough
P. Holmes, Huntcliffe Ave, Redcar
J. Holmes, Lingfield Dr, Eaglescliffe
S. L. Holmes, Buckingham Dr, Normanby
W. Holmes, Runswick Ave, Acklam
J. Holmes, Runswick Ave, Acklam
D. Holmes, Runswick Ave, Acklam
K. Holt, Aylsham Cl, Ingleby Barwick
K. Holt, Aylsham Cl, Ingleby Barwick
D. Holt, Aylsham Cl, Ingleby Barwick
R. G. Homer, Arken Terr, Norton
M. Honeyman, Beechfields, Coulby Newham
G. Honeyman, Towngate, Barnsley
Hood Family, Doimed Ct, Marton
D. Hooton, Overdale Rd, Middlesbrough
T. B. Hope, Lord Nelsons Yard, Yarm
C. W. Hopkins, Cliffe Ct, Seaton Carew
R. A. Hopkins, Cliffe Ct, Seaton Carew
M. Hopkinson, Moor Green, Nunthorpe
I. Hopkinson, Fearnhead, Marton
J. F. Horkan, Bramley Gr, Marton
M. Horncastle, Crathorne Cres, West Lane
J. Horner, Mersehead Sands, Acklam
J. Horsley, Brent Ct, Billingham
A. Horton, Church St, Castleton
H. Horton, Ainthorpe Lane, Danby
M. Houghton, Swaledale Cl, Ingleby Barwick
T. Howe, Butterfield Dr, Eaglescliffe
R. Howes, Westminster Rd, Linthorpe
M. Howes, Westminster Rd, Linthorpe
N. Howes, Southwell Rd, Linthorpe
C. Hoyland, Southfield Cres, Norton
J. Hoyland, Southfield Cres, Norton
R. Huck, Queens Rd, Linthorpe
J. Huck, Queens Rd, Linthorpe
J. Huck, Queens Rd, Linthorpe
D. Hudson, Chipchase Rd, Linthorpe
L. Hudson, Chipchase Rd, Linthorpe
J. Hudson, Chipchase Rd, Linthorpe
E. Hudson, Latham Rd, Linthorpe
P. Hudson, Southwick Ave, Middlesbrough
M. Hudson, Tamarisk Cl, Ingleby Barwick
M. Hudson, Brampton Cl, Hemlington
M. Hudson, Glendale Rd, Tollesby
P. Hughes, Clevegate, Nunthorpe
M. Hughes, Clevegate, Nunthorpe
S. Hughes, Lowfield Ave, Ingleby Barwick
P. Hughes, Green Meadows, Macclesfield
L. Hughes, Fairville Rd, Stockton
M. Hugill, Abbey Ct, Normanby
S. Hugill, Worcester St, Middlesbrough
K. Hugill, Danby Rd, Eston
I. Hugill, Danby Rd, Eston
R. Hulse, Field Close, Thornaby
A. Hulse, Hood Dr, Normanby Grange
K. Hulse, Hood Dr, Normanby Grange
A. Hulse, Hood Dr, Normanby Grange
A. Hulse, Hood Dr, Normanby Grange
A. Humble, Croxdale Gr, Fairfield
C. L. Humble, Bonnyrigg Cl, Ingleby Berwick
M. Humble, Bonnyrigg Cl, Ingleby Barwick
S. Hume, Hillcrest Ave, Fairfield
I. Humphrey, Carlbury Ave, Acklam
C. J. Humphrey, Carlbury Ave, Acklam
E. Humphries, Gatley Wk, Eaglescliffe
J. Humphries, Gatley Wk, Eaglescliffe
G. Hunt, Calluna Gr, Marton Manor
P. Hunt, Esk Mill Cottages, Castleton
G. Hunt, East Lodge Gds, Redcar
J. S. Hunt, Planetree Ct, Marton
L. Hunter, Low Grange Ave, Billingham
R. Hunter, Offerton Dr, Hemlington
C. Hunter, Offerton Dr, Hemlington
C. Hurndal, Wicklow St, Middlesbrough
R. Husband, Coulby Newham
K. Husband, Nunthorpe
K. Husband, The Causeway, Billingham
R. Husband, Oak Hill, Coulby Newham
K. Husband, Ripon Rd, Nunthorpe
E. A. Huskinson, Fonteyn Ct, Hemlington
L. E. Huskinson, Fonteyn Ct, Hemlington
S. F. Hutchinson, The Paddock, Stokesley
P. Hutchinson, Carlton Dr, Thornaby
J. Hutchinson, Eltham Cres, Thornaby
D. Hutton, Cookgate, Nunthorpe
C. Hutton, Cookgate, Nunthorpe
C. Hutton, Cookgate, Nunthorpe
M. C. Hutton, Stokesley Rd, Nunthorpe
B. Hylton, Gascoyne Cl, Marton
P. Hylton, Gascoyne Cl, Marton

I

M. P. I'Anson, Whinfell Ave, Eaglescliffe
A. N. I'Anson, Aske Rd, Redcar
M. C. I'Anson, Aske Rd, Redcar
H. Ingham, Fairfield Ave, Linthorpe
J. Ingham, Fairfield Ave, Linthorpe
G. Ingham, Park Vale Rd, Middlesbrough
W. Ingledew, East Cres, Middlesbrough
C. C. Ingoe, Lime Rd, Normanby
C. P. Ingoe, Lime Rd, Normanby
C. J. Ingoe, Lime Rd, Normanby
S. Instone, Mowbray Gr, Stockton
R. P. Instone, Mowbray Gr, Stockton
G. Instone, Mowbray Gr, Stockton
A. Irwin, Harlsey Rd, Hartburn
P. Iveson, Andover Way, Hemlington
K. L. Ivison, Park Rd. Sth, Middlesbrough
A. J. Ivison, Park Rd. Sth, Middlesbrough
A. Ivison, Park Rd. Sth, Middlesbrough

J

S. Jackson, Wordsworth Cl, Billingham
M. Jackson, Wordsworth Cl, Billingham
K. Jackson, Wordsworth Cl, Billingham
E. Jackson, Oakdale, Spencerbeck
D. Jackson, Oakdale, Spencerbeck
P. Jackson, The Broadway, Darlington
C. Jackson, North Stand
R. Jackson, Gilsland Gr, Normanby
G. Jackson, Gilsland Gr, Normanby
D. Jackson, Clevegate, Nunthorpe
M. Jackson, Clevegate, Nunthorpe
S. Jackson, Gilsland Gr, Normanby
G. Jackson, Gilsland Gr, Normanby
A. Jackson, Hawkstone Cl, Guisborough
P. Jackson, Hawkstone Cl, Guisborough
R. Jackson, Essex St, Middlesbrough
G. Jackson, Mayfield Cl, Eaglescliffe
A. Jacques, Chandlers Ridge, Nunthorpe
B. Jacques, Chandlers Ridge, Nunthorpe
L. Jacques, Chandlers Ridge, Nunthorpe
J. James, Westgate Rd, Linthorpe
A. James, Westgate Rd, Linthorpe
I. James, Houghton on the Hill, Leics.
S. James, East Cres, Middlesbrough
S. James, East Cres, Middlesbrough
C. James, East Cres, Middlesbrough
B. James, Hayling Gr, Redcar
S. James Jnr, East Cres, Middlesbrough
A. Jameson, Dovedale Rd, Norton
S. Jefferies, St. Hilda's
C. G. Jeffrey, Hylton Rd, Billingham
C. M. Jeffrey, Hylton Rd, Billingham
M. Jenkinson, St. Margarets Way, Brotton
G. Jenkinson, St. Margarets Way, Brotton
D. Jenkinson, St. Margarets Way, Brotton
M. Jenkinson, Sidmouth Cl, Tollesby Hall
P. Jennison, Runnymede, Nunthorpe
S. Jepson, Linmoor Ave, Pallister Park
G. Jessop, Ashbourne Rd, Stockton
G. Jessop, Ashbourne Rd, Stockton
M. D. Jessup, Maidstone Dr, Marton
C. D. Jessup, Maidstone Dr, Marton
L. Jewkes, Whinfield Cl, Stockton
C. Jewkes, Whinfield Cl, Stockton
T. Jinks Jnr, Oakwell Rd, Norton
T. Jinks Snr, Oakwell Rd, Norton
R. Joel, St. Austell Cl, Stainton Manor
G. Joel, St. Austell Cl, Stainton Manor
T. Joel, St. Austell Cl, Stainton Manor
T. M. Joel, Bank Sands, Acklam
A. P. Johns, Lindrick Rd, New Marske
E. Johns, Lindrick Rd, New Marske
S. L. Johns, Lindrick Rd, New Marske
D. L. Johnson, Mill St. West, Stockton
K. E. Johnson, Haverthwaite, Acklam
A. Johnson, Elwick Ave, Acklam
B. Johnson, Elwick Ave, Acklam
S. Johnson, Elwick Ave, Acklam
R. W. Johnson, Emmetts Gds, Ingleby Barwick
M. Johnson, Boscombe Gds, Hemlington
C. Johnson, Kinloch Rd, Normanby
M. Johnson, Kinloch Rd, Normanby
C. Johnson, Thackeray Gr, Acklam
M. Johnson, South Gosforth, Newcastle
D. Johnson, South Gosforth, Newcastle
C. Johnson, South Gosforth, Newcastle
A. Johnson, South Gosforth, Newcastle
L. Johnson, Foxhowe, Coulby Newham
A. Johnson, Weaverham Rd, Norton
M. A. Johnson, Weaverham Rd, Norton
B. M. Johnson, Weaverham Rd, Norton
S. Johnson, Beckenham Gr, Hemlington
E. Johnson, Eltham Cres, Thornaby
A. Johnson, North Albert Rd, Norton
M. Johnston, Trenholme Rd, Middlesbrough
S. Johnston, Trenholme Rd, Middlesbrough
M. Johnstone, Netherby Gn, Middlesbrough
A. M. Johnstone, Netherby Gn, Middlesbrough
S. J. Johnstone, Netherby Gn, Middlesbrough
A. Joly, Cadogan St, North. Ormesby
T. M. Jones, Rutland Ct, Middlesbrough
H. Jones, Thornfield Rd, Linthorpe
J. Jones, Thornfield Rd, Linthorpe
N. Jones, Weymouth Ave, Tollesby Hall
S. Jones, Weymouth Ave, Tollesby Hall
N. G. Jones, Woodlea, Coulby Newham
B. Jones, Dallas, Texas
S. Jones, Glaisdale Ave, Middlesbrough
N. Jones, Parklands Ave, Billingham
A. Jones, Parklands Ave, Billingham
C. Jones, Cochrane Park, Newcastle
S. Jones, Gayton Sands, Acklam
S. Jones, Cromwell Gn, Stockton
M. Jones, Mapleton Cres, Redcar
J. Jones, Mapleton Cres, Redcar
P. J. Jones, Kingsley Rd. Fairfield
S. J. Jones, Cardinal Gr, Stockton
M. Jones, Surbiton Rd, Hartburn
G. Jones, Mallaig View, Stockton
L. Jones, Huntcliff Dr, Brotton
D. Jones, Huntcliff Dr, Brotton
D. Jones Jnr, Huntcliff Dr, Brotton
P. Jordison, Mellor St. Stockton
J. Jordison, Mellor St, Stockton
G. Jowett, Butterfield Rd, Eaglescliffe
A. Jowett, Butterfield Dr, Eaglescliffe
J. Jowett, Butterfield Dr, Eaglescliffe
C. Jowett, Butterfield Dr, Eaglescliffe
N. Jowsey, Richmond Place, Redcar
A. Jowsey, High St. West, Redcar
D. Jowsey, High St. West, Redcar
A. Jowsey, High St. West, Redcar
D. Jukes, Ribble Cl, Billingham
J. Jukes, Ribble Cl, Billingham

K

J. Kane, Worcester St, Middlesbrough
B. Kane, Craigearn Rd, Normanby
J. Karlsson, Carlbury Ave, Acklam
D. Karlsson, Carlbury Ave, Acklam
S. Kavanagh, Brancepeth Ave, Park End
C. Kavanagh, Brancepeth Ave, Park End
E. Kavanagh, Brancepeth Ave, Park End
S. Kavanagh, Mansfield Ave, Thornaby
S. Kavanagh, Mansfield Ave, Thornaby
G. Kay, Monkland Cl, Middlesbrough
C. Kay, Monkland Cl, Middlesbrough
J. Kay, Thackeray Gr, Linthorpe
E. Kay, Thackeray Gr, Linthorpe
L. Kay, Thackeray Gr, Linthorpe
C. Kaye, Adelaide Rd, Marton
R. Keady, Golders Gn, London
J. Keenan, Malvern Dr, Brookfield
N. Keetley, High St, Swainby
B. Kelleher, East Cres, Whinney Banks
L. Kelleher, Rockliffe Rd, Linthorpe
N. J. Kelleher, Topcliffe Dr, Acklam
J. Kelleher, Norcliffe St, North Ormesby
S. P. Kelleher, Topcliffe Dr, Acklam
P. J. Kelleher, Topcliffe Dr, Acklam
A. M. Kellerman, Ash Gn, Coulby Newham
C. A. Kellerman, Chestnut Dr, Marton
D. Kelley, Thames Ave, Thornaby
D. Kelly, Craven St, Middlesbrough
J. Kelly, Lincoln Cres, Billingham
P. Kelly, Lincoln Cres, Billingham
A. J. Kelly, Chillingham Ct, Billingham
M. Kemp, Grosvener Gds, Normanby
L. Kemp, Piperknowle Rd, Hardwick
D. Kennington, Hurn Walk, Thornaby
P. Kennington, Hurn Walk, Thornaby
H. Kennington, Hurn Walk, Thornaby
M. Kennington, Hurn Walk, Thornaby
P. Kent, Kilkenny Rd, Guisborough
S. Kent, Kilkenny Rd, Guisborough
M. Kent, Kilkenny Rd, Guisborough
A. Kent, East Farm, Medomsley
N. J. Kent, East Farm, Medomsley
H. M. Kent, East Farm, Medomsley
J. Kent, Okehampton Dr, Marton
M. Kenworthy, Hunters Gate, Eston Under Nab
J. Kenyon, Bradhope Rd, Berwick Hills

J. Kenyon, Lawnswood Rd, Thorntree
T. Ketteringham, Water End, Brompton
L. Ketteringham, Water End, Brompton
A. Khan, Gresham Rd, Middlesbrough
D. Kidd, Canewood, Middlesbrough
L. Kidd, Canewood, Middlesbrough
G. A. Kidd, Canewood, Middlesbrough
A. Kidner, Lulsgate, Thornaby
C. Kidner, Lulsgate, Thornaby
K. Kidner, Lulsgate, Thornaby
S. Kidson, Meath St, Middlesbrough
K. Kilpatrick, Emerald St, Saltburn
J. J. Kilpatrick, Westbourne Rd, Whitby
G. W. King, Cotswold Cres, Billingham
V. King, Cotswold Cres, Billingham
N. King, Roseberry Cres, Great Ayton
C. J. King, Roseberry Cres, Great Ayton
P. King, Sycamore Rd, Redcar
C. King, Sycamore Rd, Redcar
J. King, Mayfield Ave, Normanby
M. King, Crawcrook Walk, Hardwick
S. Kirby, Anchorage Mews, Thornaby
K. Kirby, Eden Rd, Middlesbrough
S. Kirby, Eden Rd, Middlesbrough
S. Kirby, Eden Rd, Middlesbrough
C. Kirby, Eden Rd, Middlesbrough
P. Kirkbride, Penrith Rd, Middlesbrough
M. Kirkbride, Sadberge Gr, Fairfield
T. Kirkham, Earlsdon Ave, Acklam
N. Kirkham, Earlsdon Ave, Acklam
I. R. Kirkup, Newham Ave, Tollesby
J. Kirton, Cunningham Dr, Thornaby
P. Kirwan, Chatsworth Ct, Stockton
C. Kitchen, Whitley Rd, Thornaby
F. Kitching, Cheltenham Cl, Linthorpe
G. Kitching, Farnham Cl, Eaglescliffe
J. Kitching, Farnham Cl, Eaglescliffe
L. Kitching, Scalby Gr, Fairfield
S. Klincke, Tithebarn Rd, Hardwick
G. Knaggs, Ellerburne St, Thornaby
B. Knaggs, Cooper Lane, Potto
M. Knox, Heythrop Dr, Acklam
A. Knox, Heythrop Dr, Acklam
J. Kotch, Sunstar Gr, Marton Manor
M. Kotch, Sunstar Gr, Marton Manor
S. J. Kubaj, Harford St, Middlesbrough
M. J. Kubaj, Hartford St, Middlesbrough
S. J. Kubaj, Harford St, Middlesbrough
P. Kulscar, Woodland St, Stockton
M. Kumar, Gresham Rd. Middlesbrough

L

P. Laforge, Nuneaton Dr, Hemlington
K. Laing, Westfield Way, Dormanstown
R. W. Lake, Harrowgate Lane, Stockton
D. Laker, Millholme Cl, Brotton
M. R. Laker, Millholme Cl, Brotton
L. Lakin, Bywell Gr, Ormesby
K. Lamb, Limpton Gate, Yarm
D. Lamb, Limpton Gate, Yarm
S. Lambert, Dorothy St, North Ormesby
J. Lambert, Skelwith Rd, Berwick Hills
D. Lambert, Dorothy St, North Ormesby
A. Lambert, Dorothy St, North Ormesby
T. Lambert, Birkley Rd, Norton
G. Lambert, Birkley Rd, Norton
N. Lambson, Queensberry Ave, Hartlepool
J. Lambton, Spencer Cl, Marske
C. Lambton, Spencer Cl, Marske
G. Lambton, Spencer Close, Marske
A. Lambton, Spencer Cl, Marske
J. Lamming, Claude Ave, Linthorpe
S. Lamming, Claude Ave, Linthorpe
N. Lamming, Claude Ave, Linthorpe
A. Lancaster, Mersey Rd, Redcar
I. Lancaster, Mersey Rd, Redcar
K. Lancaster, Caldwell Cl, Hemlington
B. Lancaster, Lavender Rd, North Ormesby
J. Lancaster, Lavender Rd, North Ormesby
K. Lancaster, Lavender Rd, North Ormesby
P. Lancaster, Lavender Rd, North Ormesby
A. Lancaster, Amroth Gn, Pallister Park
E. Lancaster, Amroth Gn, Pallister Park
A. Lancaster, Mersey Rd, Redcar
I. Lancaster, Mersey Rd, Redcar
B. Land, Holmefields Rd, Normanby
S. Land, Holmefields Rd, Normanby
P. Land, Holmefields Rd, Normanby
D. Lane, St. Annes Rd, New Marske
P. Langston, The Jennings, Normanby
T. Larkin, St. Germains Ln, Marske
M. Larkin, St. Germains Ln, Marske
S. Larkin, St. Germains Ln, Marske
W. J. Laroche, Edmundsbury Rd, Linthorpe
T. Larry, Brettenham Ave, Easterside
S. Larsson, Bowness Gr, Redcar
P. Laverick, Sealand Cl, Thornaby
G. Law, Toddington Dr, Norton
S. Law, Hoveton Cl, Stockton
J. Law, Hoveton Cl, Stockton
S. Law, Hoveton Cl, Stockton
I. Lawson, Wheatlands Park, Redcar
J. Lawson, Redcar Lane, Redcar
K. Layburn, Hartforth Ave, Acklam
K. Layburn, Hartforth Ave, Acklam
I. Layton, Staindale, Guisborough
D. I. Layton, Staindale, Guisborough
J. Leach, School Ave, Whinney Banks
P. Leadbitter, Thirlmere Ave, Acklam
J. Leadbitter, Wolsingham Dr, Acklam
M. Lee, Northfields, Hutton Rudby
S. Lee, Northfields, Hutton Rudby
C. Lee, Amberley Gn, Pallister Park
J. Lee, Amberley Gn, Pallister Park
S. D. Lee, Greymouth Cl, Hartburn
B. Lee, Wimpole Rd, Fairfield
C. Lee, Wimpole Rd, Fairfield
A. Lee, Wimpole Rd, Fairfield
P. E. Lee, Sorrel Ct, Marton
J. A. Lee. Sorrel Ct, Marton
M. Lee, Ragworth Rd, Norton
K. Lee, Ragworth Rd, Norton
B. Leeson, Thorntree Rd, Thornaby
M. Leeson, Thorntree Rd, Thornaby
K. Leitch, Saltburn Lane, Skelton
M. Levitt, Bradleys Terr, Great Ayton
K. Levitt, Bradleys Terr, Great Ayton
A. Lewis, Bentinck Ave, Linthorpe
T. Lewis, Bentinck Ave, Linthorpe
J. Lewis, Deepdale Ave, Grove Hill
C. Lewis, Deepdale Ave, Grove Hill
E. Lewis, Redwing Lane, Norton
P. Lewis, Hollowfield, Caulby Newham
B. Lewis, Sorrel Ct, Marton
G. Lewis, Sorrel Ct, Marton
T. Lewis, Canon Gr, Yarm
N. Liddell, Keithlands Ave, Norton
A. Liddell, Keithlands Ave, Norton
D. Liddell, Keithlands Ave, Norton
L. Liddell, Keithlands Ave, Norton
M. Liddle, Wolviston Back Ln, Billingham
J. Liggett, Cones Ave, Thornaby
G. Liggitt, Barker Rd, Linthorpe
M. Liggitt, Barker Rd, Linthorpe
C. Lightowler, Ragpath Lane, Stockton
G. Limon, Tawney Rd, Eston
R. Limon, Tawney Rd, Eston
M. Limon, Sunnygate, Eston
F. Limon, Sunnygate, Eston
J. Limon, Sunnygate, Eston
C. Lindberg, Jubilee Rd, Eston
E. Lindberg, Prospect Terr, Eston
E. Lindberg, Jubilee Rd, Eston
K. T. Lindo, Arden Gr, Fairfield
D. Lindo, Arden Gr, Fairfield
K. S. Lindo, Arden Gr, Fairfield
J. Lings, Park Ave, Teesville
T. Lings, Park Ave, Teesville
I. Linklater, The Hall Close, Ormesby
J. R. I. Linklater, The Hall Cl, Ormesby
S. Lisle, Overdale Cl, Redcar
M. H. Lisle, Overdale Cl, Redcar
J. Livingstone, South Stand
M. Livingstone, South Stand
J. Llewellyn, Barnard Ct, Marton Gr.
R. Lobley, Marske Rd, Saltburn
M. Lofthouse, Aiskew Gr, Fairfield
M. R. Lofthouse, Aiskew Gr, Fairfield
A. Lombard, The Headlands, Marske
S. Long, Berwick Chase, Peterlee
C. Longhorn, Woodford Walk, Thornaby
C. Longstaff, Welbury, Northallerton
D. Longstaff, Welbury, Northallerton
G. Longstaff, Lowick Cl, Stockton
J. P. Longstaff, Merlin Rd, Middlesbrough
R. A. Longstaff, Merlin Rd, Middlesbrough
F. Lonsbrough, Axminster Rd, Hemlington
G. Lonsbrough, Axminster Rd, Hemlington
D. Lord, Chipchase Rd, Linthorpe
K. Loughran, Fosdyke Gn, Netherfields
A. Loughran, Fosdyke Gn, Netherfields
M. P. Love, Hall Dr, Middlesbrough
R. Love, Hall Dr, Middlesbrough
M. G. Lovell, Kirkleatham Lane, Redcar
J. Lowe, Dionysia Rd, North. Ormesby
J. Lowe, Zetland Rd, Middlesbrough
D. Lowe, Dishforth Cl, Thornaby
S. C. Ludley, Park Ln, Middlesbrough
N. Lund, Emerald St, Saltburn
P. Lynas, Mapleton Cres, Redcar
P. Lynch, Bevanlee Rd, South Bank
A. D. Lynch, Bevanlee Rd, South Bank
M. S. Lynch, Bevanlee Rd, South Bank
P. Lynch, Preen Dr, Acklam
S. Lynch, Greenfields Way, Hartburn
C. Lynch, Rievaulx Ave, Billingham
S. J. Lynch, Rievaulx Ave, Billingham
C. Lynch, Rievaulx Ave, Billingham
L. Lynch, Rievaulx Ave, Billingham
A. Lythe, Stainton Walk, Marton

M

N. Macauley, Sheraton Pk, Stockton
J. H. Macdonald, Holly Garth, Great Ayton
S. MacDonald, Fox Gloves, Coulby Newham
C. MacDonald, Fox Gloves, Coulby Newham
R. S. MacFadzean, Atwick Cl, Billingham
M. E. MacFadzean, Atwick Cl, Billingham
C. T. MacFadzean, Atwick Cl, Billingham
I. MacFarlane, Stokesley Rd. Marton
I. MacGregor, Angrove Cl, Yarm
J. Mack, Sinderby Cl, Billingham
D. Mack, Sinderby Cl, Billingham
K. Mack, Sinderby Cl, Billingham
J. Mack, Sinderby Cl, Billingham
V. Mack, Sinderby Cl, Billingham
T. Mack, Clipstone Rd, Coventry
J. Mack, Clipstone Rd, Coventry
S. Mack, Gansted Way, Billingham
J. Mack, Wisewood, Sheffield
A. N. Mack, Claude Ave, Linthorpe
N. Mack, Claude Ave, Linthorpe
E. R. Mack, Guisborough Rd, Nunthorpe
R. Mackey, The Glebe, Norton
C. P. Mackey, Cranstock Cl, Billingham
J. Mackey, Cranstock Cl, Billingham
S. Mackey, Cranstock Cl, Billingham
S. Mackin, Ferndale Ave, Brambles Farm
P. Mackin, Renown Walk, South Bank
B. Mackin, Carron Gr, Normanby
A. Mackinlay, Highgate, Eston Under Nab
C. Mackinlay, Highgate, Eston Under Nab
T. J. Maggs, Ainthorpe Rd, Eston
C. T. Maggs, Ainthorpe Rd, Eston
P. Maggs, Aire St, Middlesbrough
A. Magowan, St. James Gds, Middlesbrough
F. N. Mallon, Sinnington Rd, Thornaby
G. R. Mallon, Scampton Cl, Thornaby
M. E. Mallon, York Cres, Billingham
B. Malone, Chippenham Rd, Easterside
V. Malone, Chippenham Rd, Easterside
D. Maloney, Landsdowne Rd, Middlesbrough
N. Maloy, Queens Rd, Middlesbrough
J. Maloy, Coxwold Cl, Middlesbrough
G. Maloy, Mulgrave Rd, Middlesbrough
A. Mann, Poplar Gr, South Bank
C. Mann, Poplar Gr, South Bank
A. E. Mansell, Mayfield Cres, Eaglescliffe
P. Mansfield, St. Andrews Crest, Bishop Auckland
M. Mansfield, Endeavour Dr, Ormesby
K. Mansfield, Carisbrooke Ave, Thorntree
J. Manton, Malvern Dr, Brookfield
R. M. Mapplebeck, Dishforth Cl, Thornaby
D. J. March, Cornfield Rd, Linthorpe
C. A. Mark, The Willows, Marton
V. Mark, The Willows, Marton
D. Marlborough, Eastfield Rd, Marske
N. Marlborough, Eastfield Rd, Marske
L. Marlborough, Eastfield Rd, Marske
J. Marlborough, Blackmore Cl, Guisborough
I. Marley, Dovedale Rd, Norton
S. Marley, Dovedale Rd, Norton
P. Marquis, Eagle Park, Marton
I. Marron, Dinsdale Ave, Acklam
G. Marron, Wilowgarth, Newby
J. Marron, The Holt, Coulby Newham
C. Marron, Devonshire Rd, Linthorpe
S. Marron, Westbourne Rd, Linthorpe
C. T. J. & R. Marsden
W. Marshall, Lindrick Rd, New Marske
P. Marshall, Lindrick Rd, New Marske
J. Marshall, Lindrick Rd, New Marske
C. Marshall, Lindrick Rd, New Marske
D. Marshall, Avro Cl, Marske
C. Marshall, Ida Rd, Berwick Hills
P. Marshall, Ida Rd, Berwick Hills
P. Martin, Meath St, Middlesbrough
M. Martin, Meath St, Middlesbrough
J. Martin, Oakfield Rd, North Ormesby
C. Martin, Oakfield Rd, North Ormesby
W. Martin, Kensington Ave, Normanby
T. Martin, Kensington Ave, Normanby
G. Martin, Kensington Ave, Normanby
S. Martin, Kensington Ave, Normanby
A. Martino, Scalby Gr, Redcar
N. Martino, Scalby Gr, Redcar
T. Marwood, Mitchell Ave, Stainsby Hill
K. Marwood, Mitchell Ave, Stainsby Hill
T. Mason, Blackburn Gr, Marske
I. Mason, Westerleigh Ave, Fairfield
J. Mason, Westerleigh Ave, Fairfield
H. Mason, East Cres, Middlesbrough
L. Mason, East Cres, Middlesbrough
P. Mason, Wolsingham Dr, Thornaby
A. Mason, Wolsingham Dr, Thornaby
C. Mason, Wolsingham Dr, Thornaby
D. Mason, Brechin Dr, Thornaby
G. Mason, Pennington Ct, Billingham
M. Mason, Ashbourne Cl, Eston
M. Matterson, Weardale Cres, Billingham
D. Matterson, Weardale Cres, Billingham
D. D. R. Matterson, Weardale Cres, Billingham
M. A. Matterson, Weardale Cres, Billingham
M. Matthews, Felby Ave, Middlesbrough
A. L. Matthews, Felby Ave, Middlesbrough
L. Matthews, Sherwood Rd, Thornaby
J. Matthews, Saltholme Cl, Port Clarence
C. Matthews, Saltholme Cl, Port Clarence
D. S. Maude, Weaverham Rd, Norton
K. S. Maude, Weaverham Rd, Norton
A. J. Mawson, Hindhead, Eaglescliffe
M. J. Mawson, Oaklands Terr, Darlington
P. May, Woodrow Ave, Saltburn
P. McAvoy, Chard Walk, Middlesbrough
M. McAvoy Jr, Cherwell Terr, Brambles Farm
M. McAvoy Sr, Cherwell Terr, Brambles Farm
P. McCabe, Stoneyhurst Ave, Acklam
J. McCallan, Thorntree Rd, Thornaby
J. McCallan, Thorntree Rd, Thornaby
B. McCallay, Geltsdale, Acklam
G. McCalley, Geltsdale, Acklam
R. J. McCallion, Grasmere Ave, Acklam
K. McCallion, Grasmere Ave, Acklam
H. E. McCallion, Grasmere Ave, Acklam
M. V. McCallion, Grasmere Ave, Acklam
G. McCann, Phillips Ave, Linthorpe
L. McCann, Phillips Ave, Linthorpe
A. McCann, Phillips Ave, Linthorpe
J. McCann, Phillips Ave, Linthorpe
D. McCann, Stainsby St, Thornaby
N. McCarrick, Northumberland Rd, Thornaby
L. McCarrick, Northumberland Rd, Thornaby
C, McCarrick, Northumberland Rd, Thornaby
J. McCarthy, Dufton Rd. Middlesbrough
J. McCarty, York Cres, Billingham
K. McCormick, Delamere Dr, Marske
D. E. McCormick, Hershall Dr, Middlesbrough
T. McCormick, Chipchase Rd, Middlesbrough
N. McCourt, Rylands Gr. Fairfield
T. McCulloch, Herbert St, North Ormesby
S. McCulloch, Maltby St, North Ormesby
S. McCulloch, Maltby St, North Ormesby
S. McCulloch, Cowrakes Rd, Huddersfield
T. McCutcheon, Hillbrow Ct, Godstone
N. B. McCutcheon, East Scar, Redcar
G. McCutcheon, East Scar, Redcar
S. McCutcheon, East Scar, Redcar
G. McDermott, Franklyn Ct, Thornaby
M. McDermott Jr, Overdale Rd, Berwick Hills
M. McDermott Sr, Overdale Rd, Berwick Hills
S. McDermottroe, Warwick Cres, Billingham
S. McDonagh, Rochester Rd, Linthorpe
P. McDonagh, Easterside Rd, Middlesbrough
P. McDonagh, Easterside Rd, Middlesbrough
M. McDonagh, Trefoil Wood, Marton Manor
R. McDonald, Tweed St, Saltburn
K. McDonald, Cresswell Cl, Hemlington
A. McDonald, Geneva Dr, Redcar

M. McDonald, Geneva Dr, Redcar
J. McDonough, Montreal Pl, Middlesbrough
K. McDougall, Alvingham Tr, Netherfields
S. McDougall, Meadowgate, Eston
M. McElvaney, Fulwood Ave, Beechwood
M. McFarlane, Greenhow Rd, Berwick Hills
M. McFarlane, Greenhow Rd, Berwick Hills
S. McFarlane, Greenhow Rd, Berwick Hills
R. McGarrick, Albert Rd, Eston
M. McGeary, Barker Rd, Middlesbrough
T. J. McGee, Fir Tree Dr, Normanby
J. T. McGee, Ellerby Rd, Eston
J. A. McGee, Ellerby Rd, Eston
K. McGee, Stone Intake Fm, Chopgate
K. L. McGee, Stone Intake Fm, Chopgate
J. R. McGee, Stone Intake Fm, Chopgate
T. McGinn, Birkhall Rd, Thorntree
A. McGinn, Birkhall Rd, Thorntree
F. McGloin, Rushmere, Marton
J. McGloin, Rushmere, Marton
D. McGloin, Rushmere, Marton
R. McGloin, Rushmere, Marton
L. McGloin, Wheatfields House, Normanby
M. McGloin, The Endeavour, Nunthorpe
S. McGlynn, Bowland Cl, Nunthorpe
J. McGlynn, Bowland Cl, Nunthorpe
J. McGlynn, Bowland Cl, Nunthorpe
I. McGough, Gilmoure St, Thornaby
A. D. McGowan, Roseberry Rd, Middlesbrough
C. McGowan, Station Rd. Sedgefield
E. McGowan, Station Rd, Sedgefield
M. McGowan, Station Rd, Sedgefield
I. McGrath, Wicklow St, Middlesbrough
K. McGrath, Campion Gr, Marton Manor
W. McGregor, Ling Cl, Marton
A. McGregor, Oaksham Dr, Billingham
P. McGuinness, Campion Gr, Marton
A. M. McGuinness, Campion Gr, Morton
J. McGuinness, Campion Gr, Marton
C. McGuinness, Campion Gr, Marton
P. McGurn, Victoria Park Ave, Leeds
J. McGurn, Victoria Park Ave, Leeds
L. McGurn, Victoria Park Ave, Leeds
I. McIntosh, Lynmouth Cl, Stainton Manor
M. P. McIntosh, Honister Gr, Acklam
G. McIvor, Weardale Cres, Billingham
P. G. McIvor, Weardale Cres, Billingham
M. A. McKenna, Bristow Rd, Middlesbrough
J. L. McKenna, Skelwith Rd, Berwick Hills
L. McKenna, Clairville Rd, Middlesbrough
S. McKenna, Clairville Rd, Middlesbrough
G. McKinlay, Hawthorne Rd, Stockton
J. McLaughlan, Elvington Cl, Billingham
M. McLaughlan, Elvington Cl, Billingham
T. McLaughlan, Elvington Cl, Billingham
T. McLay, Starbeck Way, Middlesbrough
J. McLay, Starbeck Way, Middlesbrough
D. G. McLay, Wharfdale Ave, Billingham
C. McLay, Wharfdale Ave, Billingham
S. McLean, New Rd, Billingham
C. McLean, Maldon Rd, Middlesbrough
C. McLean Jnr, Maldon Rd, Middlesbrough
C. McLeary, Wolsingham Dr, Thornaby
J. McLeary, Wolsingham Dr, Thornaby
J. McLeod, High Gill Rd, Nunthorpe
S. McMahon, Langton Ave, Billingham
H. McMahon, Langton Ave, Billingham
J. McMahon, Wellspring Cl, Acklam
A. McMahon, Cliff Farm, Staithes
S. McMahon Jnr, Langton Ave, Billingham
C. McManus, Challacombe Cres, Ingleby Barwick
P. McMurdo, Swinburns Yard, Yarm
J. McMurdo, Swinburns Yard, Yarm
I. McNaughton, High St, Yarm
K. McNaughton, Ayresome St, Middlesbrough
G. K. McNaughton, Ayresome St, Middlesbrough
C. McNeil, Tollesby Rd, Tollesby
D. McNeil, Tollesby Rd, Tollesby
B. McNeil, Tollesby Rd, Tollesby
C. McNeil, Brecon Dr, Redcar
C. McNeil, Brecon Dr, Redcar
M. McNeil, Brecon Dr, Redcar
E. McNeil, Brecon Dr, Redcar
A. McNicholas, Stonegate, Eston
C. B. McNicholas, Park Ave, Teesville
J. McNicholas, Clive Rd, Eston
E. McNicholas, Edward St, South Bank
K. McNicholas, Edward St, South Bank
M. Q. McParland, Taif, Saudi Arabia
K. A. McPartland, Southdean Dr, Hemlington
S. McPhillips, South Stand
A. McPhillips, South Stand
J. W. McQuade, Fawcus Ct, Dormanstown
B. McQuade, Borough Rd, Redcar
S. McQuade, Megarth Rd, Linthorpe
J. McQuade, Megarth Rd, Linthorpe
S. McQuillan, Blacksail Cl, Stockton
K. McTaggart, Lomond Ave, Billingham
S. McTaggart, Parklands Ave, Billingham
H. McTaggart, Parklands Ave, Billingham
G. McTiernan, Diamond Rd, Middlesbrough
P. McTiernan, Diamond Rd, Middlesbrough
C. McTiernan, Diamond Rd, Middlesbrough
T. McVey, Oxfield, Coulby Newham
J. R. Mead, Harford St, Middlesbrough
A. W. Mead, Chalford Oaks, Acklam
R. Meek, Pritchett Rd, Ormesby
A. Meek, Pritchett Rd, Ormesby
K. Meek, Phoenix Park, Hemlington
B. Meek, Forber Rd, Middlesbrough
C. Meek, Forber Rd, Middlesbrough
S. Meek, Forber Rd, Middlesbrough
G. Meek, Forber Rd, Middlesbrough
D. Meek, Forber Rd, Middlesbrough
J. Meekings, Brignall Rd, Stockton
P. Meekings, Brignall Rd, Stockton
H. Melling, Wiltshire Rd, Skelton
M. Melling, Wiltshire Rd, Skelton
J. Mellon, Phillips Ave, Linthorpe
J. Mellon, Phillips Ave, Linthorpe
W. T. Mellor, The Factory, Castle Eden
H. Mellor, Worsley Cres, Marton
C. Mellor, Beckenham Gds, Hemlington
R. Menzies, Spring Garden Ln, Ormesby
P. Menzies, Meath St, Middlesbrough
C. Mescus, Ash Gr, South Bank
G. Metcalfe, Rowland Keld, Guisborough
R. Metcalfe, Rowland Keld, Guisborough
T. Metcalfe, Rowland Keld, Guisborough
A. J. Metcalfe, Torver Mt, Nunthorpe
A. Metti, Yarm Rd, Eaglescliffe
U. Metti, Yarm Rd, Eaglescliffe
S. Micklewright, Birtley Ave, Acklam
E. Middleton, Woodvale, Coulby Newham
D. Middleton, Rydal Ave, Acklam
C. A. Middleton, Rydal Ave, Acklam
C. Middleton, Cornhill Walk, Overfields
J. Middleton-Taylor, Staindale, Guisborough
D. Middleton-Taylor, Staindale, Guisborough
A. Miles, Rydal Ave, Acklam
P. Miles, Rydal Ave, Acklam
S. Milestone, Aspen Dr, Linthorpe
G. Milestone, Aspen Dr, Linthorpe
G. Milestone, Aspen Dr, Linthorpe
S. C. Miller, Norham Walk, Overfields
N. Miller, Red House, Stokesley
M. Millett, Wansford Cl, Billingham
C. Millington, Skottowe Cres, Great Ayton
A. Mills, Heselden Ave, Acklam
G. Millward, Hexham Dr, Eston
A. Millward, Hexham Dr, Eston
A. Millward, Maria Dr, Fairfield
N. Millward, Maria Dr, Fairfield
K. Mitchell, Harrogate Cres, Linthorpe
K. J. Mitchell, Costa St, Middlesbrough
M. Mitchell, Bush St, Middlesbrough
L. Mitchell, Maple Ave, Middlesbrough
W. Mitchell, Welland Cres, Stockton
V. Mitchell, Welland Cres, Stockton
N. Mitchell, Welland Cres, Stockton
D. G. Mitchell, Sandmoor Cl, Eston
G. Mitchell, Gresham Rd, Middlesbrough
R. F. Mitchell, West Dyke Rd, Redcar
P. F. Mitchell, West Dyke Rd, Redcar
A. Mitchell, Welland Cres, Stockton
A. Mitchell, Derwent Rd, Redcar
K. Mitchell, Harrogate Cres, Linthorpe
M. W. L. Mitchell, Bush St, Linthorpe
B. Mitchinson, Kildale Gr, Fairfield
S. Mitchinson, Kildale Gr, Fairfield
R. Mitchinson, Kildale Gr, Fairfield
N. Mitchinson, Kildale Gr, Fairfield
M. Mitchinson, Hollymead Dr, Guisborough
R. Moffoot, The Spinney, Milton Keynes
P. Mogie, Heythrop Dr, Acklam
I. Mohan, Corby Ave, Acklam
D. Mohan, Easson Rd, Redcar
M. T. Mohan, Quebec Gr, Middlesbrough
E. Moir, Halliwell St, Chorley
F. Monaghan, Thornaby Rd, Thornaby
P. Monaghan, Thornaby Rd, Thornaby
D. Monks, Bondene Gr, Bishopsgarth
N. Monks, Tower Ct, Saltburn
N. Moody, Eridge Rd, Guisborough
C. Moody, Beresford Cres, Thorntree
C. Moody, Beresford Cres, Thorntree
M. Moon, Queen St, Lazenby
R. Moon, Queen St, Lazenby
S. C. Moore, Ganton House, Redcar
P. Moore, Hythe Cl, Redcar
K. Moore, Darnley Cl, Meltham
A. Moore, Jameson Rd, Norton
A. J. Moore, Jameson Rd, Norton
E. J. Moore, Jameson Rd. Norton
B. Moore, Grampian Rd. Billingham
F. Moore, Grampian Rd, Billingham
D. C. Moore, Collingwood Chase, Brotton
L. Moore, Collingwood Chase, Brotton
K. L. Moore, Collingwood Chase, Brotton
J. D. Moore, Pump Ln, Kirklevington
D. Moore, Pump Ln, Kirklevington
A. Moore, Ravensworth Gr, Hartburn
J. Moore, Ravensworth Gr, Hartburn
H. Moore, Ravensworth Gr, Hartburn
L. Moore, Ravensworth Gr, Hartburn
S. Moore, Linthorpe
R. Moore, Lancaster Dr, Marske
D. N. Moore, Lancaster Dr, Marske
S. J. Morgan, Angle St, Middlesbrough
W. Morgan, Angle St, Middlesbrough
R. Morgan, Bassleton Ln, Thornaby
J. Morgan, Roseberry Dr, Stainton
S. Morgan, Beechwood Rd, Thornaby
D. Morgan, Weymouth Ave, Tollesby Hall
T. J. Morley, Langthorne Gr, Hartburn
A. Morris, Runnymede, Nunthorpe
H. Morris, Chesterton Ave, Thornaby
W. Morris, Fairfield Rd. Stockton
L. J. Morris, Fairfield Rd, Stockton
D. K. Morrison, Chadderton Dr, Stainsby Hill
D. Morrison J, Chadderton Dr, Stainsby Hill
L. F. & A. Morrissey
P R. Mortlock, Burnmoor Dr, Eaglescliffe
T. Mothersill, Megarth Rd, Linthorpe
D. Mothersill, Megarth Rd, Linthorpe
C. Mothersill, Megarth Rd, Linthorpe
R. Mothersill, Megarth Rd, Linthorpe
P. Motson, Ragpath Ln, Stockton
S. Mount, Knaith Cl, Yarm
E. Mount, Knaith Cl, Yarm
M. Moy, Heysham Gr, Redcar
J. Muirhead, Fairwell Rd, Stockton
S. Muirhead, Fairwell Rd, Stockton
A. Muirhead, Fairwell Rd, Stockton
L. Mullen, Barford Cl, Stockton
L. Mullins, Holdenby Dr, Middlesbrough
D. Mullins, Essex St, Middlesbrough
P. Mullins, Essex St, Middlesbrough
G. Mulroy, Deva Cl, Middlesbrough
J. Mulroy, Greenfield Dr, Eaglescliffe
P. Mundy, Bransdale Gr, Redcar
I. Munroe, Ridley Ave, Acklam
S. Munroe, Ridley Ave, Acklam
P. Murphy, Ullswater Ave, Acklam
I. P. Murphy, Ullswater Ave, Acklam
B. Murphy, Trefoil Wood, Marton
R. Murphy, Arlington Rd, Tollesby
J. Murphy, Arlington Rd, Tollesby
S. Murphy, Stratford Cres, Middlesbrough
C. Murphy, Central Ave, Billingham
C. Murphy, Deighton Rd, Easterside
K. Murphy, Deighton Rd, Easterside
D. Murphy, Deighton Rd, Easterside
L. Murphy, Kings Rd, Linthorpe
T. Murphy, Kings Rd, Linthorpe
J. Murphy, Kings Rd, Linthorpe
P. Murphy, Hoskins Way, Middlesbrough
A. Murphy, Hedingham Cl, Marton Grove
B. Murphy, Trefoil Wood, Marton Manor
A. Murphy, Easterside Rd, Middlesbrough
P. Murphy, Easterside Rd, Middlesbrough
B. Murphy, Easterside Rd, Middlesbrough
P. J. J. Murray, Fen Moor Cl, Stainton View
S. P. Murray, Fen Moor Cl, Stainton View
A. M. Murray, Fen Moor Cl, Stainton View
M. D. Murray, Glendale Rd, Tollesby
L. A. Murray, Glendale Rd, Tollesby
J. H. Murray, Falcon Ln, Norton
M. Murray, Falcon Ln, Norton
A. Murray, Falcon Ln, Norton
J. S. Murray, Falcon Ln, Norton
E. Murray, Edwards St, Eston
S. Murray, Edwards St, Eston
T. Murray, Edwards St, Eston
K. Murray, Edwards St. Eston
A. Murray, Bulmer Cl, Yarm
D. Murray, Bulmer Cl, Yarm
C. Murray, Bulmer Cl, Yarm
C. Murray, Bulmer Cl, Yarm
K. Murray, Bulmer Cl, Yarm
M. Murray, Kestrel Hide, Guisborough
T. Myer, Marshall Dr, Brotton
S. Myer, Marshall Dr, Brotton
L. Myer, Marshall Dr, Brotton
T. Myers, Hornsea Cl, Billingham
D. Myers, Hardwick Rd, Billingham

N

J. Nassau, Kings Rd, North Ormesby
L. Nassau, Kings Rd, North Ormesby
K. Neale, Coxgreen Cl, Hardwick
A. P. Neale, Coxgreen Cl, Hardwick
S. Neale, Fulbeck Rd, Netherfields
T. Neil, Heugh Chare, Hartlepool
T. Nellis, Andover Way, Hemlington
L. Nellist, South Stand
F. Nellist, South Stand
C. Nellist, North Stand
D. Nellist, North Stand
J. Nevison, Carlbury Ave, Acklam
D. Newsam, Whinfell Cl, Nunthorpe
S. Newsam, Whinfell Cl, Nunthorpe
D. Newsam, Whinfell Cl, Nunthorpe
J. R. Newton, Hermitage Way, Sleights
S. Newton, Hermitage Way, Sleights
M. Newton, Hermitage Way, Sleights
G. Newton, Marykirk Rd, Thornaby
M. Newton, Marykirk Rd, Thornaby
P. Newton, Marykirk Rd, Thornaby
C. Nicholas, Campion Gr, Marton Manor
S. Nicholls, Mattison Ave, Middlesbrough
A. Blakey-Nicholson, Ainsdale Way, Beechwood
J. Nicholson, Thurnham Gr, Marton
L. Nicholson, Thurnham Gr, Marton
J. Nicholson, Ricknall Cl, Acklam
G. Nicholson, Ainsdale Way, Beechwood
J. Nicholson, Windsor Cres, Nunthorpe
D. Nisbet, The Avenue, Fairfield
V. Nisbet, The Avenue, Fairfield
E. Nisbet, The Avenue, Fairfield
J. Nisbet, The Avenue, Fairfield
P. G. Nixon, Corporation Rd, Redcar
J. Nixon, Corporation Rd, Redcar
C. Noble, Manor Fields, Dalton Piercy
M. Noble, Marsden Cl, Ingleby Barwick
C. Noble, Marsden Cl, Ingleby Barwick
B. Noble, Great Busby, Middlesbrough
C. Norlund, Shevington Gr, Marton
B. Norlund, Shevington Gr, Marton
L. G. Norman, Marrick Rd, Middlesbrough
R. Norman, Palm St, Middlesbrough
B. L. Norman, Woodcock Cl, Normanby
S. Norman, Highfield Rd, Eston
A. M. Norminton, Luccombe Cl, Ingleby Barwick
E. Norminton, Luccombe Cl, Ingleby Barwick
H. Norris, Otterpool Cl, Hartlepool
P. Norton, Meadowgate, Eston
K. Noteyoung, Ormesby Rd, Normanby
P. Noteyoung, Ormesby Rd, Normanby
J. Noteyoung, Ormesby Rd, Normanby
R. Noteyoung, Ormesby Rd. Normanby
Nugent Family, Clifton Ave, Stockton

O

S. O'Brian, Rosslare Rd, Roseworth
M. R. O'Brien, Newham Cres, Marton
D. M. O'Brien, Sherburn Ave, Billingham
P. J. O'Brien, Runcorn Ave, Stockton
M. O'Brien, Ashfield Ave, Grove Hill
G. O'Brien, Allinson St, North Ormesby
B. O'Connor, Bilsdale Rd, Stockton
M. O'Donoghue, Knighton Ct, Stainsby Hill
C. O'Donoghue, Knighton Ct, Stainsby Hill
S. O'Donoghue, Knighton Ct, Stainsby Hill
J. O'Hagan, Blantyre Rd, Normanby
B. O'Hagan, Ripley, Derbyshire
B. O'Hagan, Ripley, Derbyshire
M. O'Hara, Brackenthwaite, Acklam

S. O'Hara, Brackenthwaite, Acklam
W. O'Hara, Allendale Terr, New Marske
J. O'Keefe, Burnholme Ave, Brambles Farm
N. O'Keefe, Burnholme Ave, Brambles Farm
P. O'Keefe, Armley, Leeds
D. O'Keefe, Burnholme Ave, Brambles Farm
B. O'Keefe, Burnholme Ave, Brambles Farm
C. O'Keefe, Armley, Leeds
A. O'Malley, Cayton Cl, Redcar
V. O'Malley, Cayton Cl, Redcar
A. O'Malley, Cayton Cl, Redcar
J. O'Malley, Cayton Cl, Redcar
B. O'Meara, Belfast
R. O'Meara, Belfast
F. O'Neill, Woodlea, Coulby Newham
B. O'Neill, Woodlea, Coulby Newham
C. F. O'Neill, Woodlea, Coulby Newham
C. E. O'Neill, Woodlea, Coulby Newham
J. Oakes, Keilder Rise, Hemlington
S. Oakes, Keilder Rise, Hemlington
D. Oakley, Easby Gr, Eston
N. Oliver, Church Cl, Thornaby
S. Oliver, Eden Rd, Skelton
E. Oliver, Eden Rd, Skelton
E. Oliver, Celandine Cl, Marton
D. A. Oliver, Celandine Cl, Marton
H. Oliver, Langley Cl, Redcar
G. Olvanhill, Durham Rd, Stockton
E. Oram, The Larches, Stockton
S. Ormston, Marton Rd. Middlesbrough
G. Osborne, Nairnhead Cl, Hemlington
A. Osbourne, Skiddaw Ct, Nunthorpe
J. Osbourne, Lilac Cres, Brotton
P. D. Osbourne, Lilac Cres, Brotton
A. Overfield, St. Barnabas Rd, Linthorpe
J. V. Ovington, Hoylake Rd, Saltersgill
F. A. Ovington, Hoylake Rd, Saltersgill
P. W. Ovington, Hoylake Rd, Saltersgill
C. R. Owens, Stapleford Rd, Netherfields
P. J. Oxley, Dewberry Pk, Coulby Newham
T. Oxley, Middleton Rd. Rickmansworth

P

P. Page, Moor Park, Nunthorpe
J. Page, Moor Park, Nunthorpe
J. Page, Moor Park, Nunthorpe
R. Page, Moor Park, Nunthorpe
R. E. Painter, Eagle Park, Marton
D. L. Painter, Eagle Park, Marton
D. R. Palmer, Grisedale Cres, Eaglescliffe
G. Palmer, Newbank Cl, Ormesby
G. Palmer, Ringwood Rd, Thorntree
A. Palmer, Ringwood Rd, Thorntree
C. Palmer, Ringwood Rd, Thorntree
J. Palmer, Ringwood Rd, Thorntree
C. Palmer, Waskerley Cl, Hardwick
B. Park, Barnaby Cl, Marske
C. Park, Barnaby Cl, Marske
S. Parker, Beechfield, Coulby Newham
R. Parker, Alfred St. Redcar
S. Parker, Alfred St. Redcar
R. Parker, Alfred St, Redcar
S. Parker, Alfred St, Redcar
C. Parker, New Row, Dunsdale
D. Parker, Princes Sq, Thornaby
D. Parker, Princes Sq, Thornaby
M. Parker, Princes Sq, Thornaby
G. Parker, The Pastures, Coulby Newham
J. Parker, Penryn Cl, Skelton
G. Parker, Ripon Way, Eston
G. Parker, Park Lane, Guisborough
V. Parker, Park Lane, Guisborough
N. Parker, Whittering, Cambridgeshire
S. Parker, Whittering, Cambridgeshire
C. Parker, New Row, Dunsdale
T. Parker, Mansfield Rd, Eston
A. Parker, Mansfield Rd, Eston
A. Parkes, Vancouver Gds, Middlesbrough
S. Parkin, Otterburn Way, Billingham
B. Parkin, Centenary Cres, Norton
A. Parkinson, Bristow Rd, Middlesbrough
I. Parks, Dufton Rd. Middlesbrough
K. Parnaby, Duncombe Bank, Ferryhill
E. Parry, Buttermere Ave, Acklam
K. Parry, Buttermere Ave, Acklam
M. Parsons, Fountains Cres, Eston
D. Parsons, Fountains Cres, Eston
K. Parsons, Fountains Cres, Eston
K. Parvin, Badger Ln, Ingleby Barwick
B. Paterson, Christchurch Dr, Hartburn
G. Patterson, Pallister Ave, Brambles Farm
R. N. Patterson, Jedburgh St, Middlesbrough
T. Pattison, Reeth Rd, Hartburn
D. Pattison, Upsall Rd, Nunthorpe
D. Pattison, Upsall Rd, Nunthorpe
R. Patton, Elterwater Cl, Redcar
A. Patton, Elterwater Cl, Redcar
G. Patton, Elterwater Cl, Redcar
J. Patton, Elterwater Cl, Redcar
B. Paul, Ann Charlton Lodge, Redcar
A. J. Paxton, Alwoodley, Leeds
M. Paylor, Nunnery Fields, Canterbury
C. Payne, Sedgefield Rd, Acklam
B. Payne, Sedgefield Rd, Acklam
J. L. Payne, Belmangate, Guisborough
Payne Family, The Avenue, Linthorpe
A. Peacock, Hunters Ride, Appleton Wiske
T. Peacock, Gilpin Rd, Thornaby
D. Peacock, Durham Rd, Wolviston
S. Peacock, Wolsingham Dr, Stainsby Hill
M. Peacock, Wolsingham Dr, Stainsby Hill
R. Peacock, Rushyford Ave, Roseworth
R. Peacock, Rushyford Ave, Roseworth
A. Pearce, Ravensworth Rd, Billingham
J. Pearce, Spencerfield Cres, Thorntree
J. W. Pearce, Spencerfield Cs, Thorntree
J. Pearce, Longford St, Middlesbrough
M. Pearce, Longford St, Middlesbrough
A. Pearce, Longford St, Middlesbrough
D. Pearsall, New Market Rd, Redcar
E. Pearsall, New Market Rd, Redcar
C. Pearson, Romney Cl, Redcar
F. Pearson, Kirkleatham Ln, Redcar
S. Pearson, Kirkleatham Ln, Redcar
W. Pearson, Tibbersley Ave, Billingham
D. Pearson, Stockton Rd, Middlesbrough
A. Pearson, Buttermere Rd, Redcar
J. Pearson, Cedar Rd, Norton
R. Pearson, Cedar Rd, Norton
Mr & Mrs P. F. Pearson, Brierley G, Marton
R. A. Pearson, Sittingbourne, Kent
G. Pearson, Lodore Gr, Acklam
H. Pearson, Lodore Gr, Acklam
C. Pearson, Lodore Gr, Acklam
J. Pearson, Tees Rd, Redcar
J. A. Pearson, Tees Rd, Redcar
M. Pearson, Lumley Rd, Redcar
L. M. Pearson, Thames Rd, Redcar
J. M. Pearson, Thames Rd, Redcar
M. Pearson, Stonor Walk, Park End
M. Pearson, Stonor Walk, Park End
D. J. Peart, Blantyre Rd, Middlesbrough
D. Peart, Brentford Ct, Brotton
S. Peat, Park Ave. South Ormesby
R. Peebles, Millbank Lane, Thornaby
M. Pengilley, Lancaster Dr, Marske
G. Pennington, North Dr, Ormesby
J. Percival, Westfield Rd, Normanby
L. Perkins, Riftswood Dr, Marske
A. J. Perkins, Craigearn Rd. Normanby
S. Perks, Ashton Rd, Norton
M. Perks, Ashton Rd, Norton
J. Perrott, Milburn Cres, Norton
J. Perrott, Milburn Cres, Norton
M. Petfod, Fir Tree Ave, Normanby
S. Phelps, Overdale Rd, Middlesbrough
P. Phelps, Overdale Rd, Middlesbrough
D. G. Phillips, Earlsdon Ave, Acklam
W. F. Phillips, Westbourne Gr, Teesville
T. W. Phillips, Westbourne Gr, Teesville
R. P. Phillips, Westbourne Gr, Teesville
M. Philpott, Dunstable Rd, Middlesbrough
M. Picking, The Brookes, Yarm
P. Pierce, Offerton Dr, Hemlington
S. Pierce, Offerton Dr, Hemlington
P. Pierce, Offerton Dr, Hemlington
D. J. Piggott, Tyrone Rd, Fairfield
L. J. Piggott, Tyrone Rd, Fairfield
N. Pinkham, Falcon Way, Guisborough
A. Pinkham, Falcon Way, Guisborough
H. Pinkham, Falcon Way, Guisborough
J. Pinkney, Dovedale Rd, Norton
J. Pinkney, Dovedale Rd. Norton
C. Pinkney, Dovedale Rd, Norton
J. Piper, Meadowgate, Eston Under Nab
M. Piper, Meadowgate, Eston Under Nab
D. Piper, Meadowgate, Eston Under Nab
A. Pollard, Thornfield Rd, Linthorpe
H. Pollard, Thornfield Rd, Linthorpe
T. Pollard, Thornfield Rd, Linthorpe
R. Polson, Oakley Cl, Guisborough
J. Polson, Oakley Cl, Guisborough
C. Poole, Starbeck Way, Spencerbeck
R. M. Pooley, The Pippins, Wolviston
R. D. Pooley, The Pippins, Wolviston
A. Porritt, Oakhurst Gds, Ingleby Barwick
L. Porritt, The Barass, Staithes
R. Porritt, The Barass, Staithes
J. Porritt, Coach Road, Brotton
D. Porritt, Coach Rd, Brotton
R. Porritt, Victoria, Australia
C. R. Portas, Whinfield Cl, Stockton
D. Portas, Kensington Ave, Normanby
M. Portas, Kensington Ave, Normanby
S. Porter, Beaumont Rd, North Ormesby
J. Porter, Lulsgate, Thornaby
M. Potts, Radford Cl, Stockton
B. Potts, Radford Cl, Stockton
P. Potts, Radford Cl, Stockton
V. Potts, Radford Cl, Stockton
S. Pounder, Marton Rd, Middlesbrough
N. Pounder, St Austell Cl, Stainton Manor
M. Pounder, St Austell Cl, Stainton Manor
C. Pounds, Petersfield, Hampshire
N. Povey, Stonyroyd Hotel, Stockton
A. Powell, Fairfax Ct, Hemlington
D. Power, Queen St, Redcar
S. Power, Queen St, Redcar
H. Power, Queen St, Redcar
J. Power, Luccombe Cl, Ingleby Barwick
A. Power, Ampthill, Beds.
B. Power, Adstock, Bucks.
L. Powles, Hornbeam Walk, Stockton
M. Pratt, The Headlands, Marske
C. Pratt, The Headlands, Marske
S. Pratt, The Headlands, Marske
D. Pratt, The Headlands, Marske
S. M. Pratt, The Headlands, Marske
R. Pratt, Priestcrofts, Marske
A. Prest, Bankfields Rd, Eston
T. Preston, Saltscar, Redcar
P. Preston, Muriel St, Redcar
W. Pretty, Watnall, Nottingham
G. Pretty, Walnall, Nottingham
A. Price, Braemar Gr, Teesville
A. Price, Braemar Gr, Teesville
S. Price, Surbiton Rd, Fairfield
D. Priddy, Acklam Rd, Middlesbrough
E. Priddy, Lindisfarne Rd, Peterborough
P. Pritchard, Lydbrook Rd, West Lane
S. Prouse, Warsett Rd, Marske
J. Prouse, Warsett Rd, Marske
N. Prouse, Warsett Rd, Marske
D. Prouse, Epsom Rd, Redcar
R. Prouse, Epsom Rd, Redcar
L. Prouse, Epsom Rd, Redcar
J. Pryke, Meadowgate, Eston
S. Puckrin, Tyne Rd, Redcar
R. Puckrin, Tyne Rd, Redcar
J. Pulman, Selbourne St, Middlesbrough
A. J. Purvis, Gurney St, Middlesbrough
V. Putson, Fallows Ct, Middlesbrough
C. Pyle, Clayton Park, Jesmond

Q

G. Quine, Chapel St, Marske
M. Quinn, The Old Market, Yarm
P. T. Quinn, Lorton Rd. Redcar
R. Quinn, Raisegill Cl, Berwick Hills
J. Quinn, Raisegill Cl, Berwick Hills

R

I. Race, Sandy Flatts Lane, Acklam
B. Race, Sandy Flatts Lane, Acklam
C. Race, Tasmania Square, Marton
A. Race, Lucerne Ct, Marton
S. Race, Suffolk St, Stockton
C. Race, Rawdon, Leeds
C. Raine, The Paddock, Stokesley
A. L. Ramsay, Middleton Ave, Billingham
S. Ramsdale, Aylestone Dr, Hereford
N. Ramsdale, Mount Pleasant, Whitby
J. Ramsey, Hampton St, Stockton
K. Ramsey, Hampton St, Stockton
W. Randall, St Aidens Dr, Middlesbrough
L. Randall, St Aidens Dr, Middlesbrough
S. Randall, Piperknowle Rd, Hardwick
R. Randall, Piperknowle Rd, Hardwick
R. Ransom, Springfield Ave, Hartburn
Mr & Mrs D. Ratcliff, Coniston Gr, Acklam
I. D. Ratcliff, Coniston Gr, Acklam
W. Rawlings, Pannell Ave, Acklam
J. Raybould, Brendon Gr, Ingleby Barwick
L. Raybould, Brendon Gr, Ingleby Barwick
L. Raybould, Brendon Gr, Ingleby Barwick
D. Raybould, Brendon Gr, Ingleby Barwick
S. G. Read, High West Cote, Chopgate
I. Readman, Ormesby Rd, Normanby
M. Readman, Ormesby Rd, Normanby
P. Readman, Ormesby Rd, Normanby
J. Readshaw, South Stand
M. J. Reaney, Ellerburne St, Thornaby
A. M. Reaney, Ellerburne St, Thornaby
T. Reap, Roseworth, Great Broughton
P. Redford, Hurst Park, Redcar
K. Reece, Buttermere Ave, Acklam
S. Reece, Buttermere Ave, Acklam
J. I. Reed, Lanchester Rd, Grangetown
P. Reed, Lanchester Rd, Grangetown
M. Reed, Lealholme Gr, Fairfield
J. B. Reed, Lealholme Gr, Fairfield
N. Reed, Maria Dr, Fairfield
B. Reed, Kingsley Rd, Fairfield
G. Reed, Rochdale Ave, Roseworth
G. Reed, Cotgarth Way, Bishopsgarth
D. Reeder, Holbeck Ave, Brookfield
M. Reeder, Holbeck Ave, Brookfield
G. Rees, Rochester Rd, Linthorpe
D. Rees, Maldon Rd. Middlesbrough
A. Rees, Ayresome Park Rd, Middlesbrough
B. Rees, Ayresome Park Rd, Middlesbrough
J. V. Reeve, Trimdon Ave, Acklam
R. Regan, Lambeth Rd, Linthorpe
K. Regan, Belmont Ave, Teesville
P. Regan, Belmont Ave, Teesville
C. Relph, Guisborough Rd, Nunthorpe
C. Relph, Guisborough Rd, Nunthorpe
S. Relph, Guisborough Rd, Nunthorpe
P. Remmer, Skeeby Cl, Hartburn
S. Rennie, Crossfields, Coulby Newham
D. Rennie, Crossfields, Coulby Newham
D. Reubens, Hastings Cl, Nunthorpe
D. Reubens, Hastings Cl, Nunthorpe
L. Reynolds, Abberston Walk, Middlesbrough
M. Reynolds, Zetland Rd, Redcar
G. Reynolds, Zetland Rd, Redcar
N. Rhodes, Imperial Cres, Norton
M. Rice, Montrose Ave, Nuneaton
H. Rice, Faverdale Cl, Middlesbrough
R. Richards, Beadon Gr, West Lane
A. Richards, Holyhead Dr, Redcar
D. Richards, Pinewood Rd, Marton
C. Richards, Mortimer Dr, Norton
D. Richards, Guisborough St, Eston
M. Richardson, Westbeck Gds, Linthorpe
J. Richardson, Spencerfield Cres, Thorntree
S. Richardson, Woodlea, Coulby Newham
S. Richardson, Ashkirk Rd, Normanby
C. Richardson, Ashkirk Rd, Normanby
K. Richardson, Ashkirk Rd, Normanby
G. Richardson, South Lackenby, Eston
G. Richardson, Braemar Rd, Billingham
A. Richardson, Braemar Rd, Billingham
D. Richardson, Braemar Rd, Billingham
S. Richardson, Braemar Rd, Billingham
K. Richardson, Ashkirk Rd, Normanby
S. Richardson, Ashkirk Rd, Normanby
C. Richardson, Gosforth, Newcastle
N. Richardson, Westfield Walk, Loftus
M. Richardson, Westfield Walk, Loftus
T. Richardson, South Terrace, Skelton
T. Richardson, South Terrace, Skelton
M. Richardson, South Terrace, Skelton
T. Richardson Jnr, South Terr, Skelton
L. Richman, Brignal Rd, Stockton
M. Riddle, Flodden Way, Billingham
P. Riddle, Flodden Way, Billingham
P. Rider, Woodvale, Coulby Newham
J. Rider, Woodvale, Coulby Newham
A. Rider, Woodvale, Coulby Newham
A. B. Ridgway, Cambrian Ave, Redcar
J. Ridgway, Cambrian Ave, Redcar
S. Ridgway, Cambrian Ave, Redcar
N. Ridgway, Cambrian Ave, Redcar
J. Ridley, Borough Rd, Redcar
J. Ridley, Borough Rd, Redcar
G. Ridley, Stokesley Cres, Billingham
M. Ridley, Stokesley Cres, Billingham

J. D. Ridsdale, Hawkshead Rd, Redcar
S. T. Ridsdale, Hawkshead Rd, Redcar
S. Rigg, Blackthorn, Coulby Newham
S. Riggall, Oakley Walk, Eston
L. Riggall, Sunningdale Dr, Eaglescliffe
J. Riggall, Sunningdale Dr, Eaglescliffe
S. B. Riley, Low Grange Ave, Billingham
A. N. Riley, Low Grange Ave, Billingham
C. Riley, Washington Cs, Newton Aycliffe
T. Roberts, Gilpin Rd, Thornaby
P. Roberts, Keepers Lane, Ingleby Barwick
S. Roberts, Trunk Rd, South Bank
S. Roberts, Trunk Rd, South Bank
I. Roberts, Planetree Ct, Marton
L. E. D. Roberts, Beverley Rd, Redcar
N. Roberts, Newlands Rd, Eaglescliffe
L. Robins, Barford Cl, Norton
N. Robinson, Dingleside, Stockton
J. Robinson, Rothbury Cl, Ingleby Barwick
J. Robinson, Rothbury Cl, Ingleby Barwick
D. Robinson, Rothbury Cl, Ingleby Barwick
G. Robinson, Fernwood, Coulby Newham
M. Robinson, Fernwood, Coulby Newham
J. B. Robinson, Birkley Rd, Norton
P. Robinson, Birkley Rd, Norton
M. J. B. Robinson, Cleadon Walk, Hardwick
J. A. Robinson, Cleadon Walk, Hardwick
C. Robinson, Sidmouth Cl, Middlesbrough
S. Robinson, Sidmouth Cl, Middlesbrough
S. Robinson, Waverley St, Middlesbrough
Mr & Mrs Robinson, Harwell Dr, Stockton
P. Robinson, Trenholme Rd, Longlands
B. Robinson, The Green, Thornaby
M. Robinson, The Green, Thornaby
A. Robinson, The Green, Thornaby
C. Robinson, Enfield Chase, Guisborough
D. Robinson, Enfield Chase, Guisborough
S. Robinson, Enfield Chase, Guisborough
L. Robinson, Enfield Chase, Guisborough
D. Robinson, Maria Dr, Fairfield
D. Robinson, Oldgate, Eston Under Nab
M. Robinson, Andover, Hampshire
D. Robinson, Essex St, Middlesbrough
C. Robinson, Charlotte St, Skelton
J. H. Robinson, Windlestone Dr, Park End
P. Robinson, North Road, Darlington
S. Robinson, Lydbrook Rd, West Lane
I. Robinson, Lydbrook Rd, West Lane
M. Robinson, Lydbrook Rd, West Lane
K. A. Robinson, Lydbrook Rd, West Lane
G. Robinson, Calverley Rd, Middlesbrough
R. Robinson, Beaumont Rd, North Ormesby
T. Robson, Bulmer Ct, Normanby
D. Robson, Bielby Ave, Billingham
S. Robson, Bielby Ave, Billingham
C. Robson, Brettenham Ave, Easterside
G. Robson, Station Cres, Billingham
K. Robson, Crooks Barn Lane, Norton
M. Robson, Crooks Barn Lane, Norton
P. Robson, Braemar Rd, Billingham
T. Robson, Ashdown Way, Billingham
S. A. Robson, Ravensworth Rd, Billingham
J. Robson, Foxton Dr, Billingham
M. A. Robson, Foxton Dr, Billingham
R. Rodgers, Cedar Dr, Thornton
R. Rodgers, Pritchett Rd, Ormesby
M. Roe, Sunningdale Rd, Saltersgill
D. Rogers, Mill St. West, Stockton
J. Rogers, Barle Cl, Ingleby Barwick
L. Rogers, Gainsborough Rd, Marton Manor
P. Rogers, South Mews, Shadforth
M. Rooney, Norcliffe St, North Ormesby
M. S. Rooney, Norcliffe St, North Ormesby
M. B. Rooney, Hutton Rd, Middlesbrough
D. Rooney, Breckland Walk, Middlesbrough
W. Rooney, Park End
Mr & Mrs G. Roper, Hilderthorpe, Nunthorpe
G. Roper, Hilderthorpe, Nunthorpe
J. Roper, Netherfields Cres, Netherfields
D. H. J. Rose, Moulton Gr, Fairfield
C. Rose, The Avenue, Marton
M. Rose, The Avenue, Marton
A. Rose, Hebburn Rd, Stockton
I. Ross, Latimer Lane, Guisborough
J. Ross, Latimer Lane, Guisborough
P. Ross, Bypass Rd, Billingham
P. Ross, Bypass Rd, Billingham
I. Ross, Bypass Rd, Billingham
J. Rothery, Harwal Rd, Redcar
M. Rothwell, The Argory, Ingleby Barwick
L. Rothwell, Lydbrook Rd, West Lane
S. Rouse, Trimdon Ave, Acklam
K. Rowe, Runswick Ave, Acklam
P. Rowland, Oldbury Gr, Hemlington
P. Rowland, Oldbury Gr, Hemlington
S. Rowland, Oldbury Gr, Hemlington
A. G. Rowlands
S. Rowling, Kader Ave, Acklam
G. Rowling, Whitehouse Rd, Thornaby
N. Rowney, Medbourne Cl, Eston
S. Rowney, Melbourne Cl, Eston
A. Rowntree, Layburn Gr, Hartburn
K. Roy, Thornthwaite, Acklam
M. Roy, Waterloo Rd, Middlesbrough
M. Ruane, Normanby Rd, Ormesby
J. Ruane, Normanby Rd, Ormesby
S. Ruane, Normanby Rd, Ormesby
M. Ruane, Thornton St, North Ormesby
S. Rudd, Coulby Newham
S. Ruddock, The Willows, Marton
C. Ruddock, The Willows, Marton
J. Ruddock, The Willows, Marton
N. Ruff, Ingram Rd, Berwick Hills
M. Ruff, Ingram Rd, Berwick Hills
P. Rugg, Waveney Rd, Redcar
D. Rugg, Waveney Rd, Redcar
C. Rumsey, Appleton Rd, Linthorpe
C. Rumsey, Appleton Rd, Linthorpe
J. Ruse, The Pastures, Coulby Newham
S. Russell, Coniston Gr, Acklam
B. Russell, Coniston Gr, Acklam
N. Russell, Endeavour Pub, Tollesby Hall
J. Russell, Marton Rd, Middlesbrough
W. Rutherford, Penllyn Way, Hemlington
P. Rutherford, Penllyn Way, Hemlington
G. Rutland, Cromwell Ave, Loftus
B. Rutland, Cromwell Ave, Loftus
P. Rutland, Cromwell Ave, Loftus
E. Rutland, Cromwell Ave, Loftus
B. Ryder, Barkston Ave, Thornaby
D. Ryder, Barkston Ave, Thornaby

S

D. Sadler, Rifts Ave, Saltburn
L. Sadler, Rifts Ave, Saltburn
J. Sadler, Rifts Ave, Saltburn
D. Sadler, Rifts Ave, Saltburn
L. Sadler, Rifts Ave, Saltburn
J. Sadler, Rifts Ave, Saltburn
G. Sadler, High St, Yarm
J. W. Salter, Glenfield Dr, Tollesby
J. Salter, Chippingham Rd, Easterside
C. C. Salter, Glenfield Dr, Tollesby
M. Salvati, Foxhowe, Coulby Newham
G. Salvin, Spencer Rd, Teesville
D. Salvin, Spencer Rd, Teesville
P. Salvin, Meadowgate, Eston
A. Salvin, Meadowgate, Eston
M. Sancto, Rutland Ct, Middlesbrough
L. A. Sanders, Hampton Rd, Stockton
J. Sanders, Albert Rd, Warrington
R. Sanders, Hillside Rd, Norton
M. Sanders, Hillside Rd, Norton
I. Sanderson, Braidwood, Normanby
H. Sanderson, Mitford Cres, Stockton
R. Sanderson, Mitford Cres, Stockton
M. Sanderson, Mitford Cres, Stockton
A. G. Sanderson, Stokesley Rd, Nunthorpe
D. G. Sanderson, Stokesley Rd, Nunthorpe
N. Sands, Church St, South Marske
J. Sanson, Swallow Fields, Coulby Newham
K. Sanson, Swallow Fields, Coulby Newham
D. Sargeant, Fano Gr, Acklam
J. Sargeant, Rosalind Ct, Salford
P. Sargeant, Ebury Bridge Rd, London
J. Sargeant, Swan Rd, Harrogate
D. Saul, Glentworth Ave, Netherfields
L. Savage, Tennyson Cl, Grangetown
S. Saville, Rochester Rd, Linthorpe
S. Saville, Fulbeck Rd, Middlesbrough
F. Sawdon, Park Ave, Redcar
C. Sawdon, Park Ave, Redcar
A. Sayer, Eagle Park, Marton
M. Scanlan, Thomas St, North Ormesby
A. Schofield, Glebe Rd, Stokesley
D. Scott, Adam Cl, Redcar
D. Scott, Windrush, Highworth, Swindon
S. Scott, Windrush, Highworth, Swindon
L. Scott, Scotforth Cl, Marton
D. Scott, Trefoil Wood, Marton Manor
P. A. Scott, Trefoil Wood, Marton Manor
C. M. Scott, Trefoil Wood, Marton Manor
J. Scott, Manor Ct, Wolviston
S. Scott, Manor Ct, Wolviston
D. Scott, Laurel St, Middlesbrough
P. Scott, Laurel St, Middlesbrough
G. Scott, Captain Cooks Cres, Marton
P. Scott, Captain Cooks Cres, Marton
J. Scott, Captain Cooks Cres, Marton
M. Scott, Captain Cooks Cres, Marton
P. Scovell, Skottowe Cres, Great Ayton
E. Scovell, Skottowe Cres, Great Ayton
K. Seaman, Ipswich Ave, Park End
S. Seaman, Ipswich Ave, Park End
V. Seaman, Ipswich Ave, Park End
D. M. Secker, Windsor Rd, Redcar
B. E. Sellers, Meadow Dr, Ormesby
J. Sellers, Linton Rd, Normanby
A. Senior, Jacklin Walk, Eaglescliffe
D. Serginson, Brendon Gr, Ingleby Barwick
M. Serginson, Brendon Gr, Ingleby Barwick
T. Sexton, Princes Sq, Thornaby
B. Seymour, Lapwing Ln, Norton
S. Seymour, Lapwing Ln, Norton
B. Shail, Larch Cl, Marton
J. Shail, Larch Cl, Marton
J. T. Shakeshaft, Hawkeston Cl, Guisborough
A. Sharp, Middlesbrough
C. Sharp, Wilton Way, Eston
A. Sharpe, Raysdale Rd, Thornaby
C. Sharpe, Raysdale Rd, Thornaby
M. Sharples, Aske Rd, Middlesbrough
V. Sharples, Aske Rd, Middlesbrough
P. Sharples, Aske Rd, Middlesbrough
R. Shaw, Crowood Ave, Stokesley
P. Shaw, Lamonby Cl, Nunthorpe
M. Shaw, Abingdon Rd, Middlesbrough
P. Shaw, Ripon Rd, Brotton
M. Shaw, Ripon Rd, Brotton
V. Shaw, Halstead, Chelmsford
N. Sheekey, Ash Gr, Kirklevington
A. Sheekey, Ash Gr, Kirklevington
M. J. Sheffield, Carmel Gdns, Nunthorpe
J. Shepherd, Hutton Rd, Middlesbrough
W. Shepherd, Grantham Rd, Norton
J. Shepherd, Grantham Rd, Norton
D. Shepherd, Tavistock Rd, Linthorpe
L. Shepherd, Hugill Cl, Yarm
M. Shepherd, Hugill Cl, Yarm
A, Shepherd, Hugill Cl, Yarm
H. Shepherd, Hugill Cl, Yarm
J. Shepherd, Close Fm, Wolviston
M. Sheridan, Thurnham Gr, Marton
C. Sheridan, Ormesby Rd, Normanby
K. Sherwood, Gilmonby Rd, Park End
J. Shields, Oxford St, Middlesbrough
P. Shildrick, Ingram Rd, Berwick Hills
C. Shildrick, Ingram Rd, Berwick Hills
B. Shildrick, Ingram Rd, Berwick Hills
P. Shildrick, Crathorne Cres, West Lanc
M. A. Shilham, Swaledale Ct, Ingleby Barwick
G L. Shilham, Swaledale Cl, Ingleby Barwick
Z. Shipp, Minsterley Dr, Acklam
J. Short, Crispin Ct, Brotton
M. Short, Crispin Ct, Brotton
S. Short, Crispin Ct, Brotton
R. Short, Pennyman Cl, Normanby
G. Short, Pennyman Cl, Normanby
S. Short, Pennyman Cl, Normanby
H. Short, Amersham Rd, Middlesbrough
R. Sides, Brompton St, Middlesbrough
L. Sidgwick, Sandalwood Ct, Acklam
K. Sidgwick, Sandalwood Ct, Acklam
Mr & Mrs M. Sidgwick, Ollabery, Shetland
A. Sigsworth, Trimdon Ave, Acklam
C. Sigsworth, Rainsford Cr, Thorntree
P. Sigsworth, Rainsford Cr, Thorntree
L. Sigsworth, Hood Dr, Normanby Grange
G. Sigsworth, Hood Dr, Normanby Grange
A. Sigsworth, Hood Dr, Normanby Grange
J. B. Silk, Pennyman Cl, Normanby
A. R. Silk, Pennyman Cl, Normanby
B. Sill, Birkdale Rd, New Marske
C. Sill, Birkdale Rd, New Marske
P. Simcox, Winsford Ct, Ingleby Barwick
G. Simmons, Thirlmire Rd, Redcar
G. Simmons, High Fell, Redcar
J. Simms, Linden Cres, Marton
C. R. Simpson, High Gill Rd, Nunthorpe
M. J. Simpson, High Gill Rd, Nunthorpe
D. Simpson, Merlin Rd, Middlesbrough
S. Simpson, Merlin Rd, Middlesbrough
R. Simpson, Merlin Rd, Middlesbrough
B. Simpson, Richardson Rd, Thornaby
L. Simpson, Richardson Rd, Thornaby
J. Simpson, Debruse Ave, Yarm
S. Simpson, Debruse Ave, Yarm
W. Simpson, Wetherall Ave, Yarm
C. Simpson, Kedleston Pk, Marton
M. E. Simpson, Patterdale St, Acklam
W. Simpson, Ridley Dr, Norton
D. Simpson, Ridley Dr, Norton
I. R. Simpson, Blakey Cl, Redcar
G. I. Simpson, Blakey Cl, Redcar
P. Simpson, Bankside, Yarm
C. Simpson, Bankside, Yarm
P. Singh, West Bridgford, Nottingham
E. Singh, West Bridgford, Nottingham
D. Sinnott, Lilac Rd, Teesville
A. Sinnott, Lilac Rd, Teesville
P. Sinnott, Laburnum Rd, Teesville
D. Sinnott, Lilac Rd, Teesville
A. Sinnott, Lilac Rd, Teesville
P. Sinnott, Laburnum Rd, Teesville
K. Skelton, Curson St, Eston
D. Skelton, Coulby Newham
T. Skipper, Windy Hill Ln, Marske
M. Skipper, Windy Hill Ln, Marske
D. Slasor, Brampton Cl, Hemlington
M. Slavin, Maidstone Dr, Marton
M. Slavin, Maidstone Dr, Marton
J. Slee, Cornforth Gr, Billingham
J. Slee Jnr, Cornforth Gr, Billingham
W. J. Sleight, Wharfedale Rd, Barnsley
H. J. Small, Marrick Rd, Hartburn
R. Smith, Craven Vale, Guisborough
M. Smith, Sterling Rd, Redcar
D. Smith, Bassenthwaite, Acklam
R. Smith, Bassenthwaite, Acklam
R. Smith, Craven Vale, Guisborough
M. Smith, Sterling Rd, Redcar
D. Smith, Bassenthwaite, Acklam
R. Smith, Bassenthwaite, Acklam
T. Smith, The Walk, Elwick
A. Smith, The Walk, Elwick
A. Smith, The Walk, Elwick
T. Smith, The Walk, Elwick
G. Smith, Firtree Ave, Normanby
S. Smith, Firtree Ave, Normanby
N. Smith, Nut Lane, Longlands
D. M. Smith, Macbean St, North Ormesby
L- M. Smith, Macbean St, North Ormesby
M. Smith, Back Ln, Skelton
D. Smith, Delamere Dr, Marske
R. Smith, Avon Rd, Redcar
S. R. Smith, Ashford Ave, Acklam
L. Smith, Ashford Ave, Acklam
L. L. Smith, Ashford Ave, Acklam
R. J. Smith, Ashford Ave, Acklam
I. Smith, Beverley Rd, Nunthorpe
G. L. Smith, Beverley Rd, Nunthorpe
S. Smith, Elder Ct, Middlesbrough
T. Smith, Baldoon Sands, Acklam
G. Smith, Oldbury Gr, Hemlington
T. Smith, Laburnum Ave, Thornaby
T. Smith, Thorphill Way, Billingham
J. Smith, Thorphill Way, Billingham
M. Smith, Thorphill Way, Billingham
T. Smith, Endeavour Pub, Tollesby Hall
S. Smith, Lynmouth Cl, Stainton Manor
W. P. D. P. Smith, Highfield Cres, Hartburn
E. Smith, The Granary, Wynyard Village
A. Smith, Lancaster Dr, Marske
I. Smith, Barnard Rd, Easington
R. W. Smith, Orchard Rd, Hull
C. Smith, Greenvale Gro, Fairfield
S. Smith, Greenvale Gr, Fairfield
T. A. Smith, Seaford Cl, Redcar
A. Smith, Seaford Cl, Redcar
B. Smith, Angrove Cl, Yarm
A. M. Smith, Ainsdale Cl, New Marske
C. R. Smith, Ainsdale Cl, New Marske
A. Smith, Rainsford Cres, Thorntree
D. M. Smith, Aylesbury, Bucks
M. A. Smith, Moor Park, Nunthorpe
C. J. Smith, Moor Park, Nunthorpe
A. E. M. Smith, Moor Park, Nunthorpe
A. M. Smith, Moor Park, Nunthorpe
G. Smith, Southwell Rd, Middlesbrough
T. Smith Snr, Seaford Cl, Redcar
J. Smithard, Dentdale Cl, Yarm